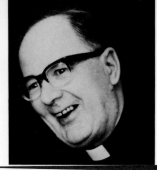

ROBERT M. DORAN and FREDERICK E. CROWE
are founders of the Lonergan Research Institute
in Toronto. They are assisted in the Collected
Works by a large international body of editorial
consultants.

COLLECTED WORKS OF

BERNARD LONERGAN

VOLUME 10

TOPICS IN EDUCATION

COLLECTED WORKS
OF BERNARD

LONERGAN

TOPICS IN EDUCATION

The Cincinnati Lectures of 1959 on the
Philosophy of Education

Edited by Robert M. Doran
and Frederick E. Crowe

Revising and augmenting the unpublished text
prepared by James Quinn and John Quinn

Published for Lonergan Research Institute
of Regis College, Toronto
by University of Toronto Press
Toronto Buffalo London

ISBN 0-8020-3440-3 (cloth)
ISBN 0-8020-3441-1 (paper)

Requests for permission to quote from the
Collected Works of Bernard Lonergan should be
addressed to University of Toronto Press.

Canadian Cataloguing in Publication Data

Lonergan, Bernard J.F. (Bernard Joseph Francis), 1904–1984.
  Collected works of Bernard Lonergan

  Partial contents: v. 10. Topics in education.
  Includes bibliographical references and index.
  ISBN 0-8020-3440-3 (v. 10: bound). – ISBN 0-8020-3441-1 (v. 10: pbk.)

  1. Theology – 20th century.   2. Catholic Church.
  I. Crowe, Frederick E., 1915–   II. Doran, Robert M., 1939– .
  III. Lonergan Research Institute.   IV. Title.

  BX891.L595 1988   230   C88-093328-3

The Lonergan Research Institute gratefully acknowledges
the contribution toward publication of this volume
of AVRIL MULCAHY, given in loving memory of her parents,
JEAN FONTAINE and JOHN MULCAHY, representative of the
innumerable little people of this world who contribute
in unrecognized ways to the progress of the human race.

Contents

Editors' Preface

Our preface will comment (1) on the series of lectures which are transcribed and edited in this volume, (2) on the record of the proceedings of the Institute in which these lectures occurred, (3) on earlier work done in transcribing and editing the lectures, and (4) on the relation of the present volume to this earlier work. We will add a few words regarding the editorial conventions that we have employed.

The Cincinnati lectures on education. Bernard Lonergan taught in Rome from 1953 to 1965, but from 1955 on returned each year to spend the summer in Canada or the United States.[1] Soon he began to receive requests for summer lectures, or for Institutes of longer duration. He had already conducted such an Institute – at Boston College in 1957 – and was booked for another at Saint Mary's University, Halifax, in 1958, when Fr Stan Tillman, dean of philosophy at Xavier University, Cincinnati, sounded him out on the possibility of an Institute at Xavier in 1959.[2] Tillman attended the Halifax Institute of 1958, and no doubt discussed the matter with Lonergan at that time. Lonergan wrote from Rome the following March with details on the proposal: the subject of the lectures was to be philosophy of education, and their mode that of a philosopher speaking on topics of concern to educators. Those to be invited, the letter adds, included members of the American Catholic Educational Association and the American Catholic

---

1 See Editors' Preface to *Understanding and Being*, Collected Works of Bernard Lonergan 5 (Toronto: University of Toronto Press, 1990) xiii.
2 Fr Joseph Wulftange, a close friend of Lonergan, mediated Tillman's request; the details are in a letter of 25 May 1958 from Lonergan to Frederick Crowe.

Philosophical Association. The routine was to involve two morning lectures Monday to Saturday for two weeks, and Lonergan was to take part in four evening sessions, two each week.[3]

The lectures actually ran from Monday, August 3, to Friday, August 14, 1959, but there does not seem to have been any kind of session on Saturday, August 8. The sources are clear on the fact that evening sessions were held.[4] But no record of them survives, either on tape or in notes of participants.

Lonergan's letter to Crowe of 3 March 1959 indicated that enrollment would be limited to fifty, as does the advertising announcement, but the final list of registrants contains fifty-five names. The same announcement speaks of the two-week period as 'an Institute on the Philosophy of Education ... under the leadership of Father Bernard J.F. Lonergan, s.j., Professor of Theology, Gregorian University, Rome' and describes it as follows:

> The Institute is planned to be co-operative in character. With this approach it is hoped that the intellectual resources of the members of the Institute as well as the director will be brought to bear on the conclusions reached. Morning sessions will be essentially the philosopher speaking to educators much as a biologist would speak to a medical doctor, a mathematician to a physicist. In these conferences it is expected the bases for a philosophy of education will be established. The evening sessions will reverse this process. The representatives of the other disciplines will test the application of the principles, refining, integrating or challenging the philosopher's stand. It is important to note that the lectures will not presuppose extensive knowledge of the field of philosophy. Rather, they will appeal to a constructive kind of intelligence capable of following the gradual assembly of the elements into an enriched and deepened view of concrete educational activity.[5]

There are interesting data on Lonergan's preparation for the lectures. Some months earlier he wrote from Rome: 'On education course: plan to

---

3 Letter of 3 March 1959 from Lonergan to Crowe.
4 They were announced both in advertisements and in a preliminary list of registrants; further, Lonergan refers one morning to a comment he made 'last night' (see below, chapter 4, note 6).
5 Lonergan made reference to this plan at least once in the course of his lectures, at the very end of the first lecture (see below, p. 25).

integrate stuff on existentialists with theory of Art in S.K. Langer (*Feeling and Form*), follower of Cassirer; eke out with *Insight,* for intellectualist, scientific side; throw in bit of theol[ogy].'[6] In an interview years later he speaks of the considerable time he gave to this preparation and also of the reading he did in Piaget at this time.[7] But the major indication of the work that went into the preparation of these lectures is found in Lonergan's own lecture notes, which were discovered among his literary remains after his death. The notes are scattered among the pages of a small loose-leaf notebook that contains other material as well. The pages are arranged in alphabetical order according to topic, and so a researcher has to move around among them to discover the notes that Lonergan actually used for those lectures. Thus, the notes on 'Art' are on pp. 4–12 of the notebook, while those on Piaget are on pp. 82–92; in between are not only notes on other topics covered in the Institute, e.g., the human good, history, intersubjectivity, new learning, but also many other pages that were not part of Lonergan's preparation for the Institute (covering such topics as *ens,* faith, God, Logos, Maritain, Newman). As will be indicated in greater detail later, the discovery of these notes greatly complicated but also greatly enriched the process of transcribing and editing Lonergan's lectures.

Record of the Institute proceedings. It seems that there was one master set of reels recording the morning lectures of the Institute, that other extant reels were copied from this master set, and that cassettes were copied from one or another of the sets of reels.

In editing the lectures we had at our disposal two more or less complete sets of reels: one of the Lonergan Research Institute (LRI), and one from Professor Emeritus W.A. Stewart, used in his philosophy courses at Saint Mary's University, Halifax; three reels from Xavier University (numbers 3, 4, and 5 of what were surely 1 to 6), running from the last part of lecture 4 to the start of lecture 9; and three reels from Terence Walsh, consisting of excerpts from various lectures, used in his philosophy courses at the University of Guelph. There is also a complete set of the lectures on cassette at the Lonergan Research Institute.

In our revision of the transcript made by John and James Quinn, we used the LRI cassettes as a working base, but for a check on their completeness made a verbatim transcript direct from the reels; there were gaps in the lat-

6 Letter of 3 March 1959 from Lonergan to Crowe.
7 See *Caring about Meaning: Patterns in the Life of Bernard Lonergan,* ed. Pierrot Lambert, Carlotte Tansey, and Cathleen Going (Montreal: Thomas More Institute Papers, 1982) 18, 54.

ter, even in the 'complete' sets, but the gaps differed, and so we were able, by switching back and forth from set to set, to find all that was recorded of the lectures.

Earlier transcriptions and editions of the lectures. Unlike the lectures of the previous year, published as *Understanding and Being,* the lectures on education have not been previously published. The earliest typescript of the lectures was done in Ireland, mainly by two members of the philosophy faculty of University College in Cork: John Dowling and Frank Dorr. William Mathews, then as now of the Jesuit House of Studies, Milltown Park, Dublin, informed Frederick Crowe of this work in a letter of 26 April 1971 indicating that two of the lectures had not yet been typed but that the rest were ready. Mathews sent the completed transcripts to Crowe at Regis College that spring through the offices of Philip McShane. The two lectures that at that time were not yet typed (6 and 7) were supplied to the Lonergan Center at Regis College in February of 1973, by William Loewe, then a graduate student in theology at Marquette University. The typescripts were quite accurate and very well organized.

In the summer of 1979 John and James Quinn, then both of Toronto, began a new transcription of the lectures. Their first version was completed in November of that year, and they presented the manuscript to Lonergan shortly thereafter for his approval and for permission to try to have the text published. Lonergan wrote to the Quinns, thanking them for their 'painstaking and excellent presentation' of the lectures, and adding a one-page list of 'suggested corrigenda.' He added, 'Had I known beforehand I would have urged you not to reproduce the staccato of my spoken word. It annoys readers but, no doubt, will provide proof of genuineness.'[8]

On 3 October 1981 the Quinns wrote to Lonergan again, indicating that they had 're-edited the entire text with an aim to smoothing out the rhythms of the spoken word.' Their new text, it appears, also took heed of all of Lonergan's suggested corrigenda. On 18 November 1981 James Quinn wrote Lonergan to tell him that the revised version of the lectures was being retyped for a camera-ready copy and that a good copy would be sent to him 'sometime after the third week in December.' Lonergan shared this copy with Fred Lawrence, professor of theology at Boston College, who prepared an additional list of changes, some substantive and some stylistic, that subsequently were introduced by the Quinns into their text.

---

8 Letter of Lonergan to John and James Quinn, 18 January 1980.

In a letter to Crowe of 18 August 1982 Lawrence stated that Lonergan had asked him also to 'do something about the advances he's made on the fourth level [of consciousness] vis-à-vis cognate issues discussed in the lectures.' Lawrence said that, with Lonergan's approval, he was proposing that there be added an appendix consisting of a condensed piece on values that Lonergan had written for the International Theological Commission in Rome, along with a brief explanatory note by Lawrence. This letter indicated as well that the only introduction Lonergan wanted to the lectures themselves would be 'a brief one mentioning the occasion for their delivery and describing the makeup of the audience, by way of explaining their narrowly *Catholic* tone.'

Meanwhile the Quinns had investigated publishing prospects, had found University Press of America receptive, and had sent Lonergan a publishing contract for his perusal and possible signature.[9] This contract seems to have been lost, so in the early fall of 1983, after consultation with the Quinns, Crowe drafted another contract and sent it to Lonergan in care of Harvey Egan, professor of theology at Boston College, asking Egan to see, in consultation with Fred Lawrence, whether it was acceptable to Lonergan, and if so, to procure the latter's signature. Egan replied on 10 October that for some reason Lonergan was reluctant to sign the contract.

The following month Lonergan moved to the Jesuit Infirmary at Pickering, Ontario. He had already appointed three executors of his literary estate (Fred Crowe, Terence Walsh, and Robert Doran), and soon afterwards, in failing health, granted Crowe power-of-attorney status. The executors were now planning an edition of Lonergan's collected works, and had begun discussions with University of Toronto Press on the project. So when, again in consultation with the Quinns, Crowe reopened negotiations with University Press of America on the education lectures, he asked for a contract that would give UPA exclusive rights for only a limited time; this, in fact, had been Lonergan's own wish at an earlier stage: that UPA have exclusive rights for only five or six years, so that after that, 'we would be free to issue an opera omnia on our own copyright, not excluded by the previous, and not rescinding the previous.'[10] UPA, however, on being contacted by telephone on 18 October 1984 was unwilling to agree to this restriction. A month later they reconsidered their position, but by that time prospects for the Collected Works project were bright indeed, and

9 Letter of John and James Quinn to Lonergan, 3 October 1981.
10 Letter of Lonergan to Crowe, 3 March 1980.

Lonergan's executors decided to pursue that option, with the hope that the education lectures might be the first volume to appear, and without further delay.

An unforeseen factor did, however, intervene to cause further delay, and so the good work done by the Quinns could not become available, the way we expected, in the first volume of the Collected Works to be published.[11] The unforeseen factor was the discovery we have mentioned of important relevant material in the Lonergan papers. Lonergan died on 26 November 1984; soon afterwards Fr John Hochban began to catalogue the contents of the boxes and filing cabinets he had left behind, and made the precious discovery of the small loose-leaf binder with the notes written for the education lectures. Without the notebook the work of the general editors might have consisted in listening again to the tapes to check the accuracy of the previously prepared text, expanding footnotes and indices where this seemed desirable, bringing the style into conformity with a Collected Works policy, and other relatively simple tasks of this sort. The discovery of the notes turned these simple tasks into a new work of editing; it was decided therefore to begin the Collected Works with other volumes (ones that would be simpler to edit, as we fondly hoped), and to proceed more slowly with the reediting of the education lectures. And so we come to the relation of the present volume to earlier work of transcription and editing.

The present volume. The discovery of Lonergan's notes accounts for the major differences between this edition and the Quinn version; other changes are minor. The context of the Collected Works, of course, has dictated that we not include Lonergan's later paper on values — it will appear in volume 21. For our context is now that of the total history of Lonergan's thought, and the present text has to take its own distinct place in that history.

With the Quinns, we have respected Lonergan's wish that the published text not be a verbatim transcription. With them, we have incorporated all of the corrigenda suggested by Lonergan and Lawrence. The changes accounted for by the discovery of Lonergan's notes are threefold. First, at times it seemed appropriate to include in the text itself a word, a phrase, a clause, even a sentence that was not spoken by Lonergan but appears in the notes. This was done wherever we judged the addition to be important, clar-

---

11 We should not, however, underrate the impact, during this period of delay, of the text prepared by the Quinns. It has been available in the Library of the Lonergan Research Institute (and elsewhere) for some thirteen years, during which time it has been consulted and quoted continually by students of Lonergan's thought on education.

ifying, or interesting enough to warrant its inclusion in the text. Wherever
such additions were made, we have indicated our editorial work in a footnote.

Secondly, at times the notes clarified the organization of Lonergan's
thought in ways that were not clear, at least immediately, from the lectures.
And so frequently we have introduced new division and subdivision headings and other organizing devices, indicating in our footnotes that this is
the case.

Third, at times it seemed more appropriate to include material from
Lonergan's notes in footnotes rather than in the text. Such instances
account for the significant expansion of the footnotes beyond what they
would otherwise have been.

In all three of these cases, of course, we have been forced to make judgment calls. But, as far as possible, we have indicated in footnotes where the
notes have influenced our decisions.

Regarding the footnotes, two other points should be noted. First, our
account of the relation of the text to the state of the recording is not as
detailed as it was in *Understanding and Being*; however, our footnotes do
indicate when coffee breaks occurred, when Lonergan spoke in an aside,
and when we have had to fill in from Lonergan's notes or from the
detailed notes of Frederick Crowe. Second, we have made every effort to
supply bibliographical data for the various works to which Lonergan
refers.

One other change needs to be indicated. We have exercised greater freedom in chapter divisions than the Quinns did, in several places moving
material from the lecture in which Lonergan delivered it either to the preceding or to the following lecture. This was done in order to preserve the
unified presentation of certain materials. Thus, the very last part of the second lecture appears here at the beginning of the third; the beginning of the
fifth lecture appears here at the end of the fourth; the beginning of the
sixth lecture appears here at the end of the fifth; and the first half of the
eighth lecture is here included in the seventh. In each case the first footnote
of the chapter indicates the change that we have made.

There is a change also in regard to editorial notes from the policy previously followed in this series: in the present volume they are incorporated
into the footnotes themselves, which are often research notes, especially
when they draw on Lonergan's notebook, and so fulfil at least part of the
intention behind the editorial notes in earlier volumes (on which see *Collection* [Collected Works of Bernard Lonergan 4, 1988] 255).

Something should be said about the title of this volume. This work has been known to many under some such title as *Philosophy of Education,* but the title *Topics in Education* was suggested by the Quinns as a result of a telephone conversation they had with Lonergan sometime in 1982. Lonergan emphasized the new situation in which the lectures will be read in contrast with the Catholic situation imposed by the conditions governing the Institute at Xavier. He suggested as a *type* of title *Topics in Education,* with the subtitle *Lectures in the Philosophy of Education,* judging that such a title might help the book reach a wider audience.[12] These would have been the title and subtitle of the Quinn edition, and we have followed their and Lonergan's wishes in this regard.

Finally, a word regarding the editorial conventions we have adopted. Some of these are already familiar to readers of the Collected Works series. Thus, we have again used the *Oxford American Dictionary* and *The Chicago Manual of Style* as guides to the minutiae of editing. We have again added a lexicon of Latin and Greek phrases and a list of the works of Lonergan referred to in our notes, with the number of the actual or anticipated Collected Works volume. We again indicate Lonergan's own citations of scripture, but add in footnotes the text of the New Revised Standard Version (NRSV). And again *PL* is our abbreviation for references to J.-P. Migne, *Patrologiae cursus completus ... Series Prima.*

Our page references to *Collection, Understanding and Being,* and *Insight* are to the Collected Works editions, with their volume numbers (CWL 4, 5, or 3) given in the footnote the first time reference to these volumes appears there.

The principal convention peculiar to this volume has to do with our use of Lonergan's lecture notes. We use the abbreviation LN, followed by the relevant page number, whenever we quote or refer to these notes. Lonergan used both sides of many of the pages in the notes, but numbered only the recto side. Where our reference is to the recto side of the page, only the page number is given, but where we quote or refer to the verso side, this is explicitly noted. Minor insertions in the text from LN were made without notice, but otherwise we have indicated that we have relied on LN for certain words, phrases, and sentences. Five of the quotations from LN that we wished to incorporate in this volume were too lengthy to be placed in footnotes, and so we have added a short appendix containing this material. Footnotes

12   Notes of a conversation between John Quinn and Frederick Crowe, 18 October 1984.

to the text refer the reader to the appendix at the relevant places. If LN contains abbreviations of words, we have, where necessary, completed the words in square brackets.

We have already mentioned Lonergan's concern about what he called the narrowly Catholic tone of the lectures. We may add (by way of explanation, not by way of apology — for the 'tone' was adapted to the audience and their situation), that those registering for the Institute were largely teachers in the Catholic school system of the United States, and that the system was fighting for survival in a not altogether friendly society. Moreover, the majority of the audience were religious who lacked the philosophic basis that Lonergan claimed would give them surety in dealing with divergent views on education; one gets a sense of this parochial climate by looking at the group picture of the participants, male and female, in the great variety of their religious habits.

We wish to thank all who have contributed to the work that has resulted in this volume, including Stan Tillman for his initiative in regard to the Institute and his painstaking recording of the lectures, John Dowling and Frank Dorr (and their helpers) for their early typescript, Philip McShane and Patrick Byrne for their advice on the mathematics and science sections, Fred Lawrence for his several helpful suggestions, and others who have collaborated in various ways: L.J. Flynn, W.A. Stewart, Terry Walsh, William Mathews, William Loewe, Michael G. Shields, Geoffrey Williams, George Schner, Robert Croken, and Marcela Dayao. And very special thanks, of course, are due to John and James Quinn (with a word too for John's wife, Marta Alina, for her work on the text), not only for their initiative and excellent work in the project of transcribing and editing the lectures for publication but also for their patience with the difficult and complicated process of bringing the volume to publication.

ROBERT M. DORAN (for the team of editors)

Philosophy of Education

Any subject involves a set of basic terms and relations

Every subject has developed and will develop : the basic terms & relations
are not a unique set but a changing set

Man is polymorphic : there are basic orientations that modify the distribution
of emphasis, the hierarchy of values, the direction of development, in the basic sets of
terms & relations : empiricist, idealist, realist; aesthetic, ethical, religious;
sensate, idealistic, identerial; mixed-up or immature & developing

Philosophies are pure expressions of human polymorphism : "philosophies of ..."
are applied expressions of the same polymorphism

Philosophy of maths, natural science, human science, history, religion, education

Philosophy of education is concerned the polymorphism of man in educational theorists,
colleges for teachers, administrators, teachers, parents, pupils, society

1. Not philosophy in sense of Wolff : abstract ens = possible; logic ontology cosmology ...
But ens = comprehensive, omnia de omnibus (as notion "concrete")
underpins, penetrates, relates, goes beyond all contents

‡1 Not philosophy as opposed to, exclusion of theology
Roman philosophy : potentially (prior to concrete) formally. (in concrete)

2. Not philosophy, as general concepts, principles — relevant to some abstract aspect.
but philosophy as comprehensive, as grounding and unifying all
particular disciplines

Part of page 20 of the notebook (LN) discussed above (Editor's Preface,
pp. xiii, xvi, xvii). Pages 20 and 21 of the notebook are printed in
appendix A to this volume (pp. 259–61).

TOPICS IN EDUCATION

Lectures on the Philosophy of Education

1

The Problem of a Philosophy of Education[1]

1   Philosophy of Education: Existence[2]

I think the first question that arises with regard to the topic 'philosophy of education' is, What is the good of it? I will argue that its value is not merely negative, but also that the discovery and articulation of its positive function calls for originality and creativity. For traditionalist responses to modern philosophies of education are inadequate, and the formulation of a truly satisfactory alternative will demand that we face complicated technical issues that take seriously the context of contemporary learning.[3]

1.1   A Merely Negative Conception of Philosophy of Education

The simplest answer, then, to the question of the value of the philosophy of education would be on the analogy of Herbert Butterfield's response to a similar question regarding the value of history. Butterfield, as you know, is a distinguished English historian who revised the previous interpretation of English history. In his *History and Human Relations*,[4] he asks whether it

---

1 The first lecture, Monday, August 3, 1959. Lonergan began by asking the participants to tell him if he was not speaking loudly enough. 'Raise your hand, and I'll raise my voice,' he said, and then added, 'I don't know what to do if it's *too* loud.'
2 This is the heading given on LN 22.
3 The previous two sentences are added by the editors, but relying on Lonergan's notes. They help give an overview of this lecture as a unit.
4 Herbert Butterfield, *History and Human Relations* (London: Collins, 1951). See pp. 171–72.

would make any practical difference if people knew no history at all, and he answers that people could probably get along just as well as they do now in the conduct of their affairs public and private even if there were no history. The trouble is, says Butterfield, there is a great deal of history that is bad history, that has disastrous effects in all directions, and this makes history a matter of the greatest practical importance: bad history must be replaced by good history. A similar negative value might be claimed for the philosophy of education, and then perhaps no more would be expected of it than such a negative value, pulling up the weeds and correcting wrong ideas.

1.2 The Influence of Dewey's Philosophy of Education

The fact is, however, that philosophy of education has had an enormous influence. In the United States, the Orient, the Middle East, and Europe, there will be a centennial celebration for John Dewey (1859–1952) in October of this year.[5] Dewey is known here and abroad for his philosophy of education. It is a philosophy of education that has exerted a profound and widespread influence. It is a philosophy of education that connects ideas on education with fundamental ideas on philosophy. Dewey conceives human knowledge as a transition from a problematic situation to an improved situation. That transition involves two components, namely, reflection and action. Either component alone he considers an aberration. Action without reflection is blind, routine, unprogressive. Reflection without action, on his philosophy, is meaningless, for according to Dewey knowing is not retrospective, not conformist, not absolute – knowing by itself is nothing – but prospective, reformist, hypothetical.[6] It is a matter of planning action and forming new hypotheses after the action has been performed. It is a continuous matter of adjustment to situations. It pertains to a process in which problematic situations are transformed into improved situations, and there is always room for more improvement, always room for more reflection.

That concept of knowledge and of reality results in the closest correlation between philosophy and education.[7] Philosophy is reflection on the human

---

5 LN 17 presents an extensive bibliography of the works of Dewey.
6 LN 22 adds, 'it is instrumental.'
7 Lonergan first said, 'That concept of knowledge and of reality is intimately linked with the notion of education,' then, 'Or, rather,' with the corrected sentence of the text.

situation at an ultimate level.[8] It is fundamental thinking about the human situation. And education is the great means for transforming the human situation.[9] It changes people's minds and wills, and it does so at the age when such change can be most easily produced – 'Get them when they're young!' Consequently, philosophy and education are interdependent.[10] Philosophy is the reflective component, and education is the active component, at the ultimate level of reflection and action in human life. Philosophy is the guide and the inspiration of education, and education is the verification, the pragmatic justification, of a philosophy. You see, then, how the two notions of philosophy and education are linked in the closest possible manner in Dewey's thought.[11]

Now it can be argued that Dewey's correlation between philosophy and education, while undoubtedly it has influenced education in this country and elsewhere to a tremendous extent, has been invalidated by the results, and this, indeed, according to Dewey's own principles. For there has been a spate of books of late, such as *Educational Wastelands*,[12] *Quackery in the Public Schools*,[13] *So Little for the Mind*,[14] *Why Johnny Can't Read*,[15] attacking what seem to be the fruits of Dewey's ideas on education; and according to Dewey, an educational philosophy has to be discarded if it is found not to work. But the fact of the matter is that Dewey's philosophy, his tendencies, are not treated simply as a hypothesis to be dropped because they are found not to work. The debate continues, and, very conveniently for us, an account of that debate has been worked out by Mortimer Adler and Milton

8 Two distinct drafts Lonergan made as he prepared these lectures read: '*Philosophy* is ultimate but practical reflection on human situation' (LN 18) and 'Philosophy is ultimate (practical) reflection on the existing human situation' (LN 22).
9 LN 18: 'Education is supreme action for changing human situation.'
10 LN 22: 'they are two moments in a single process.'
11 LN 18 adds: '*Moral good* is not just *Kantian good will* apart from results, since will is not good if there are no results; it is not utilitarian results apart from intention, and intentions are selected and made effective by motives.
    "*Moral criterion* is not Kantian category, absolute; it is not utilitarian criterion of what in past was satisfying; but it is what *will be* satisfying.
    "*Moral conflict* is not between rational and hedonistic self, not between long-term and short-term expedience, but between the self already realized and the self-to-be-realized.'
12 Arthur E. Bestor, *Educational Wastelands: The Retreat from Learning in Our Public Schools* (Urbana, IL: University of Illinois Press, 1953).
13 Albert Lynd, *Quackery in the Public Schools* (Boston: Little, Brown, 1953).
14 Hilda Marion Neatby, *So Little for the Mind* (Toronto: Clarke, Irwin, 1957).
15 Rudolf Franz Flesch, *Why Johnny Can't Read – And What You Can Do about It* (New York: Harper, 1955).

Mayer in the small book, *The Revolution in Education*,[16] where an effort is made at a logical clarification of the issues in education at the present time.

1.3 Traditionalists and Modernists

The authors divide the dissenting schools with three dichotomies. There are aristocrats or democrats, realists or idealists, traditionalists or modernists. These are simply labels for stereotypes, for logical clarification of this issue.

The aristocratic tendency is to reserve education for the few, at some level or all levels of education. The democratic tendency promotes college degrees for everyone. The realistic attitude is to keep things going, see what can be done in the concrete situations we have, and the idealistic is to move on, to do something more, always something more. But these two divisions are not the fundamental point of dissent at the present time. The aristocrats either are nonexistent in America or they are very ineffective – no one can set up a program on the basis of education for the few. Again, the realists, since they believe simply in standing pat with things as they are and making only such advances as seem concretely possible, do not need a theory, and consequently they are not in the debate. That leaves the debate to democratic idealists who are either traditionalists or modernists.[17]

The opposition between traditionalists and modernists is set forth by Adler and Mayer under three headings.[18] First, both traditionalists and modernists affirm liberal education, but the modernists hold that all questions of value, and so all questions of the aims and ends of education, must be settled by the methods of empirical science; and once they make that claim, they are excluding entirely the traditionalist view of a liberal education. Thus, while both are striving for liberal education, they mean by it totally different things. The agreement on this point is verbal and nugatory.

In the second place, both traditionalists and modernists advocate a sim-

16 Mortimer Adler and Milton Mayer, *The Revolution in Education*, with an introduction by Clarence Faust (Chicago: University of Chicago Press, 1958). Lonergan added further bibliographical information here, and gave page numbers for his references at various points in the lecture.
17 Lonergan added in an aside, 'And the word "modernist" is not used in the sense of the heresy that occurred in the church at the beginning of this century.'
18 Adler and Mayer, *The Revolution in Education* 152–56.

plification of an overloaded and congested curriculum, but their ways of going about this task are again opposed. We might say very schematically that the modernists tend to reduce mathematics and philosophy in favor of the empirical sciences, to reduce the study of languages and literatures in favor of social psychology, sociology, and current affairs, and to solve issues by moving to details, to techniques of gathering and sifting information. Against this modernist tendency, there is the opposite traditionalist tendency, which favors mathematics and philosophy, languages and literature, as the medium of education. Instead of appealing to techniques of gathering and sifting information, the traditionalist appeals to principles. So, while both groups want a simplification of the program, still they want to go about it on the basis of entirely different criteria, and they head in quite opposite directions.

Thirdly, both the traditionalists and the modernists acknowledge the relevance of the past to the present – education is not simply a new beginning; but the modernists hold that the wisdom of the past has to be reformulated as a scientific hypothesis and verified, and apart from that its value is nothing, while the traditionalists will not accept the view that all ideas are to be put into the form of scientific hypotheses and judged by the degree of empirical verification obtainable by strictly empirical methods.

Behind this thoroughgoing opposition in education there is an opposition in philosophy, and the difference between the traditionalists and the modernists on this point is that the modernists have a philosophy made specifically for educational purposes, while the traditionalists, taken as a total group, have not. It is for this reason that a positive alternative to the traditionalist response must be attempted.[19]

The modernist tendency in philosophy may be summed up under five headings.[20]

First, nothing is to be taken for granted or accepted on blind faith; everything is to be questioned.

Secondly, there is no fixed reality to be known; reality is process; knowledge is an ever changing component within the human process; there is no fixed reality and no fixed knowledge.

Thirdly, the methods of empirical science are the only valid methods; and the significant word here is *only*. These methods settle *all* questions, not

19 We have added this sentence, relying on LN 23, in order to highlight the emphasis of this lecture. See above, note 3.
20 Adler and Mayer, *The Revolution in Education* 157–62.

merely in natural science, but also in philosophy, in morals, and in religion; not only in what is common to man and the rest of the material universe, but in everything distinctively and basically human as well. In reliance on Dewey, the modernists hold for the universal and exclusive validity of the methods of empirical science.

In the fourth place, therefore,[21] there is needed a reconstruction in philosophy – Dewey has a book on the subject.[22] All the wisdom of the past, and consequently the whole traditionalist position, has to be reformulated as scientific hypothesis; it has to be cast in scientific terms, submitted to scientific testing and verification, before it can be named knowledge. Where it is named knowledge, it has just the validity that the theories and conclusions of empirical science can have. Not only is this demand for an exclusively empirical method a logical consequence of the previous point on the philosophic tradition,[23] but also it is urged on the ground that traditional wisdom is simply the product and reflection of a prescientific, preindustrial, predemocratic age and society.[24] Consequently, by the mere fact that it is the product of an age so different from our own, it is to be questioned at least, and indeed to be doubted.

Finally, on the basis of this philosophy we are told that 'experience – always in the process of being reevaluated – is not only the best teacher; it is the *only* teacher.'[25] So 'education must go either "backward to the intellectual and moral standards of a prescientific age or forward to a greater utilization of scientific method in the development of the possibilities of a growing, expanding experience." '[26]

So much for the philosophy of the modernist position. There were five points: first, nothing is to be taken for granted or accepted on blind faith; secondly, there is no fixed reality to be known – knowledge is a component

21 'Therefore' is added on the basis of LN 23 verso.

22 John Dewey, *Reconstruction in Philosophy* (Boston: Beacon Press, 1948).

23 Thus Lonergan in his lecture. LN 23 verso reads, 'Not only is this the logical philosophic requirement from the methodological assumption but also ...'

24 We have taken the words from 'but also' from LN 23 verso. In his lecture, Lonergan said, 'but also it is constantly urged that the ground of traditional wisdom is simply the product of the reflection of a prescientific, preindustrial, predemocratic age.'

25 Adler and Mayer, *The Revolution in Education* 160.

26 Ibid. 159, quoting Dewey but without reference. The two quoted passages in this paragraph are enclosed within quotation marks in Lonergan's notes (LN 23 verso) – we follow his usage.

in an ever changing process; thirdly, the methods of empirical science are the only valid methods; fourthly, these are to be applied to the whole of traditional wisdom, which is simply the product of a prescientific, preindustrial, predemocratic age and society, and consequently is not to be expected to be very relevant to our quite different times; and finally, the great appeal is to be to experience.

The traditionalist position is set out at greater length by Adler and Mayer.[27] They urge that the traditionalist would say that things exist prior to changing, and change does not eliminate all previous properties; some are permanent. Within the field of science methods differ widely, and there are still greater differences between these scientific methods and the methods proper to mathematics or philosophy or ethics.[28] Finally, there are certain truths accessible to a prescientific, preindustrial, and predemocratic age, and these truths hold for any age.

You can see that there is a weakness in that answer, at least in the way I have summed it up. An educational philosophy that appeals to the immutable elements in things, to their eternal properties, to the truths that hold in any age, and simply urges that empirical methods are not the only methods, really is defending a negative position. It is not offering a vision, an understanding, a principle of integration and judgment, and the great power that are offered on the modernist side by their close correlation between fundamental philosophic notions and educational theory.[29] If one appeals simply to what is immutable, then one appeals to what holds equally for the education of primitives, ancient Egyptians, Greeks and Romans, medieval and Renaissance men, people at the time of the Enlightenment of the eighteenth century, and people today. And that is not meeting the challenge. It grounds an abstract education for abstract human beings.[30]

It will not do, then, to ascribe a merely negative value to the philosophy of education.[31] Let us attempt, then, to grasp the idea of a philosophy of edu-

27 Ibid. 163–73.
28 Our wording here is based on LN 23 verso. In his lecture Lonergan said 'the methods proper to philosophy or mathematics.'
29 LN 22 has the two handwritten headings 'Negative Value: Butterfield' and 'Positive,' and then under 'Positive,' 'Underst[anding] Integr[ation] Judgment Power.'
30 The last sentence is based on LN 23 verso, which reads at this point, 'Not all: but seems to ground abstract education for abstract men.'
31 This sentence was added by the editors, as was the conclusion of the next sentence, from 'as providing ...' See above, notes 3 and 19.

cation as something positive, as providing the vision missing in the traditionalist response.[32]

1.4 The Renaissance Ideal and Philosophy

At the beginning of his posthumously published work *Die Krisis der europäischen Wissenschaften und die transzendentale Phänomenologie*,[33] Edmund Husserl made a point that I think will be helpful to us. He urged that 'Western man'[34] can be conceived simply as an anthropological classification, a technical term in anthropology, a geographic designation of a civilization; or, on the other hand, it can be conceived as the Renaissance conceived man. The Greeks of fourth-century Athens took current words in their culture – *epistêmê, sophia, alêtheia* – and gave them a meaning, imposed upon them an *Umdeutung*, a shift of meaning, with the result that the words came to signify

32 There are several crossed out passages on LN 22 that are relevant here. Before treating Dewey Lonergan had written about the connection of education and philosophy in Aristotelian philosophy: 'Aristotle's Metaphysics opens with a distinction between specialized instances of sophia and sophia in general.

'The educationalist needs a universal sophia: on his judgments and decisions rest the formation of the coming generation, the kinds of knowledge and the measure of each that will be had, the moral ideals and the moral habits of the people.

'Especially since educationalists hold a monopoly that is enforced by law.'

Then the notes go on to Dewey: 'Link with philosophy acknowledged not only by Aristotelians.'

After the notes on Dewey, LN 22 has (crossed out): 'The link that has been established is, not between education and philosophy of education, but between education and philosophy.

'The educationalist has to be, not just a man who has read extracts from the philosophers who happen to have said something about education, but a full philosopher, and indeed a philosopher of the most daring and thoroughgoing kind, the kind that uses his philosophy to settle the state of our schools, colleges, universities and to exert the profoundest type of influence on the mentality, ideals, and spirit of the future of the nation.

'He is the nearest approach to Plato's philosopher king. De facto, he is king; it is the hope of philosophers to help him towards philosophy.'

33 Edmund Husserl, *Die Krisis der europäischen Wissenschaften und die transzendentale Phänomenologie: Eine Einleitung in die phänomenologische Philosophie*, ed. Walter Biemel (The Hague: Martinus Nijhoff, 1954; 2nd printing, 1962) 5–14. In English, *The Crisis of European Sciences and Transcendental Phenomenology: An Introduction to Phenomenological Philosophy*, trans. David Carr (Evanston: Northwestern University Press, 1970) 7–16.

34 So expressed on LN 24 and on the tape. Husserl's expression is *das europäische Menschentum*. See, for example, *Krisis* 5.

something of which the average Athenian had no notion whatsoever. The Renaissance discovery of the ancients retrieved an idea of man that involved the negation of merely traditional power and merely traditional norms, and the affirmation of human reason and human freedom as the ultimate principles in individual life and in human society. According to Husserl, the ideal of man as endowed with reason and freedom, and as destined to base his life and the life of human society upon reason and freedom – upon reason as opposed to merely traditional norms, and upon freedom as opposed to merely traditional power – was the ideal that captured the Renaissance.

The implement and carrier of that ideal was philosophy. But since the Middle Ages philosophy has been understood in any of three quite different manners, and, I submit, none of them is satisfactory for our purposes.[35]

First, there was philosophy as it functioned in the context of the medieval symbiosis of theology, philosophy, the liberal arts, and the sciences.[36]

Second, there was philosophy as a distinct discipline and department, completely autonomous, recognizing the right and the truth of a revealed religion, but still proceeding exclusively in the light of its own criteria and its own methods. From about the year 1230,[37] the distinction between philosophy and theology was clearly drawn, but the separation of philosophy and theology emerges in full clarity in the work of Descartes. What is not clear in Descartes, of course, is the distinction between philosophy and science. He proves the conservation of momentum, for example, from the immutability of God. And while there is effectively the distinction between philosophy and science in Newton, there is not yet the verbal distinction. Newton named his great work *Philosophiae naturalis principia mathematica* – *The Mathematical Principles of Natural Philosophy*. He thought he was doing philosophy in presenting his theory of universal gravitation.

So first, you can conceive philosophy in the sense of the medieval living together with theology, and secondly you can conceive philosophy as a totally distinct and independent department that appeals to reason and acknowledges the existence of revealed truth, but that itself is something

---

35 Some editing is involved in this paragraph, based on what Lonergan would later say about these conceptions of philosophy. See below, § 3.

36 LN 24: 'mediaeval philosophy living in symbiosis with theology though distinct from theology from about 1230.'

37 The significance of this date is discussed in some detail below in chapter 10, § 4. See also Bernard Lonergan, *Grace and Freedom: Operative Grace in the Thought of St. Thomas Aquinas*, ed. J. Patout Burns (New York: Herder and Herder, 1971) 15–17, 19, and *Method in Theology* (Toronto: University of Toronto Press, 1990) 310.

different and separate. A third conception of philosophy regards philosophy as the successor to religion, as the supreme arbiter in all things. The philosophy of the *philosophes*, the thinkers of the Enlightenment,[38] was philosophy in this third sense, philosophy as an affirmation of human reason and human freedom as the ultimate basis of human life. It emphasized in particular the negation of merely traditional norms and merely traditional power, the negation that in the French Revolution dispossessed the king, the feudal nobility, and the church. The fertility of this idea, ramifying into countless fields of thought and activity, steadily promoted individualism, democracy, and state-controlled secularist education. It did so both directly and indirectly, though of course with varying degrees of consistency and efficacy. Philosophy, not merely in the sense of something distinct and separate from theology, but as the ultimate norm, an absolute self-affirmation by man, has been the inspiration of philosophies of education, as of the whole modern movement.

Philosophy in this third sense has taken two main forms: naturalism in the English-speaking world and to a large extent in France, and historicism in Germany. For the naturalists, the model of science and of all human knowledge is natural science. Specifically at the time of the Enlightenment, it was Newton's mechanics. Later the evolutionary doctrine of Darwin would replace this model. But historicism differs fundamentally from both. Here the human spirit is to be distinguished from nature. The basic category is not mechanical nor evolutionary law, but meaning. Meaning is the vehicle that brings men together, that guides their enterprises, that provides the field in which the human spirit develops and human freedom is exercised. There is a radical difference, then, between secularist thought in the German tradition and secularist thought in France, England, and the United States. The basic category does not have to do with atoms or law or evolution, but lies rather in the entirely different field of meaning. Husserl's solution to the crisis of European sciences is within the field of meaning. That historicist tendency was formulated in the nineteenth century by the German idealist philosophers and the German historians, and their heirs in this century are the existentialists.

Secularist philosophy, of course, led spontaneously to a secularist education. If the basis of human life is human reason and human freedom and

38 Lonergan here referred to the 'extremely sympathetic account of the Enlightenment by Ernst Cassirer' translated into English as *The Philosophy of the Enlightenment*, trans. Fritz C.A. Koelln and James P. Pettegrove (Princeton: Princeton University Press, 1951).

nothing else, if we are to have in 'Western man' a fundamental affirmation of human dignity as the basis of the whole of human life and society, then education simply has to be secularist. It is not quite consistent, of course, that it also be state-controlled. After all, state control is just the opposite of human freedom, since it sets up a machine. State control seems to have resulted first of all from nineteenth-century notions on economics. The tax-payer pays for education, and since politicians have control over the disposal of the revenue, they have also the duty, the obligation, to provide for and control education. If the politicians get the money, politicians have to run the schools. Second, Robert Nisbet in *The Quest for Community*[39] outlines a constant sociological tendency of the Western world for the central power to back the progressive individual against small groups. In general, groups smaller than the central power were reactionary. They were blocking the way for the new ideas of the bright individuals. The state regularly backed these individuals, broke the power of the smaller groups, and consequently, simply by backing individuals, concentrated all power into its own hands. That tendency reappears in education. Perhaps a third motive for state control is the fact that, if education were not controlled by the state, it would be ecclesiastically controlled. That is something that the secularist cannot acknowledge. Education is the affirmation of human nature, human reason, human freedom, and not of an ecclesiastical organization.

In any case, it is state control that brought to birth the function and the class of educationalists. To obtain money from taxpayers, politicians, the rich, foundations, to plan and construct buildings, their adjuncts and equipment, their libraries and laboratories, to devise curricula, set standards, impose tests, to select, train, organize, direct, inspect, hire and fire teachers and professors – for such tasks there were needed, not mathematicians nor scientists nor linguists nor litterateurs nor historians nor economists nor sociologists nor psychologists nor philosophers nor theologians nor even pedagogues. There had to be created a new caste, a priesthood of the new philosophy, the men of universal wisdom able to consult and judge specialists in any particular field. To be able to select and judge all the specialists and pass the ultimate pronouncements on all issues, there was needed a universal wisdom; and the universal wisdom that is the justification of the educationalist is philosophy of education.

39 Robert A. Nisbet, *The Quest for Community* (New York: Oxford University Press, 1953; reissued in 1962 under the title, *Community and Power*, then reissued again in 1969 under the original title). See, for example, p. 228 in the 1969 text.

The idea of the existence of that class is of course challenged by Robert Hutchins in his book *The University of Utopia*.[40] Utopia for Hutchins is very much like the United States except that it follows his ideas on education. The university would consist of about twenty-five professors selected from different fields, and 250 students. Thus there would be no need for an organizational superstructure. The president could be an active professor. Hutchins's proposal that each institute be a self-governing, independent unit would abolish the educationalists. It also would probably tend practically to eliminate the philosophy of education, though it would hardly eliminate it at least logically, since Hutchins's book itself rests upon a philosophy of education, and also since the movement of secularist philosophy, the ultimate affirmation of man as the guide of his own destiny, is not the only question involved in the notion of a philosophy of education. There are further problems.[41]

I have summarized[42] the logical presentation of the issue offered by Adler and Mayer in *The Revolution in Education*, with their antithesis between modernists and traditionalists. I have noted that a merely logical categorization of the issues is static rather than dynamic, and leaves the traditionalists at the great disadvantage of merely carrying on instead of possessing a vision of what ought to be. The nature of such a vision and some of its varieties I then attempted to illustrate briefly by starting from Edmund Husserl's concept of 'Western man' as not merely an anthropological classification but an ideal, an exemplar for mankind. With the problem thus set, I now propose to consider certain new factors in contemporary education that make it impossible simply to maintain a traditionalist view.[43] Later I will argue that one of these factors, what I am calling the new learning, points the way to an alternative that is not simply secularist. The school that I went to may have been backward, but what I was brought up on was Latin, Greek, and math-

40 Robert Maynard Hutchins, *The University of Utopia* (Chicago: The University of Chicago Press, 1953). Lonergan gave the bibliographical data.
41 The last sentence in this paragraph is provided from LN 24 verso.
42 A break was taken at this point. Before the break Lonergan said he had been treating general problems, and was going to go on to particular problems. At this point he is summing up the general problems. Some of his summary is missing from the tape. The tape begins, 'Thirdly, I gave a logical presentation ...' The notes of Frederick E. Crowe indicate that the first two items in the summary had to do with the merely negative conception of philosophy of education and the positive conception of education as a principle of power, to be found in Dewey's work.
43 The words from 'that make it ...' and the following sentence ('Later ...') are added by the editors.

ematics; that type of education is vanishing, and we must examine some of the fundamental factors tending to bring that about. They are of more concern to us. My second point, then, treats three of these factors.

2   New Factors in Contemporary Education[44]

2.1 The Masses

The first new factor is the masses. In 150 years the population of the earth has increased by 1,000 million. The increase has been possible in virtue of modern commerce, industry, and technology. To think of liquidating our industrial and technological societies is to think of liquidating the greater part of the earth's present population. As it was technology that made the increase of population possible, so the destruction of technology would mean reversing the increase in population. The masses are there, and they constitute a pedagogical problem. According to some estimates, one-third cannot learn from books; and of that one-third the really hard core cannot learn even from manual exercises. The easy solution would be to substitute a custodial system for an educational system, a place to keep children from the age of six until the industrial machine feels it can absorb them. But the ultimate issue was put by Johan Huizinga, the Dutch historian who wrote *The Waning of the Middle Ages*[45] and *Men and Ideas*.[46] In *Men and Ideas* he quotes Rostovtzeff's *The Social and Economic History of the Roman Empire*:

> ... the ultimate problem remains like a ghost, ever present and unlaid: Is it possible to extend higher civilization to the lower classes without debasing its standard and diluting its quality to the vanishing point? Is not every civilization bound to decay as soon as it begins to penetrate the masses?[47]

This is a contemporary problem that faces everyone in education.

44 The heading on LN 25 reads, 'Philosophy of Education, 2. Further aspects'.
45 Johan Huizinga, *The Waning of the Middle Ages: A Study of the Forms of Life, Thought and Art in France and the Netherlands in the XIVth and XVth Centuries*, trans. F. Hopman (London: E. Arnold and Co., 1924).
46 Johan Huizinga, *Men and Ideas: History, the Middle Ages, the Renaissance*, trans. James S. Holmes and Hans van Marle (New York: Meridian Books, 1959).
47 Mikhael Ivanovich Rostovtzeff, *The Social and Economic History of the Roman Empire* (Oxford: The Clarendon Press, 1926) 487; quoted in Huizinga, *Men and Ideas* 51. Lonergan's quotation, both on LN 25 and on the tape, is a bit different from the printed text.

2.2 The New Learning

A second contemporary development is the new learning. There has been a
succession of waves of new learning in the history of Western civilization:
the Carolingian schools, three waves introducing Aristotle in the medieval
period, the humanist movement with its discovery of Greek letters and literature, the movement of modern science. But the new learning with which
we are concerned is not merely an addition to old subjects, but their transformation. There has occurred within this century (more or less – the fundamental work was done in the last century) a revolution in the very
conception of mathematics. A second revolution has affected the conception of natural science. Relativity and quantum theory yield a notion of natural science that is quite different from the notion developed by Galileo and
Newton. Thirdly, we have witnessed the emergence and development of
modern languages and modern literatures. Renaissance-educated people
were supposed to speak Latin, write Greek, and read Hebrew, but at the
present time there is an endless number of other and contemporary languages and literatures. This transforms the whole question of the study of
language, literature, and history. Fourthly, there have been discoveries in
paleontology and archeology, the finding and decipherment of ancient
texts, and the resultant knowledge of the civilizations of Sumer and Babylon
and Assyria, of Egypt and Crete. Linear B, the third of the Cretan scripts, for
example, was deciphered within the past few years by an English architect
named Ventris. Finally, there is the advance of the human sciences, mani-
fested especially in depth psychology and genetic psychology and in the revolution that has occurred in economic thinking since the Depression.
Within the past few decades we have also witnessed the emergence of a new
type of historical thinking quite different from the nineteenth-century
approach.[48] It is illustrated by Arnold Toynbee in England[49] and by Eric
Voegelin, who has published three volumes in a series entitled *Order and
History*.[50] Voegelin gives a brilliant new interpretation of history that is very

48 LN 25: 'the emergence of broad historical thinking (Toynbee, Voegelin)'.
49 Arnold J. Toynbee, *A Study of History*, 12 vols. (London: Oxford University
    Press, 1934–61).
50 Eric Voegelin, *Order and History*, vol. 1: *Israel and Revelation*; vol. 2: *The World of
    the Polis*; vol. 3: *Plato and Aristotle* (Baton Rouge: Louisiana State University
    Press, 1956, 1957). The fourth volume, *The Ecumenic Age*, was published in
    1974, and an incomplete fifth volume, *In Search of Order*, was published post-
    humously in 1987. Lonergan added that any of us would be very proud if we
    wrote German as well as Voegelin writes English.

sympathetic to religion, though just where he stands is another question. There is, then, a new learning in mathematics and natural science, in languages and literatures and history, and in the human sciences of both the individual and the group.

2.3 Specialization

A third contemporary problem is specialization. The new learning is mountainous and unassimilated. Eric James, who was principal of Manchester Grammar School before becoming headmaster at Eton, remarks in a little essay on the content of the curriculum that when Arnold of Rugby wanted a teacher, he looked around for a Christian, a gentleman, and a scholar.[51] Today educational institutes advertise for specialists in physics, mathematics, and chemistry, not for a Christian, a gentleman, and a scholar. This specialization very easily results in a notion of education as the information belt supplying students with a great number of pieces and leaving to them the task of putting together what the professors cannot put together themselves. Einstein remarks in his autobiography[52] that things were bad enough when he was a young man, because there was so much to be prepared for examinations that it was impossible to be intelligent. He says he was lucky enough to have at hand a series of volumes that communicated a grasp of the whole. But, he says, things are infinitely worse at the present time. Intelligence is a very delicate plant, requiring favorable circumstances in which to develop. Einstein does not believe it can survive under the present setup of university curricula and examination requirements.[53]

Husserl's account of the crisis in European science is concerned, I think, mainly with the human sciences, where he finds an ever increasing multiplication of specialized fields. Each is distinct and autonomous. Each

51 We have not been able to locate this essay, and Lonergan's notes offer no clues. But James's source seems to be a letter, quoted over and over in books on Thomas Arnold of Rugby, in which he says of a form master, 'What I want is a man who is a Christian and a gentleman ...,' and adds some remarks on the desired scholarship. See, for example, Michael McCrum, *Thomas Arnold Head Master: A Reassessment* (Oxford University Press, 1989) 31–32, referring (as do other authors) to Stanley's authoritative biography of Arnold; but neither Stanley nor later biographers give a date or addressee for the letter.
52 Albert Einstein, 'Autobiographical Notes,' in Paul Arthur Schilpp, ed., *Albert Einstein: Philosopher-Scientist* (New York: Macmillan, 1940) 1–95, at 14–19. Lonergan gave some of the bibliographical data in his lecture .
53 Lonergan's remarks about Einstein have been slightly reordered and supplemented, in reliance on LN 25.

is governed by merely conventional criteria. The supreme criterion is getting results, but short of getting some new results, the criterion becomes 'the right way' – the right way to enter footnotes, to perform laboratory techniques, and so on. What makes the crisis hopeless, at least from Husserl's point of view, is the fact that any attempt at unification, at finding significance in the lot, at putting things together, is regarded as just another specialization to which no other specialist need pay the slightest attention.[54]

We have, then, three fundamental questions regarding contemporary education. First, there is the problem of the masses, of how to educate everyone. Secondly, there is the new learning, which is not merely an addition to old subjects but their transformation in one way or another – it works out differently in different fields. Finally, there is the problem of specialization; the new knowledge is mountainous, divided, and unassimilated.

3   Toward a Catholic Philosophy of Education[55]

Against this background we can reflect on the problem of a philosophy of education for Catholics. Obviously we do not want a philosophy of education in the sense of secularist philosophy, where philosophy is a successor to religion – religion is a thing of the past. In much of today's education ultimate criteria come from philosophy in the sense of human reason and human freedom as ultimate.

Again, we do not want a philosophy exclusively in the Cartesian sense of philosophy as a discipline that recognizes a certain superiority of theology but proceeds simply on its own independent criteria and in accord with its own independent methods. The fact is that what we have is a Catholic educational system, with primary schools, high schools, colleges, and universities. That is the concrete fact, and it exists because it is Catholic. Again, we agree with the democratic idealists, not for their reasons, but because we consider all men to be the brothers of Christ. That is the solid basis for all democratic idealism, and it is our basis, too: 'Love one another as I have loved you' (John 15.12).[56] Thus Fr William Cunningham's book, *The Pivotal*

---

54 Lonergan refers to Husserl in a similar context in *Understanding and Being: The Halifax Lectures on Insight* (Toronto: University of Toronto Press, 1990 [CWL 5]) 190.
55 LN 26: 'Philosophy of Education, 3. The Problem for Catholics'.
56 LN 26: 'our democratic idealism rests on the secure foundation of the mystical body of Xt; whatever for the least of these ... for me.'

Problems of Education,[57] simply takes it for granted that a Catholic philosophy of education will be supernaturalist. So we are not interested in a philosophy of education simply in the Cartesian sense of a discipline separate from and, in its methods and criteria, independent of our religion.

In the third place, a contemporary philosophy of education cannot simply be the medieval symbiosis of philosophy and theology. For such a view does not provide proximate criteria for an examination of the new learning. The new learning is what has come into being since that philosophy was worked out, and that philosophy does not offer a direct synthesis for the unassimilated mass of the new learning.

I began, then, by distinguishing three senses of the word 'philosophy,' and now I find that none of the three fits, at least proximately, what is wanted for a Catholic philosophy of education at the present time. We want not the secularist philosophy, because de facto we are interested in Catholic schools and colleges, high schools and universities; not philosophy exclusively in the Cartesian sense of a separate discipline totally distinct from the Catholic religion and Catholic theology; and not directly and simply philosophy as it was thought out in the medieval period, since that philosophy is not connected intimately enough with the new learning.

There are further difficulties, however.[58] The first has to do at least with the traditional interpretation of medieval philosophy. On this view, philosophy is philosophy *simpliciter,* not 'philosophy of ...' We hear at the present time of a philosophy of mathematics, a philosophy of science, a philosophy of nature, a philosophy of history, and a philosophy of education. This mode of speech is strange to anyone brought up on scholastic fare, where philosophy is a subject by itself, not a subject of some other subject; it consists of major and minor logic, ontology, cosmology, psychology, natural theology, and ethics; it is not a philosophy of everything else.

Now, how does one get the notion of a philosophy of ...? a philosophy of *X*? What kind of a philosophy is that? That raises a rather technical philosophic problem. I think you will see a connection between it, though, and my book *Insight,*[59] and this from two angles.

57 William F. Cunningham, *The Pivotal Problems of Education: An Introduction to the Christian Philosophy of Education* (New York: Macmillan, 1940). Fr Cunningham was in attendance at these lectures. Lonergan in an aside said, 'It's in my notes; I didn't know we'd have the honor of having Fr Cunningham with us.'
58 Lonergan said, 'There is a further difficulty, however,' and went on to speak of the problem of 'philosophy of ...' In fact, though, this was but the first of four 'further difficulties.'
59 Bernard J.F. Lonergan, *Insight: A Study of Human Understanding* (2nd rev. ed.,

Insofar as one attends merely to concepts, one can think of universals being applied to particulars: the universals would be the philosophy, and the particulars that to which they are applied. But you also have to think of understanding, insight, as the ground of conception. This understanding arises from sensible data. If we think in this way, we will see a quite different relation between intelligence and sensible data. Intelligence, understanding as insight, as the ground of conception, has a quite different relationship with the particular and the concrete from the relationship found in the abstract concepts 'the universal' and 'the particular.' There are, then, at least two ways of having a theoretical discipline connected with particulars: one through insight into phantasm, the other through the subsumption of particulars under universals. (Later we will see a further mode that can be developed out of a mathematical notion of fundamental importance at the present time, group theory.)[60]

A second difficulty is that medieval thought was not historical thought. It was concerned with eternal, timeless truths rather than with genesis, development, history. But the problem of education is the problem of education *today*, the problem of educating, not primitives, ancient Egyptians or Greeks, medievals or people of the Renaissance, but people of today. It is the problem of the development of the individual up to the level of the times, the level of development reached by Western culture and civilization.[61] How do you bring *today* into the categories of any philosophy? It cannot be done if philosophy deals simply with timeless truths. How do you incorporate into your philosophic ideas such a notion as *the present time?*

London: Longmans, Green, and Co., 1958; 5th ed., revised and augmented, Toronto: University of Toronto Press, 1992 [CWL 3]). Our page references are to the Collected Works edition.

60 The problem of 'philosophy of ...' clearly was a matter of major concern to Lonergan as he worked out these lectures. In fact 'philosophy of ...' is a category recurrent in Lonergan's thinking at this time. See the course notes *De intellectu et methodo* (Gregorian University, 1958–59, spring semester) 47, where we have the Latin equivalent 'philosophia de ...'; this may be the earliest occurrence. See also the notes from his lecture on the philosophy of history (Thomas More Institute, Montreal, September 23, 1960) p. 8 of transcript; and the 1961 paper 'Openness and Religious Experience' in *Collection*, ed. Frederick E. Crowe and Robert M. Doran (Toronto: University of Toronto Press [CWL 4]) 185.

In handwritten notes connected with these lectures – the notes are headed 'Philosophy of Education' – we find two lengthy treatments of the question. These are given below in the appendix, § A.

61 This sentence is supplied from LN 26.

Again, how do you account in your philosophy for the notion of the developing individual, the prephilosophic individual who may become a philosopher, or function as a philosopher if he is not one? What does philosophy do with the notion of the development of the individual or the development of society? If you conceive philosophy simply as a matter of eternal, timeless truths, you have no answer to such questions. Such philosophy cannot be timely; it is timeless.

Thirdly, philosophy as traditionally conceived is essentially neutral. As you know, about the year 1930 there flared up a big dispute as to whether there could be a Christian or a Catholic philosophy. An account of the dispute and a present opinion on it can be found in Maurice Nédoncelle's *Existe-t-il une philosophie chrétienne?*[62] Is there any more a Catholic philosophy than there is a Catholic mathematics? Some would answer flatly in the negative. But if there is no more a Catholic philosophy than a Catholic mathematics, then how can we have a Catholic philosophy of education?

Fourthly, the traditional Catholic conception of philosophy is not existential. It has been concerned with the per se, not with the individual coming to grips with the meaning *for him* of true propositions. It has been concerned to pick out and label which propositions are true. But to show how propositions come to have a meaning for me in my living, what is true for men as they exist in this world at the present time, is not a question proper to Catholic philosophy as it has been traditionally conceived. That belongs rather to theology, for man as he exists in this world is affected by original sin, gifted with the offer of divine grace, and faced with the alternative of accepting or rejecting this offer. All of these determinations pertain not to philosophy but to theology. How, then, can you have a Catholic philosophy of education, if you do not consider man as he is in this world? The problem is technical, but it reaches deeply into one's very conception of a philosophy. Traditionally, the issues I have been outlining are taken care of by theology, by training in ascetics, by liturgy, the sacraments, the entire life of the church. They were not questions that were discussed, though, in philosophy. If we are to have a Catholic philosophy of education, then, we need first to provide a positive answer to the question, Is there a Catholic philosophy at all?

---

62 Maurice Nédoncelle, *Existe-t-il une philosophie chrétienne?* (Paris: Librairie Arthème Fayard, 1956). In English, *Is There a Christian Philosophy?*, trans. Dom Illtyd Trethowan (London: Burns and Oates, 1960, Faith and Fact Books: 10). Lonergan gave a fair amount of bibliographical data concerning the original French edition.

Can the difficulties I have just mentioned be turned? If they are to be turned, one has to say that medieval philosophy was a moment in a *philosophia perennis*, in a perennial philosophy. One cannot think of philosophy as something cut and dried and settled for all time several centuries ago, so that all you need do on any problem is look up the books and get the answers. Once when I was attending a meeting of the American Catholic Philosophical Association, I went into a nearby cafeteria for lunch, and noticed two priests at another table. There was a famous clinic in the city, and the priests were talking about symptoms. At first I did not catch on, but assumed they were at the philosophy convention, too. Finally, they turned to me and asked if I was at the clinic. I told them I was not, and they said, 'Well, what are you doing?' I answered that I was at the philosophy convention. 'Protestant?' they asked, and I said, 'No, Catholic.' 'Well, what are you having a Catholic convention in philosophy for? You can't change first principles!' – and they went back to their symptoms. You cannot have a Catholic philosophy of education on that basis; philosophy in the past has not been thought out in terms of concrete situations and concrete developments. That type of question was taken care of by theology.

But if one conceives the medieval philosophy as a moment in a perennial philosophy, in a philosophy that remains true to itself and yet develops, that preserves its identity and yet takes over the mastery of different successive ages, then one can, I believe, develop a Catholic philosophy of education. I believe that the perennial philosophy is essentially an open philosophy, that it can take cognizance of individual and historical developments, that it can be concrete, existential in the general sense of that term (not in the sense of particular existentialist schools), and that it can be historical, Catholic, and a 'philosophy of ...' It need not be confined simply to timeless truths and conclusions from universals to particulars. I hold that belief principally as a theologian, and in fact I consider such a development essential for Catholic theology. For Catholic theology is the theology of a historical religion that was providentially prepared by the revelation given to the Hebrews,[63] that arose at a particular point in historical time, in the fulness of time, and that has developed over the course of two thousand years. If theology is to deal with theological problems of origins and development, if it is to enter into the concrete, it must have an appropriate philosophic tool. Moreover, the Catholic religion is a religion that has a mission to men of all times and all

63 LN 26: 'it was prepared by OT and by Gk culture.'

places, and so once more it is essential that Catholic theology have a philosophic tool that can differentiate itself according to the differences of men at different times and places.[64] Finally, I also believe that such a development has its roots and its fundamental justification in what is best in the medieval tradition. Any work I have done has been largely devoted to that end. I wrote a series of articles on *gratia operans* in St Thomas. The articles are based on my doctoral thesis, which deals with human will in the concrete situation of this life.[65] Again, I studied intellectual theory in St Thomas.[66] Thirdly, my book *Insight* heads in the same direction. There is more of a tendency among non-Catholic reviewers than among Catholics to find the book very traditional, but I believe that it is fundamentally an expression of traditional thinking.

It is in this light that I wish to tackle the problem of the philosophy of education: What precisely are the types of thinking and development needed to bring our philosophic thinking into contact with a host of other problems in theology and other fields, but for us during these two weeks into contact with problems of education?

So much for my introductory discussion. The last two points concern, first of all, the things that are new in our time, the concrete meaning of this talk about a traditional wisdom suited to a preindustrial, predemocratic, prescientific age and, second, the theoretical problem of a Catholic philosophy of education. The new factors that we have to cope with are the masses, the new learning, and specialization. On the theoretical side, our problem is that, as traditionally conceived by Catholics, philosophy is not a 'philosophy of ...', not a subject of other subjects, but philosophy simply. There is a host of problems connected with that shift in conception, and some of them are very technical. I believe that shift in conception can be effected on a basis strictly in harmony with the tradition, and it will be my

---

64 LN 26: 'to understand its [Christianity's] origins and its developments, the new learning is an indispensable tool to aid it in its mission to all men of all times and places, and so of our own time, need of human sciences, their development, adjustment, integration'.

65 Bernard Lonergan, 'St. Thomas' Thought on *Gratia Operans,*' *Theological Studies* 2 (1941) 289–324; 3 (1942) 69–88; 375–402; 533–78. These articles were edited in book form, *Grace and Freedom: Operative Grace in the Thought of St. Thomas Aquinas* (see above, note 37).

66 'The Concept of Verbum in the Writings of St. Thomas Aquinas,' *Theological Studies* 7 (1946) 349–92; 8 (1947) 35–79; 404–44; 10 (1949) 3–40; 359–93. In book form, *Verbum: Word and Idea in Aquinas,* ed. David B. Burrell (Notre Dame: University of Notre Dame Press, 1967).

attempt to offer some indications as to how this can be done. That will be the contribution I can make to this Institute. I am not a specialist in education, but I have suffered under educators for very many years, and I have been teaching for an equally long time. As a physicist will listen to a mathematician, and doctors to a biologist, so in a somewhat similar fashion you can listen to me as I speak about philosophy and its relation to theology and to concrete living. But most of the concrete applications, the ironing out of things, will have to be done by you who are in the fields of education and philosophy of education.

4   Manner of Presentation

I have had to resolve a problem regarding the manner of my presentation. I could begin from a study of the nature of human intelligence and of the way in which this nature is illuminated, made more precise and more rich, by the new learning. In that fashion I would be able to tackle more directly the theoretical problems involved in the concept of a Catholic philosophy of education. But the disadvantage of proceeding in this way is that it would be difficult, except for incidental remarks, to see that my presentation is heading anywhere in particular or that it is connected in any concrete fashion with the notion, aims, and content of a Catholic education, and especially of a Catholic general education.

An alternative procedure is to presuppose for the moment an indication of the solution to the more theoretical problems, and to begin from the notion of the human good, attempting to grasp in philosophic fashion in what the human good concretely consists, and how it changes from one age to another and one country to another. What are the different levels of its integration, and consequently what is the specific good that education at the present time has to have in mind? This is the approach that I shall take. It is sixty years since Dewey wrote *The School and Society*.[67] But what, concretely, is society? Your idea of the school will be a function of your idea of society, and your idea of society is connected with your notion of the good. I can begin more concretely from the notion of the human good, from the structure of human history – because my notion of the human good is interconvertible with my notion of the structure of history – and perhaps beginning that way will be more acceptable.[68]

67 John Dewey, *The School and Society* (1899. Revised edition, Chicago: University of Chicago Press, 1915, 1943).
68 Lonergan added that he would yield to the majority opinion, and would start from the more theoretical side if that is what his listeners preferred.

I will start, then, with the good as objective development. What we will be aiming at is a philosophic concept of our age. We want an education that is education not for Renaissance man or for Catholics anywhere, because primitives can be Catholics. There are missionaries working among the Pygmies and the Bushmen, and so on, and the education they give is Catholic. But we want a Catholic education for people today in our milieu. How do you tie a philosophy to so particular a concept as 'our milieu?' How do you bring the notion of the good down to the level of concrete living? I will begin, then, from the good as an objective development, and then I will consider the good as subjective development, the developing subject. I will then move on to a more detailed account of contemporary developments in the new learning that may be helpful to you from the viewpoint of educational thought.

2

The Human Good as Object:
Its Invariant Structure[1]

1   Introduction

I wish to speak about the good. My aim is to be able to provide a basis for your discussions of the end, the aim, the goal of education. Why are people educated? Well, it is for some good. But what do you mean by the good? That is the question that will occupy us today and tomorrow, and perhaps the next day.[2]

I will consider first the good as an object[3] and then the good as the developing subject. The problem is, of course, to obtain a notion of the good that is sufficiently concrete to be relevant to a discussion of education and its aims, and at the same time sufficiently differentiated so that one will be able to discuss the differences in educational aims at different times, in different cultures, in different societies. One can say, for example, that if a man knows his eternal destiny and the moral law, he knows all he needs to know to save his soul, and so he is an educated man. That education can be given to the Catholics in Central Africa without any difficulty. But that is not exactly what we are aiming at in Catholic schools and universities in the United States. How do you derive a notion of the good that enables you to

1 The second lecture, Tuesday, August 4, 1959. But we have relocated the last part of Tuesday's lecture (see below, note 4).
2 In fact, this question occupied Lonergan all three days.
3 LN 35 has the subheading 'Objective aspect of Educational Aim, Goal, Purpose,' and under this '1. Discuss at once because well to have clear in discussion of subjects, epistemology; also in view of existentialism.'

see that, although this is an essential good, it is not all that we are aiming at in our education? That is the fundamental problem, but it is stated much more briefly and simply than it is answered.

First, then, I shall make some preliminary remarks on the notion of the good. Then I shall discuss an invariant structure of the *human* good, and of the human good *in this life*. The next life is much more important and much better, but we settle the next life in this life for ourselves and for whomever we can help. Pope Pius XII spoke of the impersonalism of modern life that is destroying souls. That impersonalism of modern life is a product of social forces in this world, but it is destroying souls eternally. It will be sufficient for us to discuss the human good *in this life*, because it is in this life that we do whatever we are to do that will settle our own eternal destiny and influence the eternal destiny of others.

An invariant structure of the human good is something that can be found in any human society. In presenting this invariant structure, however, we must speak not only about the human good, but also about evil, since the human good is not apart from evil, but in tension with it. Much of our striving for the good is a matter of fighting against evil.

Secondly, I shall discuss differentials of the human good. Here I will be employing a mathematical analogy. What makes the difference in the human good at different times we will call a differential. I will discuss three differentials: the development of intelligence, sin, and God's grace.[4]

Thirdly, I will discuss levels of integration. The second topic deals with the origin of differences at different times, the third topic with the way one adds up, integrates, those differences into a description of a situation. That is a general outline of what I will say about the human good as a developing object.

2   The Notion of the Good

2.1 Not Abstract[5]

We will start from the well-known tag *ens et bonum convertuntur,* being and the good are convertible. The good exists, and what exists is good. Philosophy

---

4 Lonergan began the discussion of the differentials at the end of this second lecture, but time ran out before he got very far. We have moved the entire discussion of the differentials into the third lecture.

5 LN 35 has the following heading for this section: '2. Verum = Ens = Bonum.'

speaks of the good as a transcendental. That is to say, the good is not confined to one of Aristotle's ten predicaments. For example, it is not true to say that only substances are good and accidents are not, or that, among the accidents, only quantity or quality or relation is good. Rather, the good is found in all of the descriptive categories. The good is not an abstract notion. It is comprehensive. It includes everything. When you speak of the good, you do not mean some aspect of things, as though the rest of their reality were evil. The good is a notion that is absolutely universal, that applies to whatever exists; and at the same time it is totally concrete. This is what I mean by saying it is a comprehensive term. This is a peculiar sort of notion, but perhaps an example will prove helpful. When we use the word 'concrete,' is the concept behind that word abstract? Are you talking about an abstraction when you talk of the concrete? That is precisely what you are not talking about. But as concepts, 'abstract' and 'concrete' seem to be quite the same. Yet you are ready to admit that when you use the word 'abstract,' you are talking about an abstraction, but you are not when you talk about the concrete. There are different types of terms, then, and terms like 'concrete,' 'good,' 'being' are comprehensive. So our first point about the good is that it is comprehensive, and hence not abstract.

2.2 Not an Aspect

Next, the good is not an aspect.[6] The definition of the good that has been current since Aristotle is *id quod omnia appetunt*, what everything seeks or runs after. However, it is not only *what* is sought or desired that is good; the capacity to desire is also good, and the desiring itself is good; and having the concrete situation in which the desiring can go on to operations through which one obtains the good is also good; and having the cooperation necessary to get there is also good. So one can see that not only what is sought is good, but also the seeking, the capacity to seek, the skills that go into the process of fulfilment, and the fulfilment itself are good.[7] The definition of the good as what everything seeks does not exhaust the notion of the good. What everyone seeks is certainly good, but there is a whole set of other elements that are related to it, and they are good too.

6 This sentence is based on LN 35. See below, note 7.
7 LN 35: 'not an aspect: id quod omnia appetunt; appetites, seeking, conditions of obtaining, fulfilment; set of appetites, interdependence, transcendent goal; all are also good.'

2.3 Not Negative

Again, the good is not negative. It is not a matter of 'don't do this' and 'don't do that.' In our upbringing, perhaps, we may have developed the idea that the good is something negative, something one achieves by not doing certain things. But it is evil that is the negation.

2.4 Not a Double Negation

Again, the good is not just a double negation. The Scotist definition of being is 'not nothing,' and if the good and being are convertible, one might say on this account that the good is just 'not evil.' But that is an attempt to think of the good abstractly.

2.5 Not Merely an Ideal

Again, the good is not merely an ideal. According to an Aristotelian tag frequently repeated by St Thomas, true and false are in the mind, but good and evil are in things.[8] The good is in things; it is something existing. The ideal is relevant to the good insofar as the existing good is incomplete and in process of completion. The good is not utopia. The good is not an ideal that does not exist and is beyond possible attainment. The good is the concrete, and the ideal is the next stage in the development of the concrete.[9]

2.6 Not Apart from Evil

Again, as I have already remarked, the good is not apart from evil in this life. In his *Enchiridion* ('Handbook') St Augustine made perhaps one of the most profound remarks in all his writings, and for that matter in the whole of theology, when he said that God could have created a world without any evil whatever, but thought it better to permit evil and draw good out of the evil.[10] We must not forget that what God wants, the world God foreknew

---

8 See Aristotle, *Metaphysics*, VI, 4, 1027b 25–27; Thomas Aquinas, *De veritate*, q. 1, a. 2.

9 LN 35: 'not merely ideal: bonum et malum sunt in rebus;"ideal" the completion of what now is incomplete but in potency really, not a mere possibility, desirability (utopian).'

10 Augustine, *Enchiridion, sive De fide, spe et caritate*, c. 11 (PL 40, 236): 'Mala cur esse sinat Deus ... Neque enim Deus omnipotens ... cum summe bonus sit, ullo modo sineret mali aliquid esse in operibus suis, nisi usque adeo esset omnipotens et bonus, ut bene faceret et de malo.'

from all eternity in all its details and freely chose according to his infinite wisdom and infinite goodness, is precisely the world in which we live, with all its details and all its aspects. This is what gives meaning to a phrase that might at times be considered trite: resignation to the will of God. God does not will any sin, either directly or indirectly. He wills only indirectly any privation or punishment. What he wills directly is the good, and only the good. Yet the good that God wills and freely chooses with infinite wisdom and infinite goodness is this world. It is a good, then, that is not apart from evil. It is a good that comes out of evil, that triumphs over evil.

2.7 Not Static

Finally, the good is not static. It is not the fulfilment of some blueprint. Man develops. He is intelligent, and successive ages learn something more. St Thomas's proof that beatitude cannot be had in this life is that beatitude is rooted in intellectual perfection, and no one in this life knows so much that later generations cannot discover something more; consequently, the only people who could have beatitude, if beatitude lay in this life, would be the last generation. Moreover, the good in this world comes out of evils, and that coming out of evils is another dynamic aspect of the good in this world.[11]

2.8 The Good Known Analogously[12]

I have said a number of things that the good is not. It is not abstract, not an aspect, not a negation, not just a double negation, not merely ideal, not apart from evil, and not static. Then what is it? You recall the passage in the Gospel where the young man said to our Lord, 'Good Master,' and our Lord replied, 'Why do you call me good? One alone is good' (Mark 10.17).[13] There is a pregnant sense of the word 'good' in which One alone is good. According to St Thomas there is a strong sense of the Aristotelian *ti esti, quid sit?* what is it? that refers to a full understanding of the object. When you

---

11 LN 35: 'not static: man develops, intell = potens omnia facere et fieri (angelic knows all at once); coming out of evils (which God permits but does not cause, positively or negatively).'
12 LN 35: 'Quid sit bonum: like quid sit ens.'
13 NRSV: 'As he was setting out on a journey, a man ran up and knelt before him, and asked him, "Good Teacher, what must I do to inherit eternal life?" Jesus said to him, "Why do you call me good? No one is good but God alone."'

ask, 'What is the good?' in that sense, you are asking, 'What is good by its essence?' 'What is good?' asks for the essence, and there is only one thing that is good by its essence, and that is God. Everything else is good by participation; just as there is only one thing that exists by its essence, and everything else exists by participation. That good, that being, is known properly, as opposed to analogously, only in the beatific vision. You know what is the good, what is being, by its essence, when you have the beatific vision. Otherwise you know them only analogously. In other words, one must attend not merely to the analogous concepts but also to analogous knowledge. Analogous knowledge is what is really important. Our knowledge of being and the good, like our knowledge of God, is analogous, because God alone is and is good by his essence. You cannot know the good by its essence unless what is good by its essence is the object. The only knowledge you can have of being or of the good through beings by participation is an analogous knowledge. Consequently, as one's knowledge of finite beings and finite goods becomes more full, more perfect, more adequate, in the same proportion one has a fuller, more adequate, more perfect basis for forming an analogous notion of what the good is.

Perhaps this will help us see what lies behind the profound contrast between Plato and Aristotle. In the *Republic* Plato wants to find out what the good man would be, and seeks to answer this question by describing the good society. At the term of the argument, he says that, if the good society is to exist, the guardians will have to know the Idea of the good. Knowing the Idea of the good is the ultimate solution to all human problems.[14] But Aristotle said in his *Ethics* that whatever may be the case with regard to the Idea of the good, obviously it cannot make much difference to the goodness of concrete human living. That is a matter of acquiring the right habits. Aristotle studies things in the concrete.[15]

Now there is a sense in which both Plato and Aristotle are correct. The Idea of the good really is God himself. The divine essence is the essence of the good, and the *only* essence of the good, the only place where the essence of the good is found. And that is the measure of all other good. And the good is mysterious because God is mysterious. As Isaiah says, 'My thoughts

---

14 The argument to which Lonergan refers cuts through the whole of Plato's *Republic.* But J.A. Stewart, whose book *Plato's Doctrine of Ideas* was important in Lonergan's development, identifies book 6, and especially the section 506e to 509b as the 'locus classicus' for Plato's Idea of the Good. See Stewart, *Plato's Doctrine of Ideas* (Oxford: Clarendon Press, 1909) 49–54.

15 See Aristotle, *Ethics*, I, 6, 1096b 27 to 1097a 14.

are above your thoughts, and my ways are above your ways' (Isaiah 55.8).[16] On the other hand, anything that exists and is good by participation is finite, and because it is finite it is not perfect in every respect; it can be criticized. The possibility of noting that it is not good in every respect, that it can be criticized, is for St Thomas the basis of human freedom. One cannot choose between God and anything else, but one can always choose between finite things, because they are finite in their being and in their goodness. They are not good from every possible viewpoint. Criticism is possible. Hence one can say that what is beyond criticism is either God or an idol, because the finite good is always open to criticism. The possibility of finding fault, of seeing that something is not perfect in every respect, is the basis of liberty. Those of you familiar with Paul Tillich will recall how he extends the notion of the idol to finite *truth* and so eliminates the absolute value of the finite truth.[17] He considers any dogmatic religion to be an idolatry simply because it attributes an absolute value to finite truth. That is mistaken — though we need not go into the argument. But the finite good cannot be treated as though it were infinite and as though it were beyond criticism, and to treat it as though it were beyond criticism is to set up an idol.

2.9   The General Notion of the Human Good

Now, while most of my illustrations thus far have been from the human good, we have not yet attended to what is specific in the human good. The good is human insofar as it is realized through human apprehension and choice. Without human apprehension and choice we would not exist — we are children of our parents. We would not have our cities, and so on. Everything in human life that we know about, apart from 'the forest primeval, the murmuring pines and the hemlocks'[18] depends upon human apprehension and choice. That is the distinctive feature of the human good — it is what comes out of human apprehension and choice. Furthermore, human apprehension develops, so that one age understands things better and knows more than the preceding age; and human choice is good or evil; and so the human good is a history, a cumulative process where there is both advance of apprehension, and distortion, aberration, due to evil.

16 NRSV: 'For my thoughts are not your thoughts, nor are your ways my ways, says the Lord.'
17 See Paul Tillich, *Systematic Theology*, vol. 1 (Chicago: The University of Chicago Press, 1951) 100–105.
18 Henry Wadsworth Longfellow, *Evangeline*, opening words:
    'This is the forest primeval. The murmuring pines and the hemlocks ...'

With regard to the human good we can repeat all our negations concerning the good in general: the human good is not an abstraction, not an aspect, not a negation, not a double negation, not a mere ideal, not something apart from evil, not static. It is not just a set of negative precepts, or of very general positive precepts. It is not a system, a legal system or a moral system. It is a history,[19] a concrete, cumulative process resulting from developing human apprehension and human choices that may be good or evil. And that concrete, developing process is what the human good in this life is, the human good on which depends man's eternal destiny.

So much for our general notion of the human good.

3   The Invariant Structure of the Human Good

3.1   The Structure

We move now to our first division, the invariant structure. What is true about the human good at any place or time? We distinguish three main aspects. They are also levels: the particular good (what St Thomas frequently speaks of as the *bonum particulare*), the good of order, and value.

3.1.1   The Particular Good

The particular good is what people usually think about when you talk about the good. It is the most manifest aspect of the good, what commonly is meant by[20] *id quod omnia appetunt,* what everything seeks. In any given

19 LN 35: 'Hence, as good is not abstraction aspect negation double-negation mere ideal, apart from evil, static; so also human good is not just a set of negative precepts, of very general positive precepts, a legal or moral system, but a history (which includes emergence of systems, their partial successes and partial failures).' For Lonergan's enduring interest in the connection of the human good with history, see 'The Transition from a Classicist World-View to Historical-Mindedness,' in *A Second Collection,* ed. William F.J. Ryan and Bernard J. Tyrrell (London: Darton, Longman & Todd, 1974) 6–7: 'If at one time law was in the forefront of human development ... at the present time it would seem that the immediate carrier of human aspiration is the more concrete apprehension of the human good effected through such theories of history as the liberal doctrine of progress, the Marxist doctrine of dialectical materialism and, most recently, Teilhard de Chardin's identification of cosmogenesis, anthropogenesis, and christogenesis.' See also 'The Human Good,' *Humanitas* 15 (1979) 126: 'what we are talking about is not simply process but historical process. It is not something of the past, it is something we are part of, it is human history, it is something in which we are involved now and for the rest of our lives.'

20 The words 'what commonly is meant by' are supplied from LN 35.

instance the particular good might be a thing, such as a new car, or an event, such as someone coming or going, or a satisfaction, or an operation. The particular good regards the satisfaction of a particular appetite. It is perfectly familiar and very simple.

3.1.2 The Good of Order

The good of order is the setup. The family, for instance, is not a particular good, but a flow of particular goods for father and mother and children. Another instance of the good of order is technology-economy-polity. The most obvious aspect here is the economy. There can be a depression, and it is not for lack of raw materials, nor for lack of factories and railways, nor for lack of capital — money is going begging. Nor is it for lack of people willing to work or for lack of people willing to invest. It is just that the whole setup has simply gone awry; it just will not work. That is a case of the evil in the depression. You can see the absence of the good of order.

Again, an educational system is a good of order. An educational system is not the education of this child or this young man or this young lady. It is a flow of educations. It determines what flows and the direction in which it will flow. The church, too, is a good of order. It gets people to heaven — not just one, but a flow of people into heaven. The world of art, letters, sciences, philosophy — the world of learning — is a setup, a good of order.

Now what are the general characteristics of a human good of order? It includes a number of things. We will discuss four: a regular recurrence of particular goods, coordinated human operations, a set of conditions of these operations, and personal status.[21]

The most conspicuous aspect of a good of order is a regular recurrence of particular goods. If X is a good thing and occurs, it will recur when there is a good of order. If breakfast is a good thing, and if there is a good of order, you will have breakfast every morning. A theoretical analysis of the notion of recurrence can be found in *Insight*.[22] The good of order is not a matter of mechanist planning. Planning has to work in every single detail or everything goes awry. But the good of order is a matter of sets of alternative

---

21 The sentence 'We will discuss ...' is supplied by the editors; see Lonergan in the last paragraph of this subsection. For the later development of Lonergan's thought on the human good of order, see *Method in Theology* (see chapter 1 above, note 37) 48–50.
22 Lonergan referred to *Insight* and its index (see Recurrence, schemes of).

schemes of recurrence.[23] It is something like the way the water circulates on the surface of the earth: it goes up from the sea in water vapor and forms clouds that are carried over the land; the water then falls down in rain, which flows into brooks and streams and rivers, and finally returns to the sea. The circulation of water does not work like a machine, according to some set of rules. Rather, all along it works according to sets of probabilities. Thus, there are spots that are deserts, and others that have too much rain, and still others that have too much humidity. The regular recurrence of particular goods is a fundamental aspect of the good of order. When there is a regular recurrence of particular goods, there is a good of order behind it.

Next, that regular recurrence occurs through coordinated human operations. There is a recurrence of particular goods because men operate, and operate in some sort of coordinated fashion, with a certain interdependence. So the second element in the good of order consists in coordinated human operations.

Thirdly, you can have the coordination and the operations only if certain conditions are fulfilled. We will distinguish three parts in this third element. First, there are the habits in the subject. What do I mean by a habit? A person has a habit of mind when he does not have to learn, when he already knows, when he can operate on his own, when you do not have to take the time to teach him. A person has a habit of will when you do not have to persuade him — 'Barkis is willin'.'[24] A person has a habit of dexterity, of manual skills, when he does not have to learn how to do something. If he had to learn how to drive a car, there would be no use asking him to drive you downtown; you ask a person who already has the skill. Thus we can distinguish three kinds of habits: cognitional habits, volitional habits, and skills; not having to learn, not having to be persuaded, not having to acquire the skill. Habits are a condition of coordinated human operations. If every time something had to be done people had to take a year off to learn, or to be persuaded, or to acquire the skills, nothing would ever be done.

The second condition of effective coordination lies in institutions. Institutions are like habits, but in the objective order. Everyone in the United States comes to an agreement about a way of doing things when the government passes a law. An institution is a mechanism set up for making deci-

---

23 The phrase 'sets of alternative schemes' is taken from LN 35. In the lecture itself, he said simply, 'But the good of order is a matter of the scheme of recurrence.'

24 The phrase Barkis uses to court Clara Peggotty in Charles Dickens, *David Copperfield*.

sions. There are many such mechanisms — not only governmental, but social institutions in general. Such institutions are objective conditions that result from human apprehensions and choices and facilitate the flow of coordinated operations. But you can count on the other fellow doing it: through these institutions individuals are socialized. For example, if every time you went out for a drive you were not sure whether there might be some lad driving around with the purpose of running into people, it would be a more hazardous enterprise; but because of socialization, we can count on no one but a madman doing that.

The third condition of coordinated operation is material equipment, the material means of facilitating cooperation.[25] For example, a university without any buildings does not have the material equipment that is one element in an educational system.

The final element in the good of order is personal status. When you have coordinated operations resulting in a flow of particular goods, there arise personal relations that are congruent with the structure of the good of order. Such personal relations give rise to status. Thus, the family is a good of order; a mother fulfils certain functions within the family; she plays a determinate role in the good of order that is the family, and by playing that role, fulfilling that part, she enters into certain relations with the other members of the family. Being in those relations with other members of the family is having a status in the family, a status that arises from the personal relations that result from coordinated human operations. Similar conditions obtain for pupil and teacher, doctor and client, and so on right along the line.[26] The human good gives rise to determinate structures of interpersonal relations that result in status.

So the good of order involves four aspects: a regular recurrence of particular goods, coordinated human operations, the triple condition of these coordinated human operations — habits, institutions, and material equipment — and finally, the personal status which results from the relations constituted by the cooperation.

3.1.3 Value

The third element in the invariant structure of the human good is value. Not only are there setups, but people ask, 'Is the setup good?' They say,

25 The words 'material means of facilitating cooperation' are based on LN 35.
26 LN 35: 'mother, worker, judge, etc.'

'There is nothing wrong with him, it's the setup.' Children fight about particular goods, but men fight about the value of a good of order. The international tension that we call the Cold War exists because people in the West have a different idea of the good of order from that of the Soviets.[27] The question of what precisely is to be the good of order concretely functioning and determining the habits, the institutions, the material equipment, the personal status of everyone in every aspect of their lives — the total human good of order — raises the question of value. Is the order good?

We can distinguish three approaches to value, or, if you want, three kinds of value: aesthetic, ethical, and religious.

Aesthetic value is the realization of the intelligible in the sensible: when the good of order of a society is transparent, when it shines through the products of that society, the actions of its members, its structure of interdependence, the status and personality of the persons participating in the order.[28] You can recognize a happy home or a happy community. The good of order can be transparent in all the things made, all the actions performed, in the habits and the institutions. It strikes the eye. Thus, a man who was taking instructions in Catholic doctrine from me when I was in Toronto remarked to me that he could see the joy on people's faces as they came out of Mass on Sunday — there is a Hungarian church not far from the place where the Jesuit seminary is.[29] He was struck by the contrast between this happiness and the ordinary run of things in the city. It is aesthetic value, then, that enables people to apprehend the human good on its profoundest level or, on the contrary, to sense something wrong, in a very immediate fashion, an immediate apprehension that we may later be able to analyze a bit;[30] for the moment it is enough to recognize its existence.

Secondly, there is ethical value. It swings us beyond discussion of the good as developing object to the good that is the subject. Ethical value is the conscious emergence of the subject as autonomous, responsible, free. When we say that children reach the age of reason when they are seven, and young men become responsible before the law at the age of twenty-one, we are speaking of the development of the human person that gradually becomes aware of freedom and of its meaning and responsibilities. Because the sub-

27 In an aside, 'The people in the West don't want to risk losing theirs, and the Russians want to impose their own on everyone.'
28 Some of the expressions in this sentence are taken from LN 35 verso.
29 The Jesuit Seminary in Toronto was then located at 403 Wellington Street West, off Spadina Avenue. St Elizabeth's Hungarian Catholic Church was a few blocks north at Spadina and Dundas.
30 See below, the beginning of § 3.3.2.

ject is intelligent, rational, free, and responsible, the development of the subject consists in becoming aware of that nature – intelligent, rational, free, responsible – and taking his stand upon the criteria immanent in that nature, on absolute norms, on being guided by the true and false, right and wrong, good and evil, and devoting oneself to, even sacrificing oneself for, these criteria.[31] And it is passing through a crisis – well, it is a gradual process, but there are also critical periods in the development of any individual when one becomes aware of oneself or finds oneself. That is the emergence of ethical value – doing things, and developing the idea that things are to be done, because they are right, and saying, 'I want to do what is right.' Then one becomes a center of initiative, free and yet good. We are too apt, at least in our upbringing, to develop the false notion that being good and being unfree, being constrained, go together. But the excellence of man, the proper good of man, is precisely doing what is right because he is free. His freedom is to realize the good.

Now if one has stopped short at ethical value, one is left with a secularist philosophy of education. If one includes ethical value, of course, one has a rather high type, a very high type, the highest possible type, of secularist education. But there is also religious value. With ethical value there emerges the autonomy of spirit, the subject taking his stand upon the truth, upon what is right, upon what is good. Religious value appears when you go a step further, when the autonomous subject stands before God, with his neighbor, in the world of history, when he realizes within himself the internal order,[32] the metaphorical justice of justification, that inner hierarchy in which reason is subordinate to God, and sense to reason.[33]

I have presented an outline of the invariant structure of the human good. It is a structure that can be verified in any human situation at any level of civilization or culture. It is a general structure that consists in particular goods, the good of order or setup (which may be very compact or very differentiated), and values, which appear aesthetically, ethically, or religiously.

3.2 Notes on the Invariant Structure of the Human Good [34]

I wish now to emphasize certain aspects of the general invariant structure of

31 The words from 'and devoting' are supplied from LN 35 verso.
32 The words 'internal order' are supplied from LN 35 verso.
33 Lonergan added that these are the terms employed in the Augustinian and Thomist account of justification, of the state of sanctifying grace, and he referred to Thomas Aquinas, *Summa theologiae*, 1–2, q. 113, a. 1.
34 This heading is taken from LN 35 verso.

the human good. It is open; its three aspects are related to one another in an interlocking fashion; it is synthetic; and it is isomorphic with several other structures.[35]

3.2.1 An Open Structure

First, then, it is an open structure. Its content is unspecified. We spoke of particular goods, but we did not say what they were. They can be the particular goods of any level of development or civilization. So too, with regard to the good of order we gave general indications that have many applications. We spoke of a flow of particular goods, but did not specify what the particular goods are. We spoke of human cooperation, but did not indicate what the operations are or how they are coordinated. We spoke of habits, institutions, and material equipment, but did not specify any of these. We distinguished aesthetic, ethical, and religious values, and offered some illustrations, but again we did not pin them down. The structure of the human good is an open structure that can become more determinate by picking out sets of particular goods, types of order, the manner of realizing value. But that structure can be used in thinking about any human good from the Stone Age to the present time.

3.2.2 Interlocking Aspects

In the second place, the three aspects of the human good — particular goods, the good of order, and values — are interlocking. Particular goods are not enough. Man is intelligent; he is not satisfied with breakfast today; he wants lunch and dinner, too, and he wants them every day. Precisely because man is intelligent, the particular good leads him on to the good of order. Human intelligence insists upon some assurance of regularity, recurrence, security, so the particular good leads right into the good of order.

Again, for man as reflective and rational, any order is bound to be considered, evaluated, criticized. It is a finite good, and if it is not to be erected into an idol, it is going to be criticized, found fault with. The possibility and inevitability, so to speak, of reflecting on the order in which we live, the social system, the cultural situation, and evaluating and criticizing it appears, for example, in Nietzsche's contrast between the Apollonian and

35 This sentence has been added by the editors.

the Dionysian. Man as insisting on the good of order is Apollonian; but as ready to tear it all down he is Dionysian.[36] The same possibility is found in the distinction between classicism and romanticism. Classicists insist upon the values in the good of order, and romanticists on the fact that this is not enough for man. Reflection accounts, too, for the reactionary and the revolutionary, for enthusiasm and debunking, for the apostle who wants to transform the world and the hermit who wants to flee it as hopeless – and so on. The particular good leads man into the good of order, and the good of order leads man into reflecting on the order and evaluating it and criticizing it. In that evaluation and criticism there emerges the notion of value, Is it worth while?[37]

3.2.3 A Synthetic Structure

In the third place, the invariant structure is synthetic or unifying. While the invariant structure does not enucleate, analyze out, the precise aspects that we are going to examine later when we consider the good as the developing subject, still it is large enough a structure to include both subject and object, to unite the subjective and the objective, the individual and the social.[38] Around this point there is an interesting problem in the interpretation of St Thomas. In one place in the first part of the *Summa theologiae* (q. 47, a. 1),[39] he states that the good of order found in the whole universe is the closest approximation to divine perfection. But in another place (q. 93, a. 2, ad 3m), he states that the order in the soul, on which is based the Trinitarian analogy, provides the most intense, concentrated image of divine perfection.[40] There is a conflict between order and person. Are we interested in the order that helps persons, or in persons simply? Do you sacrifice persons for the order?[41] The law does so when people are executed and wars are fought. But the order can also be sacrificed for persons. And the

---

36 See Friedrich Nietzsche, *The Birth of Tragedy* in *The Birth of Tragedy and The Genealogy of Morals*, trans. Francis Golffing (New York: Doubleday Anchor, 1956) passim.
37 In an aside, 'After a hard day in the classroom, you ask yourself, Is it worth while?'
38 This sentence is partly constructed from LN 35 verso.
39 LN 35 verso mentions also q. 103, a. 2, ad 3m.
40 LN 35 verso adds, '*Plato* order in the soul produces order in society, and order in society is condition for order in Soul.'
41 There is a hiatus on the tape at this point. The next two sentences are based on the notes of F. Crowe.

two can also be united insofar as the person emerges with personal status within the order. Then the order is an order between persons, and the good of order is apprehended, not so much by studying the notion of schemes of recurrence and determining the schemes in which human goods occur, but by apprehending human relations. The most efficacious example of the human good of order is the family, and the family subsists on personal relations. It is in their personal relations with one another that the members of the family concretely perceive their good of order. Through personal relations there is a concrete, immediate apprehension of what the good of order concretely is. It is useful to have a theoretical structure, to be able to speak of the good of order generally, but the simplest and most effective apprehension of the good of order is in the apprehension of personal relations.[42]

3.2.4 Isomorphic with Other Structures

My final observation on the invariant structure of the human good will be to indicate a few parallels.

The first parallel is with the structure of cognitional activity.[43] We have distinguished particular goods, the good of order, and value. Our acquaintance with the particular good is mainly a matter of *experience.* But to know about the good of order, you have to *understand.* It is intelligence, understanding, insight, that is chiefly relevant to knowing the good of order. And it is when one reflects on different orders, different possible setups and systems, that one comes to the notion of value, and such reflection is on the level of *judgment.* You will recall from *Insight* that experience, understanding, and judgment are three fundamental levels of consciousness.[44] They run parallel to a fundamental division in metaphysics, according to which finite being is composed of potency, form, and act, whether substantial or accidental.[45]

The structure of the human good is also relevant to a division of men and

---

42 LN 35 verso adds, 'Existential subjects before God with neighbour in world of history make themselves and contribute to history by choosing orders of particular goods.'
   A break was taken as this point. The lecture resumed with Lonergan speaking of his 'final observation' on the invariant structure of the human good, that is, the next point.
43 This sentence is added by the editors.
44 See Lonergan, *Insight,* chapter 11.
45 See ibid., chapter 15, 456–63.

of societies. Regarding societies, Pitirim Sorokin[46] distinguished three types of society or culture or civilization: sensate, idealistic, and ideational.[47] In the sensate civilization or culture, attention concentrates on the particular goods; the good of order is a means to the attainment of the particular goods. The point to any system is not that it is good, but that it is a means to other goods. There is an expression of this mentality in Bentham's formula 'The greatest good of the greatest number,' where the greatest good is the greatest number of particular goods, and where there is sought a utilitarian calculus that would add up the particular goods and portion them out equally. The idealistic civilization or culture, on the other hand, insists upon the order itself as the great good. And the ideational culture insists upon and attends to the value.

Regarding individuals, Søren Kierkegaard distinguishes three types of existential subjectivity: the aesthetic, the ethical, and the religious.[48] The aesthetic is connected with the particular good, the ethical with order, with what is right and wrong, and the religious with the relations between man and God. Kierkegaard's religiousness is related to Sorokin's ideational culture and with value; the ethical sphere is parallel to the idealistic society and to order; and the aesthetic is interested in particular goods and a sensate culture.

The significance of this set of parallels will appear only later, when we get behind this account of the good to its foundations in the integration of subjects.[49]

We have discussed some preliminaries on the good, the invariant struc-

46 Lonergan added comments on Sorokin, mentioning that he was a long-time professor of sociology at Harvard, and before that was at Minnesota, and that, while he was definitely of the older generation of sociologists at that time, he was also extraordinarily learned and profound. On Sorokin see *Understanding and Being* 420, note *k* to lecture 9.

47 See, for example, Pitirim A. Sorokin, *The Crisis of Our Age: The Social and Cultural Outlook* (New York: E.P. Dutton, 1941; reprinted in paperback, 1957); in greater detail, *Social and Cultural Dynamics*, 4 vols. (New York: American Book Company, 1937–41).

48 The three spheres of existence are so pervasive in Kierkegaard that it would be guesswork to give a specific reference as Lonergan's source; but see the index to *Concluding Unscientific Postscript*, trans. David F. Swenson, completed and provided with introduction and notes by Walter Lowrie (Princeton: Princeton University Press, 1941) under Aesthetic, Ethical, Religion.

49 On the tape, the last clause is 'when we start getting behind the foundations of this account of the good, and the integration of subjects, and so on.' The rendition in the text here is an interpretation.

ture of the human good as an object, and certain general features of that structure. Again, it is open, interlocking, and synthetic, and it has a number of significant parallels with knowledge, society, and the status or kinds of man. Now we can make what we have said a bit clearer and more concrete if we consider evil, the negation of the good. Just as there is a whole series of aspects to the invariant structure of the good, so there is a whole series of opposite aspects that are evil.

3.3 Evil

3.3.1 Particular and Organized Evils

As there are particular goods so there are particular evils: privations, suffering, harm, destruction. But as there is a good of order, so too particular evils can become chronic; there can be a scheme of recurrence working for them, so that if they occur, they occur again, and keep on occurring. A crime wave, a depression, a war is an organized structure that keeps evils recurring.

As there are various aspects to the good of order, so there are corresponding aspects of evil at this level.[50] Thus the cooperation, the coordinated operations required for the good of order, can break down in friction and conflict, strikes and lockouts, sedition and revolution: a complete breakdown of the good of order. Again, the good of order can be sapped on the level of the conditions of cooperation. There can be mistaken or vicious habits; people can acquire skill to do not only what is good but also what is evil. There can be unsuitable, intractable institutions, excellent in a different age but now antiquated, out of date, preventing more good than they are doing. There can be institutionalized evils, setups based on error, structures geared to war.[51] There can be outdated equipment, and there can be persons without any status. Toynbee conceives 'the proletarian' as an attitude of people who are *in* the society but not *of* it; they have no concern with what happens to the good of order.[52] There can be the destruction of

50 This sentence is added by the editors.
51 In the lecture Lonergan said simply, 'There can be institutionalized evils.' We have based what appears here on the following on LN 35 verso: 'institutionalized evils (error, war).'
52 See Arnold J. Toynbee, *A Study of History*, vol. 3: *The Growth of Civilizations* (London: Oxford University Press, 1934); index, Proletariat. See the indices also of vol. 6: *The Disintegration of Civilizations, Part Two* (1939), and of vol. 10: *The Inspiration of Historians* (1954).

personal relations and status through hatred, envy, jealousy, lust, resentment, grievance. People with grievances, nations with grievances, very easily can become warped in their entire outlook.

There are, then, not merely particular evils; evil can also penetrate the good of order, and it can do so in as many ways as there are aspects of the good of order.

3.3.2 Negation of Value

There can also be evil as the negation of value. First, opposed to aesthetic value there can be ugliness. The order can exist yet not be transparent. It can be too complex, too intricate, for people to apprehend. This is a great danger and difficulty in modern society. The destruction of the significance of smaller groups makes the social system something that the average man cannot understand, cannot apprehend. For example, in feudal society, with its obvious hierarchy, it was always possible to know who was responsible for something, and so it was possible to account for evil. But in the highly intricate network of interdependence in modern commercial and industrial society, man is confronted with a vast machine that he does not understand. In Canada there was a political party named Social Credit, based upon what is simply a blunder in economics. A Montreal lawyer, talking to a man who was in favor of Social Credit, asked him, 'Do you understand how that proposal would work?' The man replied, 'No.' 'Then why are you voting for it, if you don't understand it?' The man said, 'Well, do you understand how your radio works?' The lawyer had to say, 'No.' The man said, 'Well, you turn it on, and if you like it, it sounds good, doesn't it?' 'Yes.' 'Well, Social Credit sounds good to me.' There is no comprehension, and no hope of having any comprehension, of the good of order that exists. There may be an existing good of order that is not on the human level, not on the human scale, and the average man cannot apprehend it. This point is made by Robert Nisbet in a book which I mentioned yesterday, *The Quest for Community*.[53] Things have slipped beyond the human scale, and the average man tends to find it incomprehensible. He says, 'They are doing this, they are doing that.' But who are 'they'? Nobody knows. That leads to frustration. It is very hard at the present time to form small groups of men that will work for particular purposes, because they know there is no use trying. 'You can't buck the machine; you can't get anywhere.' There is no significance to it; control and power are too centralized.

53 See above, chapter 1, note 39.

Again, besides having an order that is not transparent, there can be no order to be transparent. Here I would refer you to a book by Karl Jaspers, *Die geistige Situation der Zeit.*[54] Jaspers conceives modern society as an enormous machine that no one is running. The average man is provided with a certain number of choices regarding food, clothing, housing, vacations, amusements, and so on, and any of them is better than what he can provide for himself. If he wants to see Europe, the best thing he can do is go to a tourist agency and let them take him around; they do a much better job than he could do on his own. But there is only a certain limited number of tours, and he has to pick from among them. Similarly, everything connected with his job has been worked out for him by somebody else; he just goes through the motions. And the fellow that works it out is in the same position. He has to do an efficient job of working out the other fellow's job, or he loses his own job. This obtains right up to the head of the industrial hierarchy. The fellows at the top are no better off; they are the people that get the ulcers. They have to estimate the best possible use of the existing technical resources and anticipate future developments in the best possible way, or they are out. What is settling everything is technological possibility.[55] It is settling every aspect of the individual's private living, of the conditions of his living — what his cities are like, what his vacations are like, everything he does in his work. And who is running it? Concrete technological possibility. There is no room for personal decision, personal achievement, personal taste, personal significance. This is a case of economic determinism resulting from a lack of the existence of individuals who know their own minds and live their own lives. In other words, economic determinism as affirmed by Marx — something necessary — is a mistake; but there *is* an economic determinism resulting from people not having any minds of their own, not insisting that human intelligence and reason and free choice be the ultimate determinant of what human life is to be. If that breaks down, then human life and human society become mechanical.

The same result can appear on the level of science. Human science thinks

54 Karl Jaspers, *Die geistige Situation der Zeit* (Berlin, Leipzig: Walter de Gruyter, 1931); in English, *Man in the Modern Age*, trans. Eden and Cedar Paul (London: Routledge and Kegan Paul, 1951). Lonergan added: 'The book was published about 1931, went promptly into five German editions, and has been translated into a series of other languages including Japanese.'

55 'technological possibility': In 'Moral Theology and the Human Sciences,' a paper written for the International Theological Commission in 1974, Lonergan's aim is to go 'beyond simple conflict between natural law and technical possibility and [move] toward the enlargement of the attainable human good' (p. 2 of the manuscript).

that to be scientific it has to imitate the natural sciences. It wants to be a science of prediction. It does not want to be a moral science that would exhibit to free men their choices, the alternatives that lie before them, and leave them to choose. It wants to conceive men as atoms, find out the forces that move them, and predict what they will do whether they choose or not. There can result an estrangement of man's world from man. Man sets up an inhuman order because he conceives man as a component in a machine; and man hates that machine. Such hatred is far more apparent in Europe than in America. In America there is still plenty of room to move about, but in the old, densely populated civilizations and cultures of Europe, this hatred just leaps right out — a profound hatred of the modern world, the estrangement of man from his world. The whole world, the whole social setup, is something alien to man. This hatred is expressed in neurotic art, in a sense of frustration, of hopelessness, of 'no use trying.'

That has to do with the objective aspect of the order. But there can be alienation, a loss of order *within* a man, the negation of ethical value. One is just a drifter; he makes no choices; he does not want to be a center of intelligent, rational, free, responsible choice.[56] Insofar as he makes a choice at all, it is a choice to be like everybody else, to be one of the crowd, to conform, to be other-directed. And insofar as the number of drifters, conformists, other-directed people increases, there is called forth the complementary type with the will to power, the social engineers, the hidden persuaders, who dominate the drifting masses and do so in a way that has nothing to do with their intelligence, reasonableness, freedom, or responsibility.[57] They are controlled without their knowing it — the propaganda ministry of the totalitarian state. And there can be its equivalent in the advertising setup, big institutions for control of people's choices without their knowing it.

In the third place, there can be the negation of religious value, estrangement from God, secularism, the negation of the idea of sin, complete and full self-assertion. In the Gospel our Lord speaks of the man who neither feared God nor respected man; but if the widow came and knocked at his door and kept pestering him, he would finally give her what she wanted just to get rid of her.[58] That person who neither fears God nor respects man has

56 LN 36 adds, 'Heidegger's inauthentic man.'
57 LN 36: 'naturalistic negation of others' intelligence reasonableness freedom responsibility.' Relevant here is the section '2. Social Alienation' in 'Prolegomena to the Study of the Emerging Religious Consciousness of Our Time,' in *A Third Collection*, ed. Frederick E. Crowe (Mahwah, NJ: Paulist, 1985) 60–63.
58 See Luke 18.1–8.

had God pass out of his picture. There may have been a time when he was influenced by religion, but he got rid of it the way we get rid of scruples: 'It's the reasonable thing to do; drop it entirely; it's for children.' When that negation arises, then human history, which is the human good, the cumulative process resulting from human apprehension and choice, ceases to be man cooperating with God. Man's acceptance of this world ceases to be an acceptance of God's will. We find it hard to see that this world is good. If we cease to accept the world as the world God chose — Thy will be done on earth as it is in heaven — then the good in the world has to be the only good there is.

While some individuals can be content to stop there, it very frequently happens that others do not. There arise vast illusions. A greater part of my life, and of many of your lives, was passed in a milieu in which the idea of automatic progress dominated social thinking. Everything was inevitably getting better. That idea has been eliminated by two world wars, the Depression, and the Cold War, so that no one talks about automatic progress any more. But it was a vast illusion that possessed men's minds and influenced all sorts of decisions. The classless society promised by Marx is another such illusion, the illusion of a utopia. Nietzsche's Superman is another illusion, an illusion of the individual.[59]

Again, the calm contemplation of this world as it is, without any possibility of giving any meaning to resignation to the will of God, without seeing that beyond this world there is the good by its essence which is God, can lead to desperation and nihilism, the negation of the notion of value. Man can be conceived as the blind alley of biological evolution, as by Nietzsche. By that is meant that the highest point in biological evolution is man; further evolution has to be cultural; and when man goes in for cultural development, animal drives weaken, and man becomes decadent; he is no longer vigorous, no longer out to dominate and control and effectively bring about the good.

Finally, there can be superficiality and frivolity. People do not come to grips with the problem of good and evil in the world. Science is conceived, not only by materialists but also by as refined and in many ways as profound a philosopher as Karl Jaspers, as what everyone must accept because of palpable consequences. If there is an absence of palpable consequences that force the adhesion of everyone, then the question cannot be scientific. This

59 In LN 36 'automatic progress,' 'classless society,' and 'superman' are all examples of 'illusion of utopia.'

is a superficial notion of science that puts science on the same level as the practical techniques thought out by the primitives. Those techniques produced palpable good results, and so the ideas behind those techniques must have been right; they could be scientifically verified. But if it is only in the palpable consequences which everyone can see that there can be science, then there is no science of man, because the consequences of the really profound human errors occur only fifty or a hundred years later, and then the span of time is a bit too long for anyone to say that palpably this evil at this time is due to that man's error being propagated a century ago.

We may recall as well Husserl's account of the situation in the human sciences, where we find a constant multiplication of specialties, the acceptance in each specialty of merely conventional criteria, and no possibility of any unification, integration, or overall significance. This shows a frivolity in man's thought about man, a frivolity which seems to me to be connected with estrangement from God, alienation from God, secularism.

Briefly, then, the evil is the opposite of the good, and as the invariant structure of the good has many aspects, so opposite to each of these aspects there are specific evils.

We will next move on to our second main division, namely, the differentials of the human good. We have considered a structure that can be verified in different ways from the Stone Age to the present time, and we must consider next what makes the differences. Our third topic will be, In what way do these differences add up to give us a level of civilization? Insofar as we are able to distinguish different levels of integration in the human good, we will be able to distinguish different classes of educational goals. In general the differentials are what make a difference, and the integration is the way in which you add up these differences.[60]

---

60 LN 36: 'Classicist: motus cognoscitur ex termino; post-classicist: motus cognoscitur ex via: differential and integral

'Differential: what is done that makes a difference; integral: summation over time of differences = situation.'

Some of the second lecture has been moved to chapter 3. See p. 27 above, note 4.

3

The Human Good as Object:
Differentials and Integration[1]

1 The Differentials of the Human Good

The differentials of the human good are of three kinds.[2] The first is intellectual development. Man's intellect is *potens omnia facere et fieri*: it is infinite potentially. Moreover, it moves through incomplete acts towards more complete actuation. The angel from the first moment of its existence knows naturally all that it will ever know, but the human race exists in time, and through time cquires its knowledge. It is natural to man to have an intellect that develops in time. That intellectual development, which is accountable for progress, is a first principle differentiating human societies.[3]

The second principle differentiating human societies is sin. In sin, man is the first cause. Whenever we do good, we are just God's instruments, but with respect to the radical element in sin man is the initiator, the first cause.

---

1 The conclusion of the second lecture, Tuesday, August 4, 1959, and the whole of the third lecture, Wednesday, August 5, 1959. See note 19 below.
2 The theme of what are here called the differentials of the human good is an interest of Lonergan's that dates back at least to the student papers on history (probably written in 1937–38) that are found in File 713 in the Archives of the Lonergan Research Institute. See '*Insight* Revisited,' *A Second Collection* 271–72, for Lonergan's later recollection of his early work on the topic.
3 This sentence is partly constructed from LN 36 — the indication regarding progress.

Sin is nothing, a negation, but that is man's originality; and that makes a difference: sin is the basis of decline in human society.[4]

The third differential is redemption, victory over sin, the restoration of the order destroyed by sin.[5]

1.1 Intellectual Development[6]

1.1.1 The Development of Intelligence

As we distinguished insight or intelligence and judgment, so we shall distinguish two levels of development in the first differential. There is intellectual development, and there is reflective development. Intellectual development corresponds to civilization, reflective development to culture — if you want to distinguish between civilization and culture. Again, Hutchins in *The University of Utopia* distinguishes between the methods of discovery and the methods of discussion.[7] His distinction is approximately the same as the one I am making. Methods of discovery are scientific methods pertaining more to insight or intelligence, while methods of discussion are concerned with aims and values, educational purposes, and so on, and pertain more to the reflective level.

With regard to the first level, then, we can see the structure of civilizational development from our account of insight. The act of understanding occurs with respect to imagined or sensible data. The human situation at any time includes a set of data; someone understands something, gets a bright idea, and figures out what would happen if this idea were put into effect. He takes counsel with others or with the influential people; a policy is devised; consent is won; and human action changes in the light of the new idea. The change in human action brings about a new situation, and the new situation suggests further acts of understanding. The process functions as a wheel: situation, insight, counsel, policy, common consent, action, new situation, new insight, new counsel, new policy, and so on.[8] The wheel can

---

4 This sentence is partly constructed from LN 36 — the indication regarding decline.
5 LN 36: '(3) redemption, victory over sin, restoration, progress.'
6 LN 36 reads, 'Intellect as differential: (a) intelligence; (b) reflection.'
7 Robert Maynard Hutchins, *The University of Utopia* (see above, chapter 1, note 40) 72–74.
8 LN 36: 'Situation, insight, grasp of concrete potentiality, diffusion of idea, counsel, policy, action, new situation, new insight: circle.'

turn indefinitely. Such an analysis of process is mainly in terms of experience and insight, and also choice. The analysis can be illustrated by what Toynbee's *Study of History* says about 'Challenge-and-Response.'[9] Challenge is the situation, and response is guided by an insight into the situation. The response creates a new situation, which brings forth a further challenge, and so on as the process keeps going.

Now this process of new ideas can spread through the whole good of order. You start changing the situation at one point, but that change in the situation will involve repercussions all through the good of order. New ideas will start popping up everywhere. There will result augmented well-being, and it affects each of the aspects of the human good:[10] the flow of particular goods becomes more frequent, more intense, more varied; new equipment is produced; institutions are remodeled; new types of goods are provided; the society enjoys more democracy and more education; new habits are formed to deal with the new equipment in the new institutions; there is status for all, because everything is running smoothly; everybody is too busy to be bothered with knifing other people; there are happy personal relations, a development in taste, in aesthetic value and its appreciation, and in ethics, in the autonomy of the subject; finally, there is more time for people to attend to their own perfection in religion.

This process of change moves the situation away from the roots of chronic evils. The old evils cannot function in the new setup, simply because they pertain to the old situation, and that old situation has been changed. This process of development has no fixed frontiers. It radiates, as it were, from a center. The people in the next town, the next state, the next country start doing likewise. They can see that the new situation is good, and so they too have to change.

Secondly, who are the agents? I have spoken simply of the process — situation, insight, counsel, policy, new type of action, new situation, new insight, and the snowball effect of the entire cycle. The agents may be called a succession of creative personalities. The situation can be wholly transformed if there is a succession of personalities who are not simply sunk into the existing situation, immersed in its routines, and functioning like cogs in a wheel,

---

9   See Arnold J. Toynbee, *A Study of History*, vol. 3: *The Growth of Civilizations* (London: Oxford University Press, 1934); index, Challenge-and-Response. See the indices also of vol. 6: *The Disintegration of Civilizations, Part Two* (1939), and of vol. 10: *The Inspiration of Historians* (1954).

10 The last clause (from 'and') is added by the editors in an effort to sum up what follows.

with little grasp of possibilities, with a lack of daring.[11] They withdraw, perhaps even physically, but at least mentally.[12] They are detached; it is because of their detachment that they can see how things could be different. They may be accounted as nobodies while they are withdrawn, but when they return, they transform the world. In their withdrawal they become themselves, and they return with a mission.[13] The return, of course, may not occur in their own lifetime. The most influential man in the twentieth century — the strongest candidate at least — is Karl Marx,[14] and he spent years in the British Museum writing books that everyone else laughed at. Toynbee accounts for the process of such influence in terms of a creative minority. To begin, a creative personality influences a small group, which in turn influences other groups. Plato speaks of a spark that leaps from soul to soul.[15]

Toynbee distinguishes four periods in such a process. The first is marked by enthusiasm. In the second period people are more sedate. The third period is one of disillusion, of storm and stress. And in the fourth period, people acquiesce, and the prophets are honored by the sons of those who had stoned them.[16] Thus, insights occur to individuals; these individuals have to communicate their ideas to a minority; and the minority passes through the four periods. Others then will follow, but with limited understanding and devotion, and no initiative — Toynbee calls this 'mimesis.' They are charmed, they feel something is afoot, but they need a leader, they need to be organized, and so there develop a functional hierarchy, rule, law, loyalty.[17] The major weakness in Toynbee's analysis is that he presented

11 Some of this sentence is suggested by LN 36.
12 Lonergan referred here to Toynbee's lengthy treatment of 'Withdrawal-and-Return.' See the indices in the volumes mentioned in note 9.
13 This sentence is supplied from LN 36.
14 None of the tapes goes beyond the beginning of the comments on Marx. The remainder of this paragraph and the whole of the next are based on Lonergan's notes and the notes of F. Crowe.
15 LN 36 has, 'Spark: diffusion of idea; ready to risk for sake of idea.'
16 LN 36 reads, 'youthful period of poetry romance emotional upheaval intell ferment
      '— sedate mature period of prose matter of fact common sense systematiza[tion]
      '— disillusionment: storm & stress; all manner of friction conflict
      '— familiarity breeds acquiescence; prophets honored by sons of stoners.'
17 LN 36 verso has, 'Mimesis: those that follow with limited understanding, devotion; charmed, feel something afoot, cannot offer initiative of their own; need a leader
      'hence: organization, functional hierarchy, rule, law, set tasks, duty, obedience, loyalty.'

himself as an empirical scientist. On this point he has been severely criticized. But I find his work superb at another level, as an illustration of how
human intelligence works in history.[18]

The first of the differentials,[19] then, is intellectual development, and we
are considering it first on the level of intelligence. Aristotle divided all questions into four, and the four again into two: *Quid sit?* and, *An sit?* What is it?
and, Does it exist? The answer to the question *Quid sit?* is on the level of
intelligence. We have considered intellectual development in its social
aspect, that is, in the sense of civilizational order, the development of society. A concrete illustration of this type of development is provided in
Schumpeter's business cycles.[20] Schumpeter divides business cycles into
three types, the third and longest of which lasts about sixty years. An example is the age of the railroad. The discovery of the idea of the railroad and
the subsequent building of the railroads transformed the entire economy of
the United States — consider what things could not exist without the railroads, and what things came into existence because of them. The idea of
having railroads involved numerous concrete implications and made possible things that before were not possible. In similar fashion, we live at the
present time in an age of electronics. All sorts of developments stem from
the single idea of electronic devices and appliances. It is a fundamental idea
that, when put into practice, releases the possibility of a whole series of

18 Lonergan seems to have read the first six volumes of Toynbee's *Study* in 1940–
42, making copious notes which he filed with his student writings on history
(File 713 of his papers). At any rate references to Toynbee began to appear at
this time: in his book reviews in *The Canadian Register,* June 20, 1942, and April
24, 1943; and in the fourth of his articles on *gratia operans, Theological Studies* 3
(December 1942) 578, note 230. By the time of these 1959 lectures, he has
modified his early assessment, but he maintained to the end his high opinion
of Toynbee's ideas; the work 'can be viewed, not as an exercise in empirical
method, but as the prolegomena to such an exercise, as a formulation of ideal
types that would stand to broad historical investigations as mathematics stands
to physics.' 'Natural Right and Historical Mindedness,' in *A Third Collection*
178.
19 The third lecture actually begins at this point. Lonergan gave a very brief summary of what he had said in the second lecture on the invariant structure of
the human good, and indicated he had then moved on to the differentials.
20 Joseph Schumpeter, *History of Economic Analysis*, ed. from manuscript by Elizabeth Boody Schumpeter (New York: Oxford University Press, 1954). See subject index, *Business Cycle Analysis*, and *Business Cycle Theories*. See also Joseph
Schumpeter, *The Theory of Economic Development*, trans. Redvers Opie (Cambridge, MA: Harvard University Press, 1934, 1962, 1968) 212–55. Lonergan
gave a brief background to Schumpeter and commented favorably on his writing of English.

other ideas. Another illustration lies in motorcars and the transformation of
the roads. The roads that we have now did not exist fifty years ago, and one
of the main reasons they exist now is the existence of the motorcar. The
existence of roads followed the existence of the motorcar, and all sorts of
other things have followed from both. One idea leads to another and makes
the realization of other ideas possible. One can see this very clearly in concrete instances of the technological order, although the same sort of thing
exists, though more obscurely, in ideas of a more immaterial character.

I have used Toynbee's analysis largely, in treating the development of
social intelligence, that is, of intelligence with respect to the technology-
economy-polity: the process from situation, insight, counsel, policy, new
action, changed situation giving rise to, making possible and significant,
further insights. The cycle is ongoing, and the entire good of order of a culture or civilization can be transformed in that manner. That is just the analysis of the process, however. There are also the agents. The prime agents of
such a process are creative personalities. The immediate agents Toynbee
calls the creative minority, the people who catch on to the idea, and with
considerable risk and sacrifice devote themselves to its realization. Finally,
the rank and file, who have some notion of the idea, are led, carried on in
the stream.

The more specific developments of intelligence in a pure sense − the
development of science, mathematics, and so on − are a little too technical
for us to treat at this point without digressing too far from our present topic.
We will come back to these developments later when we consider the implements at the disposal of the educator to help him realize his purposes, and
ask about the good of different subjects in education. But at present we are
simply trying to form some notion of our ends. So we are thinking of the
good in general, in order to arrive at both a determination of what the aims
of education might be or should be and a criticism of what in fact they are.

1.1.2 Reflective Development[21]

Now, besides this first level of intellectual development, which is a development in intelligence, in the question *Quid sit?* What is it? there is also a

21 LN 36 verso: '(b) Reflection (E Voegelin, Order and History).' We have not
  been able to locate earlier references to Voegelin in Lonergan's works. The
  influence of Voegelin is apparent in this section, with its theme of progress in
  the apprehension of structural invariants, from the compactness of the symbol to the differentiation of consciousness.

reflective level of development, a development of culture as opposed to civilization. Civilization is connected with technology, economy, and the polity or state. But there is the quite different level of reflective thought. This level arises because advance in civilizational order both presupposes and results in a fresh apprehension of the structural invariants. Particular goods change, and changes arise as well in the good of order and in the concrete way in which aesthetic, ethical, and religious values are realized. The mere fact of the advance of civilizational order, the transition from one form of material civilization to another, involves some sort of new incarnation, new realization, of the structural invariants. 'Particular goods' is a general category. Cornflakes for breakfast was not a particular good in the nineteenth century, and so on all down the line. The ever new realization arises for two reasons: first of all, because the invariants, what we spoke of yesterday, are not grasped in their full generality, and secondly, because the full generality has to be concretized, realized, in a new fashion.

Now this shift in the apprehension and realization of the structural invariants of the human good is essentially different from the civilizational process. In the latter case insight leads to new discoveries, new ideas, new possibilities, and the process spreads and radiates through a whole society and extends into other societies. The accumulation of insights results in a new civilizational order.[22] But the structural invariants do not change. They are not the object of a new discovery. They are always there, operative though they are not noticed. You can stop the man on the street and ask him what he thinks of the distinctions among particular goods, the good of order, and values, and he will simply gape at you. Still, the structural invariants are operative in his life, in his ways of thinking and doing things, even though he does not advert to them explicitly. They are implicit in all human acts – in experience, understanding, reflection, freedom and responsibility. They are given some expression in the customs, the laws, the stories, the traditional wisdom of every society.

Nonetheless, there is a progress in the apprehension of the structural invariants. That progress is from the compactness of the symbol to the differentiation of philosophic, scientific, theological, and historical consciousness.[23]

22 This sentence is added from LN 36 verso.
23 LN 36 verso: 'Progress on reflective level is (1) from compactness of undifferentiated consciousness to (2) differentiation of philosophic, scientific, theological, historical consciousness.' On historical consciousness see below, note 77.

The invariants can be operative in the life of one who never thinks of them, or who thinks of them only in the vaguest way, symbolically, in images. It is to these images that the orator appeals when addressing the masses, and it is these images that the popular writer knows will strike a chord in the reader. The invariants are then implicit. They are known in a compact sort of way. The doctrine of heaven and hell contains compactly the whole of Christian morality, but the compact apprehension which Catholics are brought up on, that one must save one's soul, becomes extremely refined and differentiated in the theology of the four last things; and in between there is a series of stages, the history of theological thought upon the subject.

Not only is there the development of reflective analysis of the structural invariants of the human good; there is along with it a differentiation of consciousness. We will devote more attention to this idea later, but for now we can think of the difference between a child or a person with little education, on the one hand — they are entirely in everything that they do — and, on the other hand, Thales, who was so interested in the stars that he fell into the well. The milkmaid could not have fallen into the well because she could not be so interested in the stars. Thales is an example of the differentiated consciousness, with the whole of consciousness polarized upon an intellectual interest. Such differentiation of consciousness is necessary for the process from the compactness of symbols — which corresponds to the undifferentiated consciousness — to the enucleated, analyzed, studied account of the structural invariants that emerges in a philosophy, in human science, in a theology. Such an account is the fruit of, and conditioned by, a differentiated consciousness.

A concrete apprehension of the difference between compact and differentiated consciousness comes to light in some first-class, more or less contemporary studies of the history of culture and the history of religion. The rediscovery of the symbol is one of the main themes in contemporary thought. There is , for instance, Mircea Eliade's *Shamanism*,[24] in which he studies the medicine man in Central Asia and in the most ancient times. The hypothesis of the book, the subtitle of which is *Archaic Techniques of*

24 Mircea Eliade, *Shamanism: Archaic Techniques of Ecstasy* [Lonergan erred here, saying 'Mysticism'], trans. Willard R. Trask (New York: Bollingen Foundation, 1964). Lonergan added that *Shamanism* is Eliade's great work, but that he has also written a history of religions, entitled in its English translation *Patterns in Comparative Religion*. The translation is by Rosemary Sheed (London and New York: Sheed & Ward, 1958).

Ecstasy, is that there is a possibility of mystical experience in the most primitive peoples, and of its having an influence on society. His work uses symbols as a key to investigate cultures whose languages and histories are known imperfectly. The notion underlying Jung's term 'the collective unconscious,' namely, that there are natural, spontaneous tendencies in human consciousness toward certain types of symbols which recur irrespective of cultural and linguistic frontiers, has been taken by Eliade as a key to the study of the history of religions.

A similar sort of work on a different level is being done by Eric Voegelin in *Order and History*.[25] Voegelin's study reveals how the symbols of Babylonian and Egyptian thought were countered in the revelation given to Israel, and how the symbols of the Homeric age were transformed, upset, transcended by such philosophers as Heraclitus, Parmenides, and Xenophanes, and by the movement into explicitly rational consciousness that appears with the Sophists and particularly with Plato and Aristotle. Voegelin understands cultural development in terms of the movement away from the compactness of the symbol to differentiated consciousness.

One point to these studies of symbols is that, when ancient man or the ancient higher civilizations used symbols, the meaning of the symbol could be just as profound as the thought of later great philosophers. This has been noticed in a whole series of fields. Thus, when the primitive speaks about light, you must not assume that he means the light of the sun. He may mean much more a spiritual light, but he may not be able to distinguish between spiritual and physical light.[26] There is today, then, a genuine rediscovery of the symbol. Human development on the cultural level is from the compactness of the symbol to the differentiated, enucleated thought of philosophers, theologians, and human scientists. Study of that process of differentiation is both recent and extremely complex, requiring a detailed knowledge of what is going on.

The simplest illustration of such development for the theologian lies in the transition from the language about our Lord in the New Testament to the language of the Council of Nicea affirming the consubstantiality of the Son with the Father, and of the Council of Chalcedon affirming one person in two natures. The words 'person,' 'nature,' 'consubstantial' are not New Testament terms. There has occurred a transition from a more com-

25 Lonergan gave some information on the first three volumes in this series. See above, chapter 1, note 50.
26 Lonergan added in an aside that he could make such a statement only from hearsay, but that it provides an instance of a tendency in modern studies.

pact symbolic consciousness expressed in the New Testament to a more enucleated theological consciousness expressed in the great Greek Councils.

The notion of the transition from the compactness of the symbol to the enucleated thought of a more developed period is fundamental not only to the study of the deeper levels of human history, but also in thinking of education. Children will have some apprehension of profound truths, but their apprehension will have the compactness of the symbol.

Our first differential, then, is intellectual development. Man grows in understanding of nature and himself, and there is a consequent development in civilizational order. Intellectual development explains the conspicuous difference between the Stone Age and successive periods of human life and history. But at the same time, arising in and because of this change in civilizational order, there is an enucleation, a development, in the apprehension and the realization of the structural invariants of the human good itself.

1.2 Sin

The second differential is sin. Sin is a category not only of theological and religious thought. One of the fundamental inspirations of Karl Marx is perhaps his hatred and critique of the sins of the bourgeoisie in the nineteenth century. There is a terrific hatred in Marx, and it is a hatred of sin. Again, in Nietzsche there is a hatred and critique of the sins of the masses, of what is all too human, of their resentment against human excellence of any kind, of their desire to bring everything down to their own level. It was against this that Nietzsche was reacting in affirming his transvaluation of values and his 'Superman,' and so on. For Nietzsche, of course, the fundamental expression of the resentment of the masses against human excellence was Christianity. Nietzsche lived fully the secularism of the modern time. For him God was dead, in the sense that God no longer exerted any influence upon human social, political, and economic life. Nietzsche wanted to think things out in full coherence with that fact. His explanation of Christianity as a resentment against excellence is, of course, a tool that can be turned against him. In Max Scheler's analysis the notion of resentment is given a twist, another application. For a while Scheler was a Catholic, and at that time he upheld the thesis that Protestant, bourgeois, capitalist society was the product of resentment against Catholicism and the feudal aristocratic hierarchy. The notion of resentment, it seems, can be used in all sorts of ways.

These examples indicate that sin is a preoccupation not merely of religious and theological thought. Sin is an evident fact in human life, something one has to think of, something that accounts for the differences.

We will consider sin under three headings: sin as crime, sin as a component in social process, and sin as aberration.

1.2.1 Sin as Crime

Sin as crime is, as it were, a statistical phenomenon. Everything is not going to be perfect. Sin as crime is more or less an incidental, statistical, and relatively small departure from accepted norms. It gives rise to laws, the police, law courts, tribunals, prisons. At the same time, it generates the notion of the good as 'keeping out of jail' − You're a good man if you're not in jail; that's all we can ask of you. It brings out the further notion that to attain further good is a matter of having more laws, more policemen, more courts. Against sin as crime, then, there is the law, and the law is a fundamental element in the apprehension of the good. As St Paul states in Romans 3.20, 'Through the law there is knowledge of sin.'[27] And again in Romans 5.13 he writes, 'Before the law there was sin in the world, but the sin was not counted as sin since there was no law.'[28]

Sin as crime is a matter of the crimes of passion, of moral failure, of bad will, of incomprehension. The criminal class to a greater or lesser extent is a class of those who do not understand the social setup. Criminals establish another society of their own with its own moral standards. There is a story of a gangster who shot a policeman, and when asked why he did it said he did it in self-defense:[29] he had moral standards of his own that gave evidence of an entirely different society, with criteria and laws of its own. In any society there can arise the vertical invasion of barbarians, of people who do not understand the society as it exists and are in revolt against it. Such people come from within the society. The society has failed to bring them up to its own level, or they have refused to ascend to the level of the society. The annual crop of infants is a potential invasion of barbarians, and education may be conceived as the first line of defense.

27 Lonergan quoted the Greek as well in the lecture, and on LN 36 verso both this and the next quotation are given in Greek. NRSV: '... through the law comes the knowledge of sin.'
28 NRSV: '... sin was indeed in the world before the law, but sin is not reckoned when there is no law.'
29 LN 36 verso has, 'Dillinger.'

1.2.2 Sin as a Component in Social Process

Secondly, there is sin as a component in social process, as the opposite to the development of civilizational order. Our Lord remarks in Matthew 18.7 that it is necessary that scandals come. In fact, the good of order does not develop in the glorious fashion I outlined yesterday. It develops under a bias in favor of the powerful, the rich, or the most numerous class. It changes the creative minority into a merely dominant minority. It leads to a division of classes not merely by their function, but also by their well-being. This division of classes gives rise in the underdogs to suspicion, envy, resentment, hatred, and in those that have the better end of the stick, to haughtiness, arrogance, disdain, criticism of 'sloth,' of 'lack of initiative,' of 'short-sightedness,' or in earlier times, of 'lowly birth.' Thus in the very process of the development of civilizational order, there result from sin a bias in favor of certain groups and against other groups, class opposition, the emotional charging of that opposition, and the organization of those emotions and that opposition in mutual recriminations and criticism. In time the pendulum swings from dominance by force and class law, through palliatives and concessions, to a shift of power and to punitive laws. Income tax in England at the present time seems to be an instance of punitive law. We find a great emigration of the best young brains from England, because they foresee no possibility of getting anywhere in their own country, where there is discrimination against what once was the leading class.[30] Such a state of affairs interferes with creativity. It is not enough just to have a new idea, even if the idea is just what is wanted. The idea has to combine with power, with wealth, with popular notions, before it can be realized. It cannot simply emerge from the man on the spot, diffuse, give rise to new potentialities in a chain reaction. Developments become lopsided, curtailed. Completion of the development is demanded by disaffection, but it cannot emerge in the normal fashion of the spread of an idea. It has to come by management, from above downward, not from below upward. Management always needs more power. Without a constant increase in power, management is not able to control all the outside[31] factors that might interfere with its plans. If it cannot exclude those factors, it cannot achieve its results. And so there occurs the rise and growth of a bureaucratic hierarchy.

In spontaneous developments, the new ideas come where they may to the

---

30 Lonergan added that this was just a suspicion of his own, but that he was using it to illustrate the idea of punitive law.
31 The word 'outside' is supplied from LN 37.

man on the spot who is intelligent, sees the possibilities, and goes ahead at his own risk. But in the bureaucracy the intelligent man ceases to be the initiator. He does not have the power, the connections, the influence, to put his ideas into practice. He becomes a consultant, an expert, called in by the bureaucracy. Activity is slowed down to the pace of routine paperwork. Style and form, that are inevitable when the man who has the idea is running things, yield to standardization and uniformity. Wisdom and faith yield to eclecticism and syncretism: Pick the best ideas, and the ideas that will suit everybody, or some of those that will suit everybody. The process of mimesis, of the people who were carried on in the movement even though they did not quite understand it, changes into drudgery and routine, with no understanding of what is going on.[32] They keep on doing it because they have to live. Creativity has fewer and fewer opportunities for significant achievement. The lone individual is more and more driven onto the margin of the big process, of what is really going on.[33] The masses demand security, distraction, entertainment, pleasure, and they have a decreasing sense of shame.

In this regard, I relate a story told me by a man in Montreal. His mother came from Germany and his uncles went to Detroit. His uncles put their sons through college by spending their lives working in factories. When they retired from the factories they could not just be idle, so they set up small machine shops where they worked on their own time. Their sons with the college educations were quite content to work in the factories just as their fathers had done, and they spent their spare time watching baseball games on television. Now that is not simply an individual matter. The older men belonged to a different time, when opportunities existed for the individual that do not exist today. The supermarkets have pushed out the corner grocery store, and so on all along the line. You have to be in big business to be in business at all, and in big business you have nothing to say. Thus there is a spread of frivolity.

There is also esotericism: people retire into the ivory tower, and they have no intention of returning to the transformation of the situation. There is archaism: people preach the revival of the ancient virtues, but the ancient virtues are no longer relevant to the present situation; they were virtues once, but they are not what is needed now.[34] There is futurism: achieve uto-

---

32 This sentence is taken partly from LN 37.
33 LN 37 has at this point, 'feeling of frustration impotence hopelessness cynicism meaninglessness drift.'
34 LN 37: 'Archaism: revive the virtues of a past that is over.' The references to archaism and futurism rely on Toynbee, *A Study of History*. See the indices to vols. 6 and 10 under Archaism and Futurism.

pia by a leap; forget that the good is concrete — *bonum et malum sunt in rebus*: good and evil lie in the concrete, and the real ideal, the true ideal, is the potentiality in the concrete. There are what are called 'times of troubles,' wars to arouse social concern, to give people a stake in the nation, to give them the feeling that they belong together in one nation. There are the outer and inner barbarians growing to ever larger proportions. And finally, there is the universal state as an outward peace to cover over inner emptiness. Sin as a component in the social process lets the material development go ahead, and at the same time takes out of it its soul.

1.2.3 Sin as Aberration

Thirdly, there is sin as aberration, as the evil that is opposite to cultural development, to development on the reflective level, that is, to development in the apprehension of the invariants of the human good. On sin as aberration, the New Testament is rather abundant. See Romans 1.18–32, 2.12–24. Romans 5.21 tells us: 'Sin reigned in the world.'[35] John 1.9[36] has: 'He came unto his own, and his own received him not.' In John 3.19–21, we read, 'All that love the light come to the Son, but those whose works are evil refuse to come to the light, because they do not wish their works to become manifest.'[37] Again, in John 8.42–47 and 12.37–41, there is word of the blindness of Israel.[38]

Now how can sin be aberration? What does that mean? Human history is like human consciousness: if I may use a metaphor, both of them float. Human consciousness is not a fully determined function of sensitive impressions and hereditary equipment. Consciousness also depends upon an orientation within the subject that is accepted and willed by the subject. There is such a thing as freedom of consciousness — principally, of course, in the sense that acts of will are free, but also and by way of a precondition in the sense that consciousness itself is not something determined uniquely by external objects or internal objects, by biological or sensitive conditions and

---

35 Thus quoted here by Lonergan. NRSV: '... sin exercised dominion in death.'
36 Thus cited by Lonergan. Actually the verse is John 1.10. NRSV: 'He was in the world, and the world came into being through him; yet the world did not know him.'
37 Thus quoted by Lonergan. The relevant verses are actually John 3.20–21. NRSV: '... all who do evil hate the light and do not come to the light, so that their deeds may not be exposed. But those who do what is true come to the light ...'
38 LN 37 on sin as aberration lists the following passages: Romans 1.18–32; 2.12–16, 17–24; 5.21; John 1.9; 3.19–21; 8.42–47; 12.37–41; Isaiah 6.8–11.

determinants. You think of what you please. In that sense, consciousness floats. It selects. What comes to your attention depends not merely upon the thing's being there to be attended to, but much more upon your being interested. And just as consciousness floats according to the orientation of the subject — these are points on which we shall have to go into more detail later — so also history has its orientation. There is such a thing as the spirit of an age, and that spirit of an age can be an aberration, it can be folly. Whom the gods destroy they first make blind.[39] As aberrant consciousness heads to neurosis and psychosis, similarly aberrant history heads to cataclysm.[40]

In what consists the aberration of consciousness and of history? We will deal with this in more detail later,[41] but for the moment it will suffice to distinguish between the ideal tendencies of the human spirit to what is true, to what is right, to what is good, and on the other hand, what in the concrete individual is conjoined with these spiritual aspirations, that is, his concern. His total concern includes his ideal aspirations, but it includes more as well; and it can deform, misdirect, those aspirations. Every closing off, blocking, denial of the empirically, intelligently, rationally, freely, responsibly conscious subject is also a closing off, a blocking, of the dominance of the higher aspirations of the human spirit and the human heart.[42] Again, his-

39 This is the form in which Lonergan more than once quoted the proverb (see also § 1.3 below and 'The Ongoing Genesis of Methods,' in *A Third Collection* 158). It had gone through many forms in both Latin and English (deriving, it seems, from a Greek fragment), but we have not noticed any with Lonergan's plural 'gods' or with his 'blind' for 'mad.'
40 LN 37 has, 'Sin can be aberration because history, like consciousness, floats: neither determined uniquely by situation, but also by orientation of consciousness, by Spirit of the Age
    'Individual life and historical pluralities of lives emerge in and through apprehension and choice: as aberrant consciousness heads to neurosis psychosis, so aberrant history to cataclasm [sic].'
41 See below, chapter 10.
42 LN 37 has, 'Aberration: Sorge as functionally conflicting with pure desire to know
    'pure desire: openness to full understanding, truth, right, good, God, Christ, Church
    'Sorge as conflicting: limited horizon; whom the gods destroy they first make blind; excaecatio
    'Mt 15.14: caecus autem si caeco ducatum praestet, ambo in foveam cadunt
    'Heidegger: productive imagination is the a priori that unifies the a priori forms of sensibility with the categories of understand[ing] Kant und das Problem der Metaphysik; not pure desire to know
    'Every closing off blocking denial of the empirically intelligently rationally conscious subject, its unlimited range, its potential Existenz.'

torically, every failure to unblock is but the means towards the clarification of the issue for the discerning: By their fruits you shall know them.

According to the theologians, there is proof that man in this life without divine grace cannot long avoid grievous sin. That incapacity to avoid sin without grace is moral impotence. The moral impotence of man creates in man a demand for false philosophies in our day, for a high-level rationalization,[43] just as it created a demand for degrading myths in ancient times. The objectification of sin in social process provides the objective empirical evidence for the false philosophy or degrading myth.[44] The incomplete development and the sins of the philosopher or the bard make them incapable of conceiving and expressing[45] a true philosophy or a true symbolic vision of life. Moreover, those who do uphold what is true give scandal by acting and writing unworthily. Again, the refutation of n false philosophies, where n is as big as you please, does not exclude — in fact it invites — the creation of the $(n+1)$th false philosophy. There is in man a demand for false philosophy, for degrading myths, because of his moral impotence. What is needed in man to break away from the aberration of sin is a leap — not a leap beyond reason, as irrationalist philosophers would urge, but a leap from unreason, from the unreasonableness of sin, to reason. That leap is not simply a matter of repeating, pronouncing, affirming, agreeing with the propositions that are true, while misapprehending their meaning and significance. That is just what lies behind the decadence of philosophic schools.[46] The leap is rather really assenting to, really apprehending — Newman's distinction between real and notional apprehension and real and notional assent. What is wanted is something existential — real apprehension and real assent to the truth.

Now what I have said of philosophy and myth is true of all departments: of human science, of natural science, of arts and letters. All are expressions of the orientation of the human soul and the social situations produced by souls and expected in the future from souls.[47] All are determinants of, and determined by, the social situation, which is simply the result of the influence of the group on the individual, and of each individual on the group. To surrender to this aberration produces a series of lower syntheses. Hegel

43 The phrase 'high-level rationalization' is supplied from LN 37 verso.
44 This sentence is supplied from LN 37 verso.
45 Lonergan said, 'conceiving and expressing'; LN 37 verso has 'reaching and teaching.'
46 The last two sentences are partly constructed from LN 37 verso.
47 This sentence is partly supplied from LN 37 verso.

spoke of the series of ascending syntheses, but one can design without any great difficulty a series of descending syntheses as well: medieval unity shattered at the Reformation on the struggles between church and state; the wars of religion disgusted men with all supernatural religion, and led to rationalism, the guidance of life not by any divine revelation but simply by man's own reason; the fact that men could not agree effected the transition from rationalism to liberalism and tolerance; and the fact that, when people merely tolerate one another's views, they cannot have any common view, and they cannot act effectively to deal with social evils, gives rise to totalitarianism. And so we can discern in that progress, which is the progress of modern thought in one of its aspects, a succession of lower syntheses. In the face of that succession of lower syntheses, the Catholic can wish to retire into an ivory tower, to condemn the new good because it is associated with new evils; but that is just another form of the aberration.[48]

1.3 Redemption

The third differential, redemption, can be conceived in various ways.

It is a break with the past, the dead hand of the past, its institutions, the mentalities it produced, the resentments and hatreds it accounted for. Mircea Eliade, in *The Myth of the Eternal Return*,[49] sees in the rites of the vegetation cults, the Dionysian cults, the Roman *Saturnalia*, a symbolic wiping out of the past. The orgies connected with these rites were given the significance of wiping out the enmities, the resentments, the debts, the obligations to which the past had given rise, and making possible a new start. That idea of a new start is an element in confession, in the sacrament of penance. It involves the emergence of new men in a new situation.[50] Eliade criticizes these rites as a flight from history, but one can also think of them as a primitive means on the symbolic level to deal with and dominate history. It is true that man is historical, but he is historical in the sense that his apprehensions and choices form a cumulative process; and there is no contradiction between the historical and the use of apprehension and choice to dominate and control that process in some manner. In that sense the myth

48   LN 37 verso has at this point, 'Catholic Right.' The coffee break was taken here. Nothing seems to have been lost on the tape.
49   Lonergan is referring to a translation of Mircea Eliade, *Le mythe de l'éternel retour: Archétypes et répétition* (Paris: Gallimard, 1949); a more recent English translation is entitled *Cosmos and History: The Myth of the Eternal Return*, trans. Willard R. Trask (New York: Harper, 1959).
50   This sentence is supplied from LN 37 verso.

of the eternal return, the return to the new situation, to starting afresh, can be thought of as a symbolic technique on a rather primitive level for dealing with the fundamental problem of history. History dominates man enough without his attempting to free himself from it.

Another type of redemption is what Toynbee calls 'New Soil.'[51] A corrupt civilization disintegrates. New people take over the achievements of the past without the memories and hatreds, the false ideas and degrading myths. Or again, there can be new soil in the more literal sense of immigration to new lands. When such an immigration occurs the society begins afresh. The cumulative problems created by sin as a component in social process and as aberration are undercut. There is a new start.

There is a redemptive aspect in revolution, the violent destruction of existing institutions, existing habits, existing material equipment, and the persons that are the carriers of the institutions and the habits of a culture. Thucydides provides a terrifying description of the revolution at Corcyra,[52] where the people were divided into the rich and the poor, and the rich were simply wiped out, mercilessly and completely. The French and Russian revolutions were more or less complete liquidations of the past of a country. In Marxism there is a Jewish eschatological element combined with the idea of revolution, a sudden, quasi eschatological[53] transformation of the situation, produced by the revolution.

There is an element of the notion of redemption that is illusory, in archaism with its revival of ancient virtues, in futurism with its leap to utopia, in esotericism with its attitude of 'Let the world go by, at least we shall live our well-regulated and happy lives by ourselves,' and, of course, in the more recent illusion of automatic progress, which is simply a denial of the problems created by sin.

However, when I spoke of redemption, what you all first thought of was redemption in Christ Jesus. That redemption was not what was expected: an eschatological transformation of this world, a complete destruction of the unjust, and a millennium of peace and prosperity for the just. The redemption in Christ Jesus does not change the fundamental fact that sin continues to head for suffering and death. However, the suffering and death that fol-

51 See Toynbee, *A Study of History*, vol. 2: *The Geneses of Civilizations, Part 2*, 73–100, 395–99. Toynbee's expression is 'New Ground.'

52 See *The Complete Writings of Thucydides: The Peloponnesian War*, the unabridged Crawley translation with an introduction by John H. Finley, Jr (New York: Random House, 1951), book 3, chapter 10, esp. pp. 188–92.

53 The expression 'quasi eschatological' is supplied from LN 37 verso.

low from sin attain a new significance in Christ Jesus. They are no longer the sad, disastrous end to the differential of sin, but also the means towards transfiguration and resurrection. Beyond death on the cross, there is the risen Savior. The antithesis between death and resurrection runs through the writings of St Paul in a series of different forms. There is the symbolic death of baptism and the symbolic life of the Eucharist; there is the ascetic death of mortification, of dying to sin, and the ascetic resurrection of the exercise of virtue. They are all spoken of by St Paul with the compactness of the symbol.

Faith is the fundamental answer to the problem of sin not only in the next life but also in this life. Against sin as aberration, that is, the sin that verifies the old Greek proverb 'Whom the gods would destroy they first make blind,' faith reestablishes truth as a meaningful category. Pilate asked our Lord, 'What is truth?' The modern human scientist does not ask that question if he is preoccupied with imitating the techniques of the natural sciences. For then knowledge is science only in the measure that it can verify and enable one to predict. The reestablishment of truth as a meaningful category is also a liberation of intelligence and reason.

Again, against sin as a component in the social process, sin as changing social process from a matter of freedom and creativity to routine and drudgery with all its determinisms and pressures and in the limit violence, there arises hope, which liberates the pilgrim in us,[54] and which enables us to resist the pressures and the determinisms that are, as it were, the necessity of sinning further. Pius XII spoke of the fact that the modern world creates situations in which people have to be heroic to avoid mortal sin. To have that heroism there is needed the virtue of hope; and without that heroism there is no victory over the cumulative effects of sin as a component in social process.

Finally, against sin as self-perpetuating, as a chain reaction, there is love of one's enemies and the acceptance of suffering. Sin as a chain reaction has two bases. It has a basis first in the hearts of men, where sin leads to ever further sin insofar as hatred arises. But Christ teaches us, 'Love your enemies, do good to them that hate you.' Secondly, there is a chain reaction of sin in the logic of the objective situation,[55] and against that aspect Christianity teaches the acceptance of suffering. 'The servant is not better than his master.' 'Do not resist evil, but overcome evil with good.' The acceptance of

54 This clause is supplied from LN 37 verso.
55 LN 37 verso: 'in concrete logic of evil.'

suffering puts an end, at least at one point, to the chain reaction of sin that spreads throughout a society. When everyone is dodging suffering, when no one accepts it, the burden is passed ever further on.

Redemption in Christ Jesus is the answer to the problem created by sin as a component in social process and as fundamental aberration, but it has not merely a negative office. It comes through the grace of our Lord Jesus Christ, through a personal communication of the life of the ever Blessed Trinity to mankind. 'In the fulness of time, God sent his Son, born of woman, made under the law, that those who were under the law might be redeemed and receive the adoption of sons. And now that you are sons, to show that you are sons, he sent the Spirit of his Son into our hearts, crying, "Abba, Father!" ' (Galatians 4. 4–6).[56] The mission of the Son and the mission of the Holy Ghost is the basis of a new society in Father, Son, and Holy Ghost, in which there is communicated to us personally, through the person of the Son and through the person of the Spirit, a participation of divine perfection, a participation of the order of truth and love that binds the three persons of the Blessed Trinity.[57] Sin, suffering, and death remain, but in Christ they have become transition points to an ever fuller life on this earth with God the Father and the Son and the Holy Ghost, with whom we aspire to live in eternal life. The process of redemption, then, as conceived by the Catholic, is first of all the radical answer to sin — not the answer to sin that eliminates sin, but the answer to sin that endures its consequences and nullifies them and transforms man into a child of God, with a participation in the sonship that God the Father acknowledged when Jesus was baptized at the Jordan: 'This is my beloved Son. Hear ye him.'[58] In baptism we become adopted sons as Christ was the natural Son of the Father.[59]

56 Thus quoted by Lonergan. NRSV: '... when the fullness of time had come, God sent his Son, born of a woman, born under the law, in order to redeem those who were under the law, so that we might receive adoption as children. And because you are children, God has sent the Spirit of his Son into our hearts, crying, "Abba, Father!" '

57 LN 37 verso has at this point a theme that runs throughout Lonergan's work:
   'The Blessed Trinity: God as Rational Consciousness
   'Procession of the Word: as rational judgment from grasp of unconditioned: eternal Truth (sense of criterion)
   'Procession of the Spirit: as act of love from rational judgment of value and infinite understanding of identity of understanding, truth, being, good
   'Perfection of act; perfection of order (interpersonal as in society; immanent in a single consciousness as in Imago Dei).'

58 Thus quoted by Lonergan. Actually none of the accounts has the words 'Hear ye him.'

59 LN 38 has at this point, 'Body of Christ is the personal communication of a par-

So much for the three differentials of the human good. We set up an invariant structure, and then we noticed that the structure was realized differently at different times, and we distinguished three differentials: intellectual development on the two levels of civilization and culture; sin contradicting, deforming both those types of development; and finally, redemption. That analysis of the good, of course, makes it obvious why we want Catholic education. The fact of sin is not any private opinion of Catholics, but something to be noted by all. Our notion of the good cannot prescind from the tension between the good and evil. If we have an answer to the problem of evil, it will influence our education in all its aspects, because it influences our very notion of the good.

1.4 Notes on the Differentials

Certain notes on the differentials are perhaps in order. First, they have been described in isolation; I considered first intellectual development, then sin, and finally redemption; but in the concrete all three function together. They are intertwined. They do not exist in isolation, but they have to be described separately before they can be considered together. In particular, I spoke first of sin and then of redemption. But that does not mean that there are not sin and the effects of sin in the church; there are sins of the faithful, of priests and religious, of bishops and popes.

Again, as we have already said, the apprehension of sin in its real ugliness has occurred not only within the church but also outside it. There is a developing understanding, reflective differentiation,[60] and penetrating criticism of sin outside the church. It is not true in all respects, but nonetheless it is a real awareness of sin. It is illustrated in Marx and Nietzsche. It makes knowledge of sin no private prerogative of Catholics.

Again, the good is not apart from the true. We have not been operating yet on the level of a differentiated consciousness, where consciousness is concerned solely with the true, but we may note at once that the good and the true are bound together and isomorphic.[61] In undifferentiated consciousness they are just distinct moments in a single concrete process. But the good is willing the true, and the true is not known without the individ-

---

ticipation of divine perfection to the elect: individual and social; human and divine; life and death; joy and suffering; Truth and Goodness.'

60 The expression 'reflective differentiation' is supplied from LN 38.

61 The words 'and isomorphic' are suggested by LN 38.

ual's becoming good. The true can be repeated in propositions, but its meaning is not really grasped without a harmony between the subject and the truth he acknowledges.

Again, the natural and the supernatural are really distinct, as distinct as matter and form, soul and body, but in the concrete order of divine providence in this world they are united dynamically. You will notice that we went beyond philosophy when we went into our third differential and discussed the category of redemption as it occurs outside the church, as for example in the revolutionary doctrines which are having such a great influence on our time, and when we went on to the Catholic doctrine of redemption. Consequently, while one must always maintain the distinction, the real difference, between the natural and the supernatural, it does not follow that one should think and talk about the supernatural only on Sundays, or when one is doing theology, and forget all about it if one is talking about the concrete philosophically.[62]

Finally, as Pius XI said in his encyclical on the education of Catholic youth, Christ is the Way, the Truth, and the Life. I think our account of the differentials of human history, of the concrete human good, gives some insight into that truth.[63]

2   Levels of Integration

We spoke first of an invariant structure of the human good and secondly of three differentials — what makes the differences? My third main point on the good as object regards levels of integration. At any particular time we have a cumulation of differences from the past. Is there some integration of those differences? One can speak of integrations within the individual, and

62 LN 38 adds here, 'Precept of loving God above all and neighbour as oneself is functionally analogous to unfolding, implications, of pure desire to know
    'Distinction always; separate treatment does no harm in the measure that an integrated differentiation of consciousness is attained.'
63 Handwritten into LN 38 at this point is the following: 'V-P. Univ. of Toronto, Canadian Journal of Education (?), education must concentrate on its proper aim and function: time to forget demands for training in driving motorcars, religious instruction, and such trivia.' The reference is almost certainly to Dr Murray G. Ross, Vice-president, University of Toronto, 'The Role of the School in a Changing Society,' *Canadian Education: Official Publication of the Canadian Education Association* 14:3 (June 1959) 12–23; see especially pp. 13–14, where the language and positions correspond closely to those we find in Lonergan's notes. Lonergan would presumably have seen this journal in Halifax, in the month prior to the Cincinatti lectures.

of integrations within a given national culture or group of national cultures, such as the European group, and so on. What we want is a fundamental, very general distinction between levels of integration. Consequently, we begin with the notion of common sense, and proceed to a fourfold differentiation of levels of integration of the human good. The third and fourth levels will help us grasp perhaps a little more exactly and clearly what is the essential difference between modern education and classical education.

2.1 Common Sense

What is common sense? Fundamentally, it is an accumulation of insights resulting in an intellectual habit. In that respect it is like learning a science. Knowing a science — knowing physics, knowing chemistry, knowing psychology — is a matter of accumulating acts of understanding — understanding this and this and this and this — and gradually building up a habit of understanding so that you get the point right away — you do not have to learn any more. But the specific object of the intellectual habit of common sense is that on all ordinary occasions an individual is able to grasp just how to behave, just what to say, what to do, how to do it. A person who is lacking in common sense does not know what to do in this concrete situation; he is lost; he does not understand the concrete milieu in which he lives.

That accumulation of insights with regard to concrete behavior is the fundamental and common development of human intelligence. It involves no sharp differentiation between sense and intellect, body and soul, sign and signified, apprehension and appetition. People understand; but don't bother asking them why — things are so, they know, and that is all there is to it. This is the normal development of human intelligence. If you go by more than common sense, people say you are becoming technical.

When I say that in common sense there is no sharp differentiation between sense and intellect, I do not mean that different words do not exist to denote body and soul, sense and intellect. But the different words denote moments in a single concrete process or a single concrete reality rather than elements that admit specialized development.[64] There is not the sharp differentiation that arises when one moves, for example, to a metaphysics or to scientific thought. Again, I said that common sense was an accumulation of insights, and in that respect like a scientific habit. However, it has not the

64 The words from 'rather than' are supplied from LN 39.

same structure as a scientific habit. Common sense does not include accurate definitions. If you ask a man of common sense what a dog is, he will say that a dog is any animal that looks sufficiently like this to be called a dog by people of common sense. That is the only definition he has. Common sense does not go looking for accurate definitions that are valid *omni et nullo*.[65] It does not have the Socratic impulse to find out what fortitude is and what justice is, and so on. The people of Athens were people of common sense; they could not put up with Socrates' nonsense, so they gave him the hemlock. So too, people of common sense will reason, but they do not go in for long chains of reasoning; their arguments are short. Nor does common sense attempt to formulate universal principles; to do so it would need to have accurate definitions, and it does not go in for accurate definitions. Rather, it formulates proverbs, paradigmatic instances, illustrative stories.[66] Proverbs are like rules of grammar in that they have many exceptions. Still, the rules are well worth knowing, well to bear in mind in a whole series of situations. A stitch in time saves nine; look before you leap; and so on.

What is, then, the structure of common sense? It may be compared to a universal tool. People who are mechanically minded can purchase a handle into which you can fit a hammer, a screwdriver, a chisel, an awl, or a wrench – one tool that can be adapted to a whole series of purposes. Similarly, common sense is an accumulation of insights that, with a good look round and a shrewd eye on this and that person, will decide just what's up and what's to be done. There is a general nucleus equally relevant to all the situations in which a person is likely to find himself. But that nucleus does not correspond to some set of universal truths and premises from which you can deduce all the conclusions, as in a science. Common sense does not proceed that way. It takes a look round and adds a further insight, adjusting the general store to this concrete situation, and then goes ahead. So common sense is a fundamental accumulation of insights that by the addition of one or two further apposite insights is able to deal with any of the situations that are likely to arise.

Again, common sense is egocentric. It is not concerned with the general question of how anyone is to behave, but with how I am to behave; not with what anyone is to say, but with what I am to say; not with what is to be done

65 In 'Dimensions of Meaning,' *Collection* 236, Lonergan defines an *omni et soli* definition in a way that accurately reflects his use here of the expression *omni et nullo*: one that 'had to apply to every instance of the defined and to no instance of something else.'
66 The words 'paradigmatic instances, illustrative stories' are taken from LN 39.

by so and so, but with what I am to do and how I am to do it. It is like grammar. In grammar, place is always relative to my place — 'here' is my 'here' — and time is always relative to my time — I 'am,' and what is not at the same time 'was' or 'will be.' Persons, too, are relative to the first person. What is the second person? Not myself but the one I am talking to. And what is the third person? Somebody else. Common sense is egocentric in the same fashion.

Finally, common sense is the mode of all concrete understanding and judgment. When you get really down to the concrete, *you* are in the situation, and the situation is before *you*, and to deal with the situation you do not want some universal science; and in fact complete analysis is impossible and undesirable.[67] You want to make the ultimate adjustments to the concrete, beyond the generalities of science. In a way, common sense is prelogical. Lévy-Bruhl, the French sociologist, introduced the term 'prelogical' in describing primitives.[68] I do not wish to use the term in that sense, but rather to mean that common sense does not use terms, propositions, and syllogisms as a technique for the clarification and development of intelligence.[69] It proceeds in a much more direct fashion. The Greek discovery of the *logos* was the discovery of language, and consequently of concepts and judgments, and attention was drawn to the words, to the propositions, to the arguments, as a means, a tool, to make intelligence more complete and more adequate.

2.2 Four Levels of Integration

By my formulation of common sense I have provided myself with a general basis for distinguishing four levels of integration.

2.2.1 Undifferentiated Common Sense

The first level of integration is undifferentiated common sense. Undifferentiated common sense characterizes the primitive. Here there occurs the same development of intelligence in all the members of the tribe or clan. Thinking is a community enterprise. The clan or the tribe may be fruit gath-

---

67 The clause 'and in fact ...' is supplied from LN 39.
68 Lucien Lévy-Bruhl, *Les fonctions mentales dans les sociétés inférieures* (Paris: Presses Universitaires de France, 1951).
69 LN 39 has, 'prelogical in the sense that speech is not a systematically exploited tool for bringing to light defects in understanding.'

erers or gardeners or hunters or fishers. They will have developed skills, a language, some tools. They will have their art and their myths and their taboos. Tribes will differ from one another — there are enormous differences between the Eskimos and the pygmies or the bushmen — but in any given group there is a common intelligence. Common sense is common in the sense that it is common to many.

The relation between undifferentiated common sense and the idea that thinking is a community enterprise may have some connection with a phenomenon at the present time, the tendency of teenagers to conformism. An education whose ideal is adjustment does not proceed much beyond undifferentiated common sense. Conversely, if one's development is merely an undifferentiated common sense, people will have to conform.[70]

2.2.2 Differentiated Common Sense[71]

The second level of integration is differentiated common sense, differentiation of common sense by the division of labor. We may associate this level of integration with Egypt, Crete, Sumer, Babylon, Assyria, the ancient high civilizations of the Indus Valley and the Hwang Ho Valley, of the Mayas of Central America and the Incas of Peru. In those civilizations there existed large-scale agriculture, there was a great differentiation of arts and crafts, there were writing, arithmetic, bookkeeping, engineering, surveying, astronomy. There was a social hierarchy and law. There was what Voegelin calls the 'cosmological myth.'[72] The divine order, the ultimate realities, the gods, were, as it were, incarnated in the social order, so that at least in Egypt and to some extent in Mesopotamia — I don't know about the others — the king was the god or the son of god. In later stages in these civilizations there emerged another aspect of differentiated common sense in the form of a wisdom literature. This stage is illustrated, for example, in the book of Proverbs. And in the breakdowns of these civilizations there occurs the emergence of individualism.

---

70 Lonergan added in an aside something like 'That's a hypothesis, merely remote value, suggestion.'
71 In § 2.2.3 Lonergan will speak of the differentiation of consciousness, meaning by this expression something beyond common sense. In later writings he speaks, not of differentiated common sense, but of the brands of common sense. See, for example, *Method in Theology* 276: 'There are as many brands of common sense as there are languages, social or cultural differences, almost differences of place and time.'
72 See, for example, Eric Voegelin, *Israel and Revelation* 82–85.

So there is a differentiation of common sense by the division of labor; there are different kinds of common sense for people in different walks of life. This specialization leads to a high development of arts and crafts and practical sciences such as astronomy, engineering, and surveying. Building the pyramids, for example, was an extraordinary achievement in engineering.

2.2.3 Classicism and the Differentiation of Consciousness

The third level of integration involves the differentiation of consciousness, the emergence of the intellectual pattern of experience. We will name it the pure development of human intelligence.[73] This is what is meant by classicism in its best sense, the Greek achievement.

We will consider first the general characteristics of this level of integration. The individual appeals to immanent norms, to what is true against the false, to what is right against the wrong, to what is good against the evil. The autonomy of the human spirit emerges. There is a development of argument, definition, science, the critique of gods, of myths, of magic, of taboos, of institutions and manners, of aims and values. These features are all exhibited in the Sophist movement of the fifth century B.C. and the philosophic movement of the fourth century B.C. in Greece. The individual asserts his freedom to be himself. He liberates aesthetic, intellectual, scientific, moral, and religious activity from traditionally restricted functions within the collectivity.[74] Prior to this pure development of intelligence all of these features existed except science, but they were functional parts within the concrete totality. In the ancient high civilizations such as Egypt or Crete, there was differentiated common sense, where the integration comes through the concrete integration of the members of society. But there was not a theoretical integration beyond the differentiated common sense of individuals engaged in different tasks and leading different kinds of lives.

The emergence of individualism, of critical thought,[75] gives rise to what Marx called the superstructure. There are discussion groups, wandering teachers, the formation of academies, schools, libraries, universities, universalist tendencies in intellectual, political, and religious fields. There is

73 The heading for this section on LN 39 is 'Pure Development of Intelligence and Judgment.'
74 The words 'from ... collectivity' are supplied from LN 39.
75 There is a brief break on the tape at this point, but it does not seem that anything has been omitted.

the pursuit of wisdom and culture for their own sake. This pure development of intelligence is not practical; it is[76] proudly useless; it is the enrichment of mind, the advance of knowledge, the ennobling of will, the rationalization of manners, all for their own sake. But it involves a tendency as well to be limited to a particular class, to classical models, the depiction of ideals, the per se, the legal. It offers tables of virtues and vices, settled art forms and literary genres, types of polity, all in static concepts, principles, systems.

2.2.4 Historical Consciousness[77]

There is needed, then, a fourth level of integration, one that involves both further pure development and the transition to applied development and practicality. There is further pure development in the move from abstract formal objects to genetic method and to groups of operations. There is applied development in the advance of technology and in industry, in the education of the masses, in the rise of modern medicine as applied science. Even philosophy can be applied; historical consciousness emerges when there is grasped the relevance of human intelligence and wisdom to the whole of human life. Then the entire fabric of human existence appears as a historical product, as the result of man's apprehension, judgment, choice, action. Moreover, what has been made by man can be changed and improved by man.[78] We have come to realize that we are more the masters of our own destiny than we had thought. The self-assertion of modern man contains a notable measure of truth: man is responsible for his history; man

76 All tapes end here. The remainder of this chapter is constructed from the notes of F. Crowe and from Lonergan's notes.
77 The heading for this section on LN 39 verso is 'Further pure development and transition to applied development.' This section presents an early, possibly Lonergan's earliest reference to historical consciousness. From his student days he had been keenly interested in the structure of the history *that happens*, with its three simultaneous moments of progress, decline, and redemption. Further, throughout his career as professor he was concerned to bring into theology the history *that is written*; but he first dealt with this history as an object — that is the case even in the course *De systemate et historia* that followed the present lectures (Gregorian University, 1959–60); in other words his 'turn to the subject,' so evident in his 1957 lectures on existentialism, did not automatically introduce him to 'historical consciousness'; that is only now emerging as a category.
78 LN 39 verso: 'cf. back to Husserl: *Western Man anthropological classification or exemplar of mankind.*'

is largely what man has made of man. But this self-assertion has been left largely to the initiative of the secularists, and the result has been the de-Christianization of the modern world. Even so-called Catholic countries are to a great extent either backward or de facto non-Catholic. This should not surprise us: it is not merely the Bourbons who forget nothing, learn nothing, and like things that way. But also, Christianity is a wisdom, and wisdom enters on the scene only when what is going forward becomes clear. The idea of historical consciousness arose outside the church and produced disasters, but we have to consider it seriously. In Hegel's words, 'Only with the fall of twilight does the owl of Minerva take wing.'[79] The church moves slowly but surely.

The self-assertion of modern man has been implemented by philosophy, or, where philosophy deserted the scene, by empirical human science. There has developed a philosophy of human science, a philosophy of politics (the *philosophes*, the French Revolution and its *liberté, fraternité, égalité*), a philosophy of economics (the nineteenth-century iron law of wages, and the transition to a more or less managed economy after the Depression). There is a philosophy of history, as in Vico, who began a new phase different from that which held from Augustine to Bossuet. There is the move from Vico, with his insistence on the priority of poetry and the compact symbol, vis-à-vis differentiated consciousness, to Hegel, Marx, and Troeltsch.[80] Through Marx, there is the influence of the philosophy of history on later Russians and Chinese. There is the philosophy of education – already we have mentioned Dewey's influence not only in the United States but worldwide. And today there is the rediscovery of the symbol in depth psychology, in the work of Eliade and the history of religions, in Cassirer's *Philosophy of Symbolic Forms*,[81] in Voegelin's interpretation of the ancient Near East, Israel, and Greece, and in the phenomenologists and existentialists. But there are also the social engineers and the hidden persuaders, the propaganda ministries and the advertising industry.

79 'The owl of Minerva spreads its wings only with the falling of the dusk.' G.W.F. Hegel, *Philosophy of Right*, trans. T.M. Knox (London: Oxford University Press, 1967) 13. Quoted by Lonergan also in 'The Role of a Catholic University in the Modern World,' *Collection* 112: 'only with the fall of twilight does Minerva's owl take wing.'
80 See Ernst Troeltsch, *Der Historismus und seine Probleme* (Tübingen: J.C.B. Mohr, 1922).
81 Ernst Cassirer, *The Philosophy of Symbolic Forms*, trans. Ralph Mannheim, vol. 1: *Language*, vol. 2: *Mythical Thought*, vol. 3: *The Phenomenology of Knowledge* (New Haven: Yale University Press, 1955, 1957).

Ernst Cassirer in his *Essay on Man*[82] states that from the viewpoint of the phenomenology of culture, man is *animal symbolicum*, not a rational animal. This claim in fact poses succinctly the challenge of our age: Are we to seek an integration of the human good on the level of historical consciousness, with the acknowledgment of man's responsibility for the human situation? If so, how are we to go about it? These are the fundamental questions for a philosophy of education today. There is a need for a philosophy on the level of our time,[83] a philosophy that is concrete, existential, genetic, historical, a 'philosophy of ...,' and Catholic. There is required, too, an education that is on the level of our time.[84]

82 Ernst Cassirer, *An Essay on Man: An Introduction to a Philosophy of Human Culture* (New Haven: Yale University Press, 1944). The original preface to *Insight* reflects a similar concern with Cassirer's claim. See Lonergan, 'The Original Preface of Insight,' *Method: Journal of Lonergan Studies* 3:1 (March 1985) 6.
83 LN 39 verso has here, in parentheses, 'Ortega y Gasset.' Ortega is mentioned also in the original preface to *Insight*: '... if I may borrow a phrase from Ortega y Gasset, one has to strive to mount to the level of one's time.' A possible source for this reference is chapter 3 of *The Revolt of the Masses* (London: Unwin Books), which is entitled 'The Height of the Times.' This book is also a possible background source for some of Lonergan's ideas in these lectures on education.
84 LN 40 recto and verso treat many of the same problems, but do not seem to have been used directly as sources for these lectures. They are included in the appendix, § B, under the heading 'Operations and Culture.'

4

The Human Good as
the Developing Subject[1]

The last two days we have been concerned with the human good as a developing object. Our presentation serves to define any human aim i n this life, at least in general lines. Today we move on to a complementary aspect of the human good, namely, the human good as the developing subject.

1   Transitions[2]

1.1 'Being a Man': From Essence to Ideal [3]

I ended up yesterday by noting Ernst Cassirer's remark in his *Essay on Man* that from the viewpoint of a phenomenology of human cultures, man is not a rational animal but a symbolic animal. You can see from the fact of sin, which is an irrationality, that there is reason for doubting the rationality of man. On the other hand, all men use symbols, and so 'man as a symbolic animal' provides a universally true definition.

There is something to the notion of man as a rational animal that

1 The fourth lecture, Thursday, August 6, 1959, and the beginning of the sixth lecture, Friday, August 7, 1959. See note 73 below.
2 Lonergan did not give the major subheading here. We insert it on the basis of his later remarks on three transitions (see § 1.3 below). On the same basis we have made insertions in the subheadings of §§ 1.1 and 1.2.
3 'From Essence to Ideal' is added on the basis of § 1.3 (see above, note 2).

includes more than any given man may happen to be. When we defend the notion of man as rational animal we appeal to what man is potentially. The Greeks defined man as *zôon logikon, animal rationale,* the animal that is a logical animal. If the logical, rational part of the definition is regarded as something in potency, then it is something that is common to mewling infants, to people that are asleep or unconscious, to morons[4] and Ph.D.'s, to drifters and conformists and individuals facing heroically a crisis in their lives.[5] With respect to man's logical essence, namely, that he is a rational animal where 'rational' means 'in potency,' man does not develop.

However, as I noted last night, everyone understands what is meant when one hears the phrase used by President Eisenhower, 'We have to be men.'[6] The man that one has to be is not what one necessarily is. It is something that follows, not from having a birth certificate or citizenship, but from a decision, from the use of one's freedom, from a use of freedom that occurs despite a measure of uncertainty. We do not know all about everything, and if we try to find out all about everything, we become hesitating Hamlets; we do not decide. To decide we have to take risks, and the risks regard objects and other people and ourselves.

Moreover, once one makes a decision, one has not exhausted the content of being a man. One has done so just for that occasion. The challenge remains with us perpetually. There are decisions and choices that have to be made all along the line, and at any time we can fail. We can be 'the man' today and fail tomorrow. Being a man is something that, if we are it, we are so only precariously. It is a *continuous* challenge. Time enters into the essence of being a man. And so Heidegger entitled his celebrated work *Sein und Zeit, Being and Time,*[7] and Gabriel Marcel has a book entitled *Homo Viator,*[8] man the pilgrim.

It is that notion of man on which the existentialists insist, that aspect of being a man, that is relevant to our question of man as a developing subject.

4 Lonergan said, 'high-grade morons,' but we interpret 'high-grade' as a false start.
5 LN 41 has in parentheses the word 'martyrs.'
6 LN 41 has, ' "We have to be men." Eisenhower to press, Egyptian crisis, about 3 yrs. ago, fleet into Eastern Mediterranean.' Lonergan is referring to the Suez Canal crisis of 1956. See also *Understanding and Being* 190, note 16. The reference to 'last night' probably indicates a discussion period of which we have no record.
7 Martin Heidegger, *Sein und Zeit* (Tübingen: Max Niemeyer Verlag, 7th ed., 1953); in English, *Being and Time,* trans. John Macquarrie and Edward Robinson (London: SCM Press, and New York: Harper & Row, 1962).
8 Gabriel Marcel, *Homo Viator: Prolégomènes à une métaphysique de l'espérance*

If you consider man as a rational animal, where the word 'rational' is understood potentially, then there is no development; it is eternally true of every man no matter what he does, how intelligent or stupid he is, how wise or silly, how saintly or wicked — he is a rational animal in that sense. But there is another sense, being actually rational, that carries the implications emphasized by the contemporary group of philosophers known as existentialists.[9] Their reasons for doing so are, first of all, that they want to get away from positivism; being a man in that deontological sense is something outside the field of positivistic research. Again, they also want to get away from idealism. The transcendental ego of the idealists is neither male nor female, Greek nor barbarian, Jew nor Gentile, bond nor free. It does not suffer, and it does not die. But we do. What has to be a man or a woman is what suffers and dies, what has the limitations of male and female, bond and free, Jew and Gentile, and so on. So they want to break from idealism and from positivism, and insofar as they want that break, they are with us.

1.2 'We,' 'I': From Substance to Subject[10]

Who is a man? Who is to be a man? The answer is 'I,' 'We.' That use of the first person supposes consciousness. What has to be a man is not just any instance of rational animal. It is one that is awake. Moreover, insofar as he is concerned with being a man, he is aware of potential triumph or potential failure, and aware of his own freedom and responsibility.

Such awareness is consciousness,[11] and that consciousness is not to be thought of as thinking about oneself. One is conscious no matter what one is thinking about. Consciousness means that one is *doing* the thinking.[12] Cognitional and volitional activity not only deals with objects, but also reveals the subject and his activity.[13] To get hold of the notion of consciousness it is well to begin from the word 'presence.' One can say that the chairs and tables are present in the room. They are not outside; they have not been

(Paris: Aubier, 1945); in English, *Homo Viator: Introduction to a Metaphysic of Hope*, trans. Emma Craufurd (Chicago: Regnery, 1951, and New York: Harper & Row, 1962).

9 In an aside, 'with or without their consent; Jaspers is the only one who accepts the title, as far as I know; perhaps also Berdyaev.'
10 'From Substance to Subject' is added on the basis of § 1.3 (see note 2 above).
11 This first clause in the sentence is taken from LN 41.
12 We have added this sentence on the basis of LN 41.
13 This sentence is taken from LN 41.

folded and stacked in the basement; they are present in the room, they are here. Again, I am here to you, and you are there to me. You are present to me, and I am present to you. That is a second sense of the word 'presence.' Presence in this further sense includes knowledge: if I were asleep you would not be present to me, and if you were asleep I would not be present to you. There is a third sense of the word 'presence': for you to be present to me I have to be already present. No one can be present to me if I am not present to myself, if I am unconscious. But that being present to myself is not the presence of an object to the subject; it is the subject being there, conscious. Similarly, I would not be present to you unless you were already present to yourselves. When you are in dreamless sleep you are not conscious, you are not present to yourself in that third sense of 'presence.' You are present to your bed in the same way as the chairs are present in the room. But when you begin to dream, not only is there the flow of images, but there is also a spectator. That spectator is there, not as an object, but as the one looking on — and conscious. Consciousness is precisely that being the spectator.

There are, of course, different levels of consciousness. First, there is merely *empirical* consciousness: you hear the sounds but you are not worried about any meaning in them. Next, there is *intellectual* consciousness. Aristotle remarks that wonder is the beginning of all science and philosophy.[14] One asks, What is it? Why? What does he mean? Where is he going? What is he up to? Then not just anyone is present, but someone intelligent is present. Empirical consciousness is simply presence in the third sense, but in intellectual consciousness, someone intelligent is present, actually intelligent, actively intelligent, wondering why and what and how and whither. Thirdly, there is *rational* consciousness. You get an idea of what someone is up to, but you do not jump to conclusions. You think it over, and ask, Is it right? Is it something true? That is a further step beyond intellectual consciousness. Finally, these three levels are simply cognitional, but knowing heads for doing, and *I* do the doing, *I* choose, *I* will. The *I* in the choosing intervenes: the choice is *my* choice. And so when you move on to doing, willing, choosing, you get a fourth level of consciousness, *self-consciousness*. One is involved oneself as soon as one starts to will.

1.3 From Faculty Psychology to Flow of Consciousness

We have effected two transitions, and we now have to make a third. Our first transition was from the logical essence — 'rational animal' in the sense of something common to infants, morons, geniuses, and heroes — to the ideal,

14 Aristotle, *Metaphysics*, I, 2, 982b 12–18, 983a 12–18.

the is-to-be, the ought-to-be: we have to be men.[15] Again, by speaking of consciousness, we effected the transition from substance to subject. The subject is a substance that is present to itself, that is conscious. When I say 'I,' I am already conscious, I am a subject. But if I say 'he' or 'she,' I may be talking of someone who is asleep, not conscious, just substance but only potentially subject. We are dealing not with logical essence and substance, but with the subject and his ideal, what he has to be.

The third transition is from faculty psychology to flow of consciousness.[16] There is nothing wrong with faculty psychology, but it is not enough for our present purposes, because it does not take us near enough to the concrete. You have to be in the concrete if you wish to study development. Abstractions do not move, do not develop, do not change.

Now the flow of consciousness has a fundamental autonomy. Consciousness is not a market place into which there enters anything whatever, according to its own laws, and from which there departs anything whatever, according to its own laws.[17] Consciousness is a structured unity. It is true that things force themselves upon us, upon our consciousness. The well into which Thales tumbled forced itself upon his consciousness. Again, it is true that consciousness is not *completely* autonomous, that it cannot run off in any direction it pleases. The limits to the autonomy or freedom of consciousness are exhibited in psychic illness.[18] The orientation of consciousness can get out of touch with the demands of the nervous system. So there are two extremes: things can be forced upon consciousness, and consciousness cannot run off in any direction whatever. But normally consciousness is a directed organization of selected data. And governing that direction and selection is our concern, what we care about, care for, are interested in, aim

15 LN 41 adds, 'l'homme se définit par une exigence,' a phrase which Lonergan used regularly without reference. See *Understanding and Being* 99, note 11.

16 Lonergan's positive view on faculty psychology is illustrated in the use he continues to make of it, not only in the 1964 edition of *De Deo trino* (2: 59) but also in quite new work that same year, for example, the 1964 lecture '*Existenz and Aggiornamento*,' in *Collection* 225. The negative side is the inability of faculty psychology to deal with the existential subject, 'a notion that is overlooked on the schematism of older categories that distinguished faculties ... or different uses of the same faculty ... or different types of human activity' ('The Subject,' in *A Second Collection* 79). As Lonergan later realized, already in *Insight* he was beyond faculty psychology and into intentionality analysis. See 'An Interview with Fr. Bernard Lonergan, S.J.,' ed. Philip McShane, *A Second Collection* 222.

17 LN 41 has, 'consciousness is not a market-place into which comes whatever pleases, out of which passes whatever decides.'

18 LN 41 reads, 'an excessively repressive censor ends up in psychic illness.'

at.[19] Heidegger's term is *Sorge,* care; 'concern' is the ordinary English translation. The same notion reappears in such words as 'attention' and 'interest.' One can walk along the street with a friend and in the midst of all sorts
of street noises hear just that thin trickle of sound that are his words. Meaning makes his voice audible.[20] That is an example of the selectivity of consciousness. There are all sorts of impressions made upon our sensitive
apparatus, our sense organs, but not all of them get into consciousness. It is
what you are interested in that gets into consciousness. Consciousness
selects; it floats upon the series of demands for attention.

In the flow of consciousness there is not only the subjective side, the concern, what concerns me, but also its correlative, the world — not *the* world
but *one's* world. There is the world of teachers, pupils, parents, inspectors,
principals — the educational world. There is another world of priests,
parishioners, sacristans, altar boys, bishops. There is another world of doctors, nurses, orderlies, and another world of lawyers, judges, policemen, jail-
ors. There are all sorts of worlds in this sense of *one's* world. And the world in
which one lives corresponds to one's concern.

What is this world? We will begin with a distinction between profile and
horizon. The distinction can be made clear if I ask you whether you have
ever seen Brockman Hall.[21] You might all say, 'Yes,' but at any moment of
looking, what you saw was Brockman Hall in some perspective. At no time
did you see all four sides, the roof and the basement, and all the rooms
inside. What is seen at any instant is just a profile of the object. When you
recognize Brockman Hall it is because you have seen a sufficient number of
profiles to be able to recognize it as Brockman Hall. What is that sufficient
number of profiles? To speak of it, we can use the word 'horizon.' A horizon
is a total series of possible profiles, any one of which would suffice for you to
be sure that this is Brockman Hall. The horizon, then, is an organization of
possible selections of profiles. The horizon is not something you ever see; it
is a collection of possible profiles.

The distinction I have just drawn is Husserl's distinction between *Abschattung* and *Horizont.*[22] *Abschattung* is, as it were, the shadow; 'horizon' will do

19 The end of the sentence ('what ...') is taken from LN 41.
20 This sentence is taken from LN 41.
21 Brockman Hall is a building on the campus of Xavier University. The evening
    sessions of the Institute were held there.
22 Some references to *Abschattungen* (profiles) are given in Robert Sokolowski,
    The Formation of Husserl's Concept of Constitution (The Hague: Martinus
    Nijhoff, 1964) 61, 123–24, 220–21. On horizon and the alteration of perspec-
    tives (but without reference to *Abschattung*) see *Krisis* (see above, chapter 1,
    note 33) 161 (*The Crisis of European Sciences* 158).

for *Horizont*. But now we want to think of a horizon of the second degree. We have spoken of a horizon of Brockman Hall, or of any object that you cannot see the whole of in a single look. But what is one's world? It is a horizon of horizons. It is the totality of objects like Brockman Hall, the organized whole of intelligibly varying objects in which I happen to have any interest, for which I have any concern.[23] And that totality is a totality that we construct out of our experience, where the construction is governed by our concern. Just as one does not see the horizon of Brockman Hall, so one never sees one's world. What is his world? Well, you don't see it. It is a construction of constructions. What you see is the profile. The horizon is an envelope containing all possible profiles, and also the knowledge of how many profiles you need in order to recognize the object. (This is an analytic account, of course, a simpler statement of the things that go on.) One's world is a horizon of horizons, a horizon of the second degree, the totality of objects for which one has any concern. Again, one can say that *my* world is the part of the universe determined by the horizon of my concern.

Thus we have four terms, four moments in concrete existence:[24] subject, concern, horizon, world. The subject's concern determines his horizon, and his horizon selects his world. With that notion of subject-concern-horizon-world, one can move from the child's world to the world of the man. These notions thus give us something that we can deal with when we speak of the developing subject.

2   Differentiation and Horizon[25]

We now have to consider differentiations of the flow of consciousness. Later we will give more detail on the genesis of differentiation; but we want to present at once some notion of the differences.[26] We have, more or less, a structure: the flow of consciousness is the subject with his concern constructing a horizon that selects his world. But this is not always expressed[27]

23 The words from 'the organized whole' are taken from LN 42.
24 The words from 'four moments' are taken from LN 42.
25 LN 42 has much of this material under the subheading 'Differentiation of the Flow of Consciousness.' In distinct but related subsections Lonergan moves to the topic of horizon. We have put the two under one heading, understanding them both as preparatory to the discussion of development.
26 This sentence is based on LN 42. For some details on the genesis of differentiation, see below, § 3.
27 Lonergan said 'done,' but the point is that different philosophers have expressed differently the structure that Lonergan has been engaged in detailing.

in exactly the same way. The scholastics, following Aristotle, distinguished speculative and practical intellect, and Kant distinguished pure and practical reason. While I have no objection to the distinctions, they do not fit in with our concrete concern with the flow of consciousness. Thus, while we do not mean anything very different from speculative and practical intellect, pure and practical reason, still we speak of different patterns of experience, different patterns of the flow of consciousness.

2.1 The Intellectual Pattern of Experience

The consciousness of a man who can fall into a well because he is extremely interested in the stars is not an ordinary pattern of experience. When Newton was working out his theory of universal gravitation, he lived in his room for weeks on end. A bit of food was brought to him now and then, but he had very little interest in it, and he slept only when necessary, but as soon as that was over he was back at work. He was totally absorbed in the enucleation, the unfolding, of his idea. Insofar as it is possible for a man, he was living totally in the intellectual pattern of experience.

When consciousness moves into the intellectual pattern of experience, one's concern becomes the wonder that Aristotle spoke of as the beginning of all science and philosophy.[28] In the measure that that wonder is the dominant concern in consciousness, experience takes on a pattern of its own that is dictated by the exigences of that wonder. Archimedes made his famous discovery of the principles of specific gravity and of displacement, not when he was trying to think the problem out, but when he was doing something else, when he was trying to forget about it. The preconscious sets to work on the problem and throws up the images that will lead to the insight. Again, when one is making a judgment, one's imagination runs through all the possibilities, and memory recalls all the facts, that might contradict the judgment one is thinking of making. There is a spontaneous cooperation of everything in the man to the end of that intellectual wonder. At the same time, all other concern apart from the wonder falls into the background. That falling into the background of other concern is what we call impartiality, intellectual detachment, intellectual curiosity,[29] intellectual interest. There are all sorts of degrees of the absorption of the individ-

28 See above, note 14.
29 The word 'curiosity' is taken from LN 42.

ual into the intellectual pattern of experience,[30] but you can see that this pattern is an organized whole that has its own characteristics, and that it is quite distinct from the ordinary pattern of experience in which we are dealing with persons and mastering things. In the intellectual pattern of experience, consciousness is dominated by wonder, by the pure desire to know, by intellectual detachment and impartiality. One wants to know, What is it? and whether one's answer to that question is true.

What is the relation between the intellectual pattern of experience and activities such as willing, choosing, doing? In a first instance, the intellectual pattern of experience is spontaneous. But in a second instance, men can organize the conditions of their lives and the order of their work in a way that favors the intellectual pattern of experience. Once that step takes place, willing, choosing, and doing come into the picture. The organization of the conditions of the intellectual pattern of experience and the creation of tools and implements for favoring it yield the fundamental meaning of such terms as 'logic' and 'method.' In that case the will is willing the good, but the good it is willing is the good of intellect, the true. The true is a good, and the good is true. And insofar as the subject is willing the true, the subject himself and his other concerns are placed in abeyance. The subject's responsibility contracts to arriving at truth.

The significance of this point can be discovered by investigating the objections that are made against intellectualism. It is well to note just what the state of the question is. It is true that the intellectual pattern of experience withdraws man from ordinary practical concerns. He is concerned with understanding and truth, and that is his end. He is involved, but as involved he is subordinated to the ideals and norms of intelligence, to the immanent concretion within himself of the principles of logic, scientific aspiration, and method.[31] He is not committing himself in the way in which he has to commit himself when he is dealing with the good in a more ample sense than the good of truth. His responsibility is contracted to saying just what he knows, no matter how little. His responsibility is for his judgment, and that is a limited responsibility.[32] He is committed to explicitness, to exactitude, to distinguishing known certainty from known proba-

---

30 LN 42 has, 'Degrees of absorption, capacity for concentration: Newton; student enters prof's room.'

31 This sentence is constructed from LN 42; after 'logic' Lonergan writes, '(logos that enlightens everyman).'

32 This sentence is based on LN 42, which reads, 'Subject is responsible: his judgment is his, and personne ne se plaint de son jugement; but it is a limited responsibility.'

bility,[33] to carrying out the precepts that formulate the meaning of the intellectual pattern of experience. Still, the significance of moving into the intellectual pattern of experience is that, when concern is purely intellectual wonder, the correlative becomes the universe. As long as consciousness is directed by whatever concerns one may have, one is in one's world, but insofar as the intellectual pattern of experience is dominant, one is concerned, not with any private world, but with the universe. This is the meaning of the traditional notion that intellect is *potens omnia facere et fieri.* The object of intellect is *omnia,* everything, and an object that includes everything is not restricted to any genus of things. That object must be being. And so, while concern has as its correlative a private world, the intellectual pattern of experience has as its correlative the one universe, everything.

This does not mean, of course, that one tries to know everything at once. Seriation is of the essence of method. But it does mean that one never brushes issues aside, never says to any relevant question, 'I could not care less.'[34]

2.2 Horizon

There is, then, a deeper meaning to Heraclitus's statement that when men sleep each lives in a private world of his own, in his dreams, but when they wake up they live in the common world settled by the *logos,* by reason.[35] Insofar as one lives in one's own world that is settled by one's own concern, by the *Sorge* at the root of one's flow of consciousness, one is in something of a private world, one is something of a sleepwalker, even though one's eyes are open and one goes through all the acts of ordinary human living. It is

33 The expressions 'known certainty' and 'known probability' are taken from LN 42. In the lecture itself Lonergan said, 'to distinguishing certitude from probability.'
34 This paragraph is taken from LN 42.
35 See G.S. Kirk and J.E. Raven, *The Presocratic Philosophers: A Critical History with a Selection of Texts* (Cambridge: Cambridge University Press, 1957) 187–88, Fragment 1: 'Of the Logos which is as I describe it men always prove to be uncomprehending, both before they have heard it and when once they have heard it. For although all things happen according to this Logos men are like people of no experience, even when they experience such words and deeds as I explain, when I distinguish each thing according to its constitution and declare how it is; but the rest of men fail to notice what they do after they wake up just as they forget what they do when asleep.' Fragment 2: 'Therefore it is necessary to follow the common; but although the Logos is common the many live as though they had a private understanding.'

when the intellectual pattern of experience is realized that one ceases to be a sleepwalker and confronts being, the universe. So the private worlds selected by the horizon of concern are all parts of a universe.

The purely intellectual pattern is intermittent even in the most intellectual persons. It is not the whole of life, but it is an important, because guiding and directing, part. Moreover, not only is it intermittent, if one attains it at all, but attainment of it and acceptance of that attainment are not universal.[36] So let us now turn to the more practical aspect of the matter, to an application, which is the goal towards which we have been heading in drawing these distinctions of subject, concern, horizon, world, wonder, and universe.

We can distinguish the known, the known unknown, and the unknown unknown. The distinction is applicable to any stage of development,[37] and it gives us a tool that enables us to speak briefly about development in the subject.

The known is the range of questions that I can raise and answer. It is settled by the series or group of questions I can ask and answer. Beyond the known, which is the first circle, as it were, there is the known unknown, the things I know I do not know. That is a much broader circle. There is a range of questions that I can raise, find significant, consider worth while, have some idea of how to answer. But at the moment I cannot answer them. At the moment I may feel quite certain that I never really will be able to answer them myself, but still I know about these questions, I recognize some possibility of their being answered, and so I know about something that is unknown to me. That is the known unknown, the range of my *docta ignorantia*. Thirdly, there is the unknown unknown, the range of questions that I do not raise at all, or that, if they were raised, I would not understand, or find significant,[38] or, if I understood what is meant, I would see no point in asking them. I would not consider it worth while finding out what the answer was. I could not care less whether there is an answer to such questions or not. This is the realm of the unknown unknown, the field of *indocta ignorantia*. And how big it is we do not know.

The horizon is the boundary, the frontier, between *docta ignorantia* and *indocta ignorantia*. What is beyond my horizon is meaningless for me, though it may not be meaningless in itself. It is not worth while for me, but it may be worth while in itself. One's horizon, the boundary between one's *docta* and

---

36 The first part of this paragraph, to this point, is taken from LN 42.
37 This part of the sentence is based on LN 42.
38 The words 'find significant' are taken from LN 42.

indocta ignorantia, corresponds to one's concern, and one knows about one's horizon only indirectly. To know about a horizon one has to have a larger horizon within which one can define the smaller one. But if this is one's horizon one does not have the larger horizon within which one can grasp where the limits lie for the individual. One's own horizon is the limit, the boundary, where one's concern or interest vanishes. As one approaches the horizon, one's interest, attention, concern is falling off to the vanishing point. At the horizon it has ceased altogether. What one does not attend to at all, ever, one knows nothing about, and that settles one's horizon.

Moreover, the matter of going beyond one's horizon is not simple. There is an organized resistance to going beyond one's horizon. Within one's horizon, one's ready-made world, one is organized, one has determinate modes of living, feeling, thinking, judging, desiring, fearing, willing, deliberating, choosing. But to move beyond one's horizon in any but the most casual and insignificant fashion calls for a reorganization of the subject,[39] a reorganization of his modes of living, feeling, thinking, judging, desiring, fearing, willing, deliberating, choosing. Against such reorganization of the patterns of the subject, there come into play all the conservative forces that give our lives their continuity and their coherence. The subject's fundamental anxiety, his deepest dread, is the collapse of himself and his world. Tampering with the organization of himself, reorganizing himself, gives rise to such a dread.

In a moment we will go on to the topic of the development of horizon, and we will illustrate it in brief summary with thematic illustrations of scientific development, philosophic development, and most of all moral development.[40] Preparatory to this discussion of the human good as the developing subject, we worked out a framework within which the notion of the developing subject can be discussed. Thus we effected a transition from the logical essence of man that is verified in every man to the deontological, the ideal, that is expressed in 'We have to be men.' Next, we moved from substance to subject, to what can say 'I' or 'We.' That presupposes consciousness, and we distinguished levels of consciousness. Thirdly, we effected a transition from faculty psychology to the flow of consciousness and worked out an analysis, first of all, of the empirical situation. In the general case, the subject and his concern determine a horizon that selects out of the universe a world. But

39 Some of the terms in the sentence thus far are taken from LN 43.
40 A coffee break was taken at this point. The remainder of this section § 2 consists of material that Lonergan presented at the beginning of the second half of this lecture.

there is also an intellectual pattern of experience, and correlative to it is the universe, all that exists. The intellectual pattern of experience that corresponds to the universe is beyond any particular horizon. As long as it exists, it is orientated upon totality, upon being, upon everything. But the moment the intellectual pattern of experience ceases to be dominant, then one can shift back to a narrow concern. To move into the practical pattern of experience without contracting one's horizon presupposes perfect charity. There is an intimate correlation between the natural and the supernatural, according to the doctrine of St Thomas. According to St Thomas, there is a natural desire for the beatific vision, a desire to know God by his essence. When consciousness is rooted in the pure desire to know, and when one knows of the existence of God, one asks what God is. To ask, What? is to desire to know something by its essence, and to know God by his essence is something that is attained only through the beatific vision. Thus the pure desire to know includes in its range the supernatural goal to which de facto we are destined in this life. St Thomas's doctrine causes difficulty chiefly, I believe, to those whose presuppositions are not Thomist but Scotist. I cannot go into that question here and now, except to say that there is no doubt that this is St Thomas's position. He develops it over thirty-five chapters or so in the third book of the *Summa contra Gentiles*, and it recurs at all the key points in the *Summa theologiae*.[41] The natural moves into the supernatural; grace is the perfection and completion of nature. Such is the position in the Thomist analysis, where 'Thomist' means 'of St Thomas,' not the Thomistic school, which has various opinions on the matter. And that supernatural end correlative to the desire[42] to know is charity. Thus it is by charity that we can move into the practical pattern of experience without contracting our horizon.

3   Development

We now have to consider development. We note first of all that not every

---

41 Some years before in a still unpublished Latin work, Lonergan very conveniently gave precise references for what in the present lecture he calls 'thirty-five chapters or so in the third book of the *Summa contra Gentiles* ... and key points in the *Summa theologiae*.' After noting that Thomas does not treat the question in his earlier writings, he continues as follows. 'In operibus posterioribus saepius et explicite affirmatur tale desiderium: *C. Gent.*, 3, cc. 25–63 (speciatim 25, 48, 50, 57, 63); *Sum. theol.* 1, q. 12, a. 1; a. 8, ad 4m; q. 62, a. 1; 1–2, q. 3, a. 8; *Comp. theol.*, c. 104.' *De ente supernaturali*, Regis College Edition, ed. Frederick E. Crowe, Conn O'Donovan, and Giovanni Sala, p. 35.

42 Lonergan said, 'correlative to it.'

change of a horizon is a development. If one gives up driving a truck and goes to work in a factory, one is doing different things, and in a sense one is living in a different world, but there is very little development involved, if any. In general, a change from one occupation to another, from one place to another, from one group of friends and acquaintances to another just substitutes for one horizon a new horizon of about the same size. Newman comments — I think in *The Idea of a University*[43] — upon the sailor who has traveled all over the world and known all manner of men and places, but is not thought of as an educated man. There can be a broadening of a merely material horizon, and it involves no development in the sense that concerns us here. Development depends upon, and is measured by, not so much the external objects with respect to which one operates as the organization of one's operations, their reach, their implications, the orientation of one's living, of one's concern. Development retains all that was had before and adds to it, and it can add to it enormously. It eliminates previous evils by finding a higher integration in which the problems solve themselves. It finds this higher integration by working, not at the periphery but at the root, at the *Sorge*, at the concern, and by effecting the shift from the concern that is all too human to the spiritual aspiration of man that has its fundamental and first appearance in the pure desire to know that grounds the intellectual pattern of experience and sets the standards for one's morality.[44]

We now have to consider and make a little more concrete the notion of development, and as I said we will consider three illustrations: scientific, philosophic, and most of all moral development.

3.1 Scientific Development

By 'scientific development' I mean development in mathematics or natural science. The scientific horizon recedes, expands, when there occurs a crisis in existing methods, procedures, theories, assumptions which are seen to

43 John Henry Newman, *The Idea of a University Defined and Illustrated* (London: Longmans, Green & Co., 1929) 136: 'Seafaring men, for example, range from one end of the earth to the other; but the multiplicity of external objects, which they have encountered, forms no symmetrical and consistent picture upon their imagination.'

44 The words from 'that grounds' are taken from LN 43, which reads, 'It eliminates previous evil, and it does so not at the periphery but at the root, and the root is the divergence between one's concern (Sorge) and the pure desire to know that grounds the intellectual pattern and sets the standards for one's morality.'

fail. They cannot handle known results, known observations or data,[45] known conclusions. The crisis arises from a fundamental conflict between basic assumptions or methods or presuppositions and, on the other hand, something that within that order of investigation has to be accepted, something of the order of fact or inevitable conclusion. Upon this crisis there follows a radical revision of basic concepts, postulates, axioms, methods, and a consequent new mathematical or scientific structure.[46] Thus we have the triple revolution of Copernicus, Darwin, and Freud; the revolutions effected by Galileo, Newton, Einstein, quantum theory; the revolution in mathematics that began with analytic geometry and the calculus, went on to Riemannian geometry, and then to the developments in algebra due to Galois and to later developments.[47] In these cases there was a radical revision in concepts.

Now such a recession of the horizon within the scientific field meets with resistance. The subject dreads to change, to remodel the organization that is himself, his living in the scientific world. Max Planck, who made the fundamental discoveries connected with quantum theory (black-body radiation), asked in his autobiography what it is that puts a new scientific theory across. Is it the clarity of the observations or the exactness of the measurements or the coherence of the hypothesis or the rigor of the deduction or the decisiveness of the observational or experimental results? No, he said, it is none of these; they have nothing to do with it. Rather, a new scientific theory gets across when the present generation of professors is retired.[48]

However, though there is a resistance within the field of mathematics and science, still, after a relatively brief lag the resistance is overcome universally

45 In the lecture Lonergan said 'observations' but LN 43 has instead 'data.'
46 The words from 'and a consequent' are taken from LN 43.
47 At first sight this sentence calls for editing, since the work of Galois, who died in 1832, predates that of Riemann (1826–66). On the advice of Philip McShane, however, we leave it as spoken, because it seems to hit off uncannily a direction of modern mathematics close to Lonergan's interest. McShane refers to E.T. Bell, *The Development of Mathematics* (New York: McGraw-Hill, 1940, 1945) as suggesting (p. 197) that Galois was more modern than Gauss (1777–1855), of whom Riemann was a pupil (ibid. 305). The works of Galois, who coined the name 'group' (ibid. 240) were not published until 1846. See also § 2.5 of chapter 5 below.
48 Lonergan referred to the index of *Insight* under Planck for the exact reference. It is Max Planck, *Scientific Autobiography and Other Papers*, trans. F. Gaynor (New York: Philosophical Library, 1949) 33–34; this book was reprinted in 1968 and 1971 by Greenwood Press of Westport, CT.

and permanently. First, it is overcome universally: a recession in the scientific horizon is not followed by a splintering into schools, where the schools endure indefinitely, where there are fruitless debates or such an impossibility of communication that there is no debate at all. A broadening of the scientific horizon becomes accepted by all the scientists. There is not a division of scientists into certain schools, after a certain lag. Secondly, that universal acceptance is also permanent: there is no tendency to revert to earlier positions; what has been achieved is retained, and a higher viewpoint is introduced that includes all that was had and adds to it; there is no going back. It is this property of scientific development that commands the great esteem in which science is held. Scientists will disagree; they will fight; the period of crisis and reformulation presents a spectacle of insecurity; but, usually within a relatively brief period of time, these problems are overcome, and when they are overcome, the achievement is universal and permanent.

3.2 Philosophic Development

Philosophic development is different. By philosophic development I mean developments in philosophy, in human science, in theology. In those fields there occur crises and developments[49] of the same type as in the scientific field. Parmenides' attention to being was such a development; Heraclitus's attention to the *logos* was such a development; Plato's distinction between sensible and intelligible, *aisthêta* and *noêta*, was such a development. Aristotle's characterization of the intelligible as the *causa essendi* in the sensible — the *noêton* is the *aition tou einai* immanent in the sensible, form immanent in matter — was going beyond Platonic modes of thought. When Aquinas went beyond hylomorphism, the composition of substantial form with prime matter, to posit a third metaphysical entity – *esse*, existence – he was going beyond Aristotle in a profound and radical fashion.[50]

Similarly in theology, the introduction of the term *homoousion* in the fourth century caused among Catholics a series of splits on different levels and of different types. The introduction of the term 'consubstantial' was a movement from a commonsense, symbolic, intersubjective mode of thought to a technical mode of thought. You find in that fourth-century

49 The word 'crises' is taken from LN 43. In the lecture he said instead 'developments.'
50 LN 43 adds, 'Descartes separates phil from theol.'

movement the same sort of phenomena as you find in the field of scientific or philosophic developments.[51]

In the human sciences the phenomenon has been that this problem is evaded by conducting human science according to the same principles as obtain in natural science. Man is considered as though he were an electron.[52] The result is that the human science is really not human.

So there are crises and real developments within the philosophic field, just as there are in mathematics and science. However, the difference in the philosophic field is that the recession of the horizon does not result in a universal and permanent difference. The new horizon is accepted by some and not by others, and this division in acceptance is something that extends down the ages. There is a family resemblance between the empiricists, idealists, and realists of ancient Greece, of the Middle Ages, and of our own time.[53] They talk different languages, of course, and there is a far greater subtlety of analysis in the modern philosophers; but the fundamental differences are essentially the same. Similarly in the history of the church and in the history of the development of dogma, every basic development has been accompanied by a corresponding permanent heresy. The definition of the consubstantiality of the Son was accompanied by Arianism. The affirmation of one person in two natures in Christ was accompanied by Nestorianism and Monophysitism. The working out of the doctrines of the sacraments, grace, and the church in the medieval period was followed by the Protestant negation of all of these developments at the time of the Reformation. The moments of development within this field do not result in universal and permanent achievement.

Not only is the new development accepted by some and rejected by others – there is the formation of schools – but the new schools[54] then tend to splinter, to have periods of decay and revival. What is happening in a period of decay within a school? The words of the master are faithfully repeated, but the meaning has been devaluated and contracted[55] to fit into a narrower

---

51 More examples are provided on LN 44: 'homoousion; dyphysism; supernatural; sacraments; church
    'Theology integrated with Ar[istotelian] phil and sc; theology to be integrated with existential philosophy and human science.' Some of these examples are treated elsewhere in these lectures.
52 This sentence is based in LN 44.
53 The reference to the Middle Ages is based on LN 44. In the lecture he mentioned only the ancients and the philosophers of our own time.
54 In an aside, 'Here we have to distinguish; I think it's more complicated within the theological field, but the phenomena are similar.'
55 LN 44 has 'devaluated,' while in the lecture Lonergan said 'contracted.'

horizon, a lower stage of development.[56] These periods of decay are followed by periods of revival, a restoration of the original meaning. What is happening is a revival in *subjects* who have horizons large enough to follow the thought of the original inspiration. And so we have neo-Platonism as well as Platonism, neo-Aristotelianism as well as Aristotelianism, neo-Thomism as well as Thomism, neo-Kantianism as well as Kantianism, neo-Hegelianism as well as Hegelianism. So instead of the universal and permanent achievement of a recession of the horizon that is had in the scientific field, a new development in the philosophic field means a new splintering into schools, and the history of the schools is a series of waves of decay and revival.

The ground of this difference between the scientific and the philosophic developments is not hard to find. The scientific development involves a transformation of the object, a rethinking of basic categories, postulates, and axioms. Similarly in the philosophic field. However, the difference between the scientific and the philosophic is that in the case of the philosophic the subject is also one of the objects. The subject can accept the transformation in the conception of the object only if he effects a transformation in his own living. Because the subject is one of the objects, there can occur the transformation of the object only on the condition that there occurs a radical[57] conversion, a real development, in the subject. That real development in the subject is something that every subject dreads. Because of that dread of subjects there can be found down the centuries a family resemblance between materialists, between idealists, between realists, that is independent of the purely intellectual development that has been occurring. There is a fundamental philosophic difference of subjects themselves, of the capacity of subjects to broaden their horizon to the point where it includes the universe.

3.3 Moral Development

3.3.1 The Difficulty of the Subject

Now we move to a third consideration of development, namely, moral development. It is a type of development that is extremely complex not only in itself but also in thought about it. I cannot give you any simple illustrations of it such as are possible when one contrasts scientific and philosophic development.

55 LN 44 has 'devaluated,' while in the lecture Lonergan said 'contracted.'
56 The phrase 'a lower stage of development' is taken from LN 44.
57 The word 'radical' is taken from LN 44.

Moral development is development in the good that is one's concern. But one's emphasis or concern can fall upon particular goods, 'what's good for me'; it can fall upon the good of order; and it can fall upon values. And one's apprehension of values can be aesthetic or ethical or religious. These differences give rise to the possibility of a great variety of modes of organization of the moral subject, the possibility of different bases of moral orientation.[58]

Moreover, it is very difficult to draw sharp distinctions. There is a natural line of development in man. The child has to develop not only spiritually but also as an animal. The two developments are required, and both are good, both are natural. In the early stages the development of the animal side occurs at a more rapid rate than the development of the spirit, and it is a condition for the development of the spirit. When the rate of the development of the spirit outdistances the rate of the development of the animal, there arises naturally a shift in the center of gravity, a shift in the orientation, a shift in the concern of the subject. This type of process of development is fixed by natural conditions, but effecting it is an important indirect effect of the education of intelligence.[59]

There is also a logical interconnection between the different ways in which one's apprehension and willing of the good can be organized. One can start from the will of God. The will of God is the order of the universe and order within the human soul. It implies the good of order and ethical values, and the good of order includes the particular goods that are due to each individual.[60] The three — the divine will, the good of order, and particular goods — are connected logically if you start from the supreme value. But inversely the three are connected from the opposite end. Thus, the good of order is implicit in the particular goods. People can will explicitly and with full attention just the particular good, and never think explicitly of the good of order, yet full respect for the good of order may be implicit in the way they will the particular good. They respect the good of order by the manner in which they will, desire, seek particular goods. There is nothing disordinate in their willing the particular good; they are willing implicitly the good of order, even though they have not the differentiation of consciousness that would enable them to think of it explicitly. Similarly, just as the good of order is implicit in particular goods and can be willed implicitly

58 The last part of this sentence is taken from LN 44. The notes read, 'Provide a variety of possible centres of organization, different bases of orientation of subject.'
59 From 'but' to the end of the sentence is from LN 44.
60 Parts of the last two sentences are taken from LN 44–45.

by willing the particular good, not disordinately but in an orderly fashion, so also to will the will of God is implicit in willing the good of order. This inverse implication may be present simply in the mode in which one wills. But it can also be apprehended in many ways. It can be apprehended philosophically, through such an analysis as we have attempted, but it can also be apprehended in a more symbolic, compact fashion, in which emotionally charged image, understanding, judgment, and will all function simultaneously, without the subject's capacity to analyze just what is going on.[61]

Again, practice may be better or worse than theory. If the theory is very bad, the practice is apt to be better, and if the theory is very demanding, the practice is apt to be worse.

Finally, theories themselves may or may not be coherent. A good man may not be a good logician, and there can be as many theories as there are horizons in people's attitudes towards life.

So what I have been saying is that the question of moral development is very complex, and one must not jump to conclusions about particular individuals. A person may be apprehending symbolically a very high morality even though he seems to be apprehending nothing but the particular good; he may be living according to a very high morality even though all his explicit thinking is concerned with particular goods. Here applies by analogy[62] the advice Einstein gave to epistemologists and philosophers of science. He told them to pay no attention to what scientists say but to watch carefully what they do.[63] Similarly, in judging people morally, do not ask them what they think about morality, but watch what they do.

Now let us turn to something more concrete. I have been expressing the general difficulty of the subject, but now I want to move to particular considerations that will help to clarify the matter. I cannot offer here a course in moral philosophy and theology, but I can touch on a few illustrative themes that have to do with moral development.[64] I will consider first of all Piaget's study of the moral ideas of children and then I will speak about the intellectual crisis of adolescence.[65]

---

61 LN 45 adds here, '(importance of art and literature in moral education as basis for moral philosophy, as a complement for a philosophic ethic, as equivalent for philosophic ethical apprehension).'
62 The phrase 'by analogy' is added by the editors.
63 See Albert Einstein, *Essays in Science* (New York: Philosophical Library, 1934) 12.
64 This sentence is taken from LN 45.
65 LN 46 includes outlines on two other topics which he did not address in the lecture: dimensions of choice and apprehensions of obligation. See below, note 72. These notes are given in full in the appendix, § C.

3.3.2 Piaget on the Moral Ideas of Children

In his book, *Le jugement moral chez l'enfant*,[66] Piaget studies children from the poorer districts of Geneva and Neuchâtel. He is concerned with their ideas on the right way to play marbles. He distinguished three groups. For those from the ages of five to seven, the rules of the game were absolute and immutable norms, but the boys did not understand them and might have mistaken their meaning. They simply did not comprehend the game. Even the question, 'Who won?' was answered, 'Both of us!' In a later period it was all right to change the rules if all agreed, but then they felt they were not playing marbles anymore, and were committing a kind of injustice to the game. For those from the ages of twelve to thirteen, it was again all right to change the rules if all agreed, but now there was no thought of cheating or of injustice to the game. The boys had a terrifically complicated jurisprudence. Every possible eventuality had been thought of and solved just as elaborately as in the most complicated legal system we can imagine. Piaget's comment, of course, was that it is nonsense to say that there is anything we cannot teach children if we go about it in the right way. They knew how to handle every possible eventuality in an extremely complicated game of marbles. (The girls did not go in for this sort of thing, incidentally.) Piaget also noticed that, while the boys at an intermediate age listened to the oldest boys, they would not go along with their moral relativism. Only the oldest boys were capable of changing the rules according to their desires on any given occasion.

Piaget's second investigation regarded children's ideas on punishments. How should a boy who disobeyed be punished? Piaget found that the very young felt that the stiffer the punishment, the more just it was and the less likelihood there was of the disobedience recurring. 'Wouldn't it be better to reason with them?' 'Oh no, that wouldn't be just at all.' The thing to do is punish, and the severer the punishment the less the likelihood of the thing recurring. Older boys, an intermediate group, said that if the father reasoned with the boy he was a nicer man but not a juster one; the juster man was the one that handed out the punishment. Finally, the oldest boys held that reasoning would be not only more just, but also more effective. So there occur change and development in the moral ideas of children.

---

66 Jean Piaget, *Le jugement moral chez l'enfant* (Paris: Alcan, 1932); in English, *The Moral Judgment of the Child*, trans. Marjorie Gabain (London: Routledge and Kegan Paul, 1932).

Piaget's conclusions call for some reflection from the standpoint of a philosophy of education. He interpreted his results in terms of a transition from an absolute morality based upon unilateral respect for the law handed down from above, to a morality arrived at by mutual consent and based upon mutual respect. That analysis is part of the truth, but it does not have all the implications that Piaget gives to it. One can note in the childish apprehension of the rules something absolute going back to Adam and Eve: the compactness of the symbol in the apprehension of the absoluteness of morality. There *is* a symbolic apprehension of the absoluteness of morality, and it is something that the child is not to lose. Piaget's blind spot for religion prevents him from doing justice to that element.[67] There is an element there that is to be preserved.

Again, the rules for playing marbles are a matter of convention. It is not properly a matter of moral law, and consequently the boys of twelve or thirteen, who were ready to change the rules in any way at all as long as people agreed, were making the morally right judgment about the rules of marbles.

Finally, morality reached by mutual agreement and based upon mutual respect is an important part of human morality, the part of morality that arises when the subject moves to the level of ethical value, autonomy of spirit, realization of his own freedom and responsibility, and respect for the freedom and responsibility of others. It flowers in human cooperation, in concrete enterprises, and in civic virtue. It is very subtle. It cannot be put into simple rules or laid down as the law, yet it is very much a part of the law given us by Christ: Love one another as I have loved you. It is also a part of morality in which Catholics are thought to be deficient. When Catholics are in control of a local or provincial government, in fact in Catholic countries in general, the standard of civic morality is often found to be lower than among non-Catholics. There is a problem here, I think, that deserves the attention of Catholic educators.

3.3.3 The Intellectual Crisis of Adolescence

A second point — I am just touching upon the question of moral development from different angles — is the intellectual crisis of adolescence. There are two adolescent crises, one affective, the other intellectual. Georges Cruchon, professor of pedagogical psychology at the Gregorian University,

---

67 LN 45: '... unilateral respect: P's blind spot for religious view of life; God respects man's freedom and asks for his love.'

in two articles in the *Nouvelle Revue Théologique* in 1951 on the development of the human ego in the light of contemporary biopsychology,[68] indicates a correlation between the Freudian distinctions of superego, ego, and id, on the one hand, and, on the other hand, distinct areas in the brain. Such a correlation would partially justify Freud's distinctions. The area about the pituitary gland controls the secretion of hormones. It is, as it were, the brain of endocrinal secretions. It controls all such secretions, and they have a great influence upon appetites, hunger, thirst, and so on. That surrounding area of the brain (the third ventricle, I think it is called) is connected with very fundamental images and has some rough correspondence with the Freudian id. The ego has a correspondence with the back part of the brain, where the various areas are connected with sensation. The subject forms visual, auditory, and tactile images of the world of sensation, and consequently of himself as a sensible object. In the frontal lobes are located the controls and the integration of nervous activity, and there is a correspondence between this part of the brain and Freud's superego. The account of the superego, the ego, and the id in terms of their neural foundations in the brain removes some of the mythical thinking connected with Freud's theories, and at the same time enables us to draw on what is useful in his distinctions.

Now the formation of the superego, which on its neural side entails the development of the frontal lobes of the brain, keeps occurring through childhood with the world of 'do' and 'don't.' And the intellectual crisis of adolescence is the period in which adolescents reject the set of precepts and evaluations that were imposed externally through precepts at a time when they were not able to think for themselves. They go through a period of disorientation due to that rejection, and to the need in that period in which they commence to reconstruct for themselves the precepts, the evaluations, the ideals that they really accept, that are theirs. They become themselves. Education has to prepare them to go through this period in which they become their own masters. They are not going to throw out everything that was given them in childhood, but if they are to be themselves, their actions cannot be simply the result of the spontaneous tendencies and images that were necessary to control them in childhood. They have to move to some autonomy of their own, and they do so. One value of their education, and something that is universally needed and therefore relevant to the problem

68 Georges Cruchon, SJ, 'Genèse et structure du moi humaine à la lumière des sciences biopsychologiques modernes,' *Nouvelle Revue Théologique* 73 (1951) 261–74, 364–84.

of the education of the masses, would be to provide adolescents with the help and preparation they will need in that period to do a good job in becoming themselves, in that self-affirmation that occurs during adolescence. The first manifestation of the crisis is a complete revolt, a total rejection of all that has been imposed from outside. They have to become themselves. But the more their education has been a broadening of horizon towards a real apprehension of the human good in all its dimensions, the better they will be prepared.

And what is meant by a real apprehension? It involves, first, ascending from the particular goods that they know to the order that they can see within and conditioning those particular goods; next, going from that order to the notion of value, which they can see by comparing different orders. Education moves up from what is most easily apprehended to what is more subtle. And it includes some apprehension of the dimensions of choice, of the fact and significance of autonomy – because that is what is occurring at that period – and of the relation between autonomy, their being themselves, and religion. Religion is their being themselves before God.[69]

The real apprehension need not be philosophic, scientific, analytic. It can be symbolic, global, synthetic, aesthetic. The affective ideals of a culture are usually not philosophically expressed. They are exemplified in the *kalokagathia* of the Greeks, the *uomo universale* of the Renaissance, the gentleman of nineteenth-century England, and so on. Here, I think, is relevant Whitehead's remark that moral education is impossible without the constant vision of greatness.[70] Moral education communicates that vision in unnoticed ways. The vision gathers the way dust gathers, not through any massive action but through the continuous addition of particles that remain.

We can provide an illustration of the significance of the way such a vision can be communicated, even if in this case we are dealing with a very limited vision. It has been said that in the nineteenth century, despite the absence of telegraph and wireless and airplanes and any rapid communications

69 LN 45: 'Real apprehension: ascend from particular goods to the good of order, and from disputes about order and subjective possibility of order to supernatural religion. Some apprehension of the dimensions of choice, of the fact and significance of autonomy, of relation between autonomy and religion.'
70 We have not been able to locate a specific remark to which Lonergan may have been referring. But cognate ideas are to be found in many of the essays in Alfred North Whitehead, *The Aims of Education and Other Essays* (New York: Free Press, 1957).

between England and India, when the people at the colonial office in London heard news of some sort of trouble or uprising at some spot in India, they would know immediately just how the man on the spot would react, because they knew the moral training given to the public-school boys, and the people that had the administrative posts were the public-school boys. The people in London knew the mentality of the colonial administrators. But when these posts passed to the victors in competitive examinations, what was known about these people was that they were good at passing examinations, period! Even all the modern means of communication did not give the home office an understanding of what the situation was likely to be tonight and tomorrow. I offer this example simply as an illustration – it is not the aim of Catholic education to produce colonial administrators! What the example shows is that there is an ethos, something very concrete, that is communicated indirectly, and that it is enormously efficacious.

It is not enough, then, for moral education to teach people how to make a good confession, to give them an abstract[71] classification of all the acts that are bad, and which ones are mortal sins and which venial. There *is* an ethics of law and it is essential, but it does not make saints and it does not make heroes. There is also an ethics of achievement, and its basis is the precept of charity. You cannot tell what the good is going to be, because the good is not any systematic entity. The good is a history. It is what we tried to indicate in bold lines in the last two lectures. An ethics of achievement is suggested, taught, insofar as one gives some idea of the good.[72]

4   Corollaries in Education[73]

We began from the good as the developing object and went on to the good as the developing subject, where that development was conceived concretely in terms of the broadening horizon of the subject. Insofar as the broadening of the subject's horizon occurs through the development of the intellectual pattern of experience as scientific, it does meet with resistance, but that resistance is overcome universally and permanently. On the other hand, the broadening of the horizon in any matter that concerns the sub-

71 'abstract' is taken from LN 46.
72 Lonergan's notes regarding *dimensions of choice* and *apprehensions of obligation* appear at this point on LN 46 (see above, note 65). They are given in the appendix, § C.
73 The fifth lecture, Friday, August 7, 1959, began with this section. Since the material concludes the treatment of the good, we have moved it in the text to this point.

ject himself not only involves a transformation of concepts, of the notion of the object, but also postulates a development in the subject himself. Here we find standard levels of resistance that go down through the ages and are not overcome simply on the intellectual level. So it is that there result differences between the philosophic schools, and those differences ramify into all fields.

I think there are a number of corollaries that can be drawn at once with regard to education from that consideration of the horizon of the subject. I will mention them briefly. It is more for you to work out the fuller applications. Then I will proceed to a consideration of the new learning, to a consideration of what the intellectual pattern of experience is and what is distinctively new in contemporary thought.

4.1 Active Methods

First of all, what we had to say about horizon indicates an element of fundamental truth in what are called active methods in education. The fundamental element of truth in active methods is that education helps the subject construct *his own* world. What he cannot assimilate and use to develop *his* world and broaden *his* horizon is something that will be alien to him, something you can force upon his attention and oblige him to pass exams in, but something that he will slough off afterwards as a snake drops its skin. One has to build on the foundations, whatever they are, in the mind of the pupil. One has to take people as they are and start from there. Moreover, subjects, and particularly the young, are extremely interested in that developing of *their* world. The questions of children are simply endless. The problem is to teach them that the answers to questions are not as easy as they think, and to do so without discouraging and stopping the flow of questions.

Since the real basis of the active method is the subject constructing his own world, active method does not necessarily entail external activity. One has to distinguish between external activity and active method in general. In the measure that consciousness is undifferentiated, in the measure that there cannot be an apprehension without there being also an external act — people have to act it out — in that measure active method includes not merely listening and looking but also talking and moving about. A perception has to have some sort of expression, because a perception is part of the subject's constructing of his world. But in the measure that consciousness is differentiated, that expression need not be accompanied by any external sign. However, the child seems to need at least some sort of symbolic expression really to perceive. Thus, if the child wants to perceive a church, he will put up his two hands to represent the steeple, and say, 'I'm a church!' The suggestion of the object in the expression can be extremely remote, purely symbolic, but that element is part of the perception. Thus the younger the pupil is, the more need there is for an externalization of the construction.

Education helps the subject construct his world and broaden his horizon, but such a development cannot be achieved simply on the basis of the *attained* organization of the student. Insofar as one's teaching is based only on the already attained interests of one's students, one is not broadening the horizon but just helping them organize things within the horizon that already has been attained. Broadening the horizon cannot appeal to attained or developed interests, but has to appeal to more fundamental potentialities represented, for example, by the wonder of desiring to understand, a wonder which is unlimited in its scope, and by its corollaries in the affective field and in the field of the will.

Consequently, while there are fundamental potentialities in the subject that can be appealed to, still going beyond the attained horizon is normally indirect. Just as the scientist drops his present theory because he finds it does not work, so in general finding that things do not work within a given horizon is one of the means for moving on beyond it. Again, there is an indirect moving beyond the attained horizon insofar as developments occur that force the broadening. Much education, and the real fruits of education, are for that reason indirect. The development of intelligence effects a shift in the center of gravity of a person's orientation.[74]

4.2 Should Education Be Moral?

Next, the question is often raised, Should education be moral? As long as education is dealing with undifferentiated consciousness, there is not the distinction between will and intellect. The whole person is functioning. Only insofar as the student is in a specialized intellectual pattern of experience will there be a distinguishing of the intellectual and the moral. That type of development occurs rather late in education. Consequently, as long as education is dealing with undifferentiated consciousness, as for example in art, in language study, in literary study, in historical study, the moral element is

---

74 This sentence is based on LN 47, which adds at this point, 'again, appeals to him, motivation, can be presented not only in analytic form (which would be beyond him) but in symbolic form, aesthetically
    'ethos: the totality of direct and indirect motivation
    'sense of style, sense of shame; efficacy but narrow.'

always present, at least implicitly. It is only when one moves on to the purely philosophic or mathematical or scientific side of education that moral education would become something distinct; and then it takes a specialized form of its own and may be handled by the religious side of education.

I repeat here what I have already said. One can conveniently distinguish between an ethics of law and an ethics of achievement. While an ethics of law regards rules of conduct — don't do this, don't do that — an ethics of achievement reveals that there is the world and that there is something for me to do in it. It includes the idea of vocation, not simply in the sense in which we use the word 'priest' but also in a general sense, and of development in the apprehension of the good. An ethics of achievement is more positive than an ethics of law.[75]

4.3 Philosophy of Education and the Horizon of the Educationalist

Finally, with regard to the philosophy of education itself, the fundamental problem is the horizon of the educationalist – of the person or group that has the power and the money, that runs the bureaucracy, that makes the decisions – and the horizon of the teacher. Insofar as their horizons are insufficiently enlarged, there will be difficulties all along the line. So the genuine function of a philosophy of education is to bring the horizon of the educationalist to the point where he is not living in some private world of educationalists, but in the universe of being.[76]

75 LN 47: 'ethics of achievement, many presentations, from concrete imagined emotionally charged to more analytic reflective.'
76 Lonergan has handwritten onto LN 47 at this point,
    '(1) Undifferentiated common sense
    '(2) C.S. differentiated to division of labour – specialists information belt
    '(3) Pure intellectual development
    '(4) Historical consciousness
        'A Positivistic pragmatic   Part. good
        'B Idealistic   Good of order
        'C Realist   Value
    'Easier for PhilEd to lower level of society than to pull it up.'

5

The New Learning: Mathematics[1]

We now have to consider the new learning. For one of the objections raised against traditional education is that it was thought out for a prescientific, predemocratic, preindustrial age, and insofar as there is a new learning, there is at least a question raised by that objection. We have to know what the new learning is. As I have said, what is significant is what is new, not insofar as there are material additions to what was known before — the encyclopedias are bigger — but in the sense that the very idea of learning itself, of knowledge itself, of the structure of knowledge, has been developed, transformed. The contemporary idea of geometry, of mathematics, of science, of philosophy is a new idea. There has been development, for example, not just in the sciences but in the very notion of science itself. In that respect there can be a challenge from the new learning to education for our time.

I will presume you are all familiar with scholastic theories of intellect, and will make that my starting point, to express, in the first place, what was known about intellect prior to the new learning, and in the second place, what developments have arisen from the new learning.

1 Most of the fifth lecture, Friday, August 7, 1959 (on the beginning of the fifth lecture, see above, chapter 4, note 73) and the beginning of the sixth lecture, Monday, August 10, 1959.

1   **Knowledge of Intellect Prior to the New Learning**

1.1 Scholastic Theories

The ontological structure of intellect in the writings of St Thomas may be represented schematically as follows.[2] There is an *intellectus agens*, on the one hand, and there are senses, imagination, phantasms, *re*-presentations of the data of sense, and an *intellectus possibilis*, on the other hand. The agent intellect illuminates the phantasm and uses it as an instrument to impress upon the possible intellect an intelligible species. The possible intellect, determined by the species, has an act, *intelligere*, understanding,[3] and from that act there proceeds an inner word. It is a simple inner word, not a judgment, since in itself it is neither true nor false. The standard illustration of such an inner word is the definition. This simple inner word is followed by a reflective process, an activity named *reductio ad principia*, a reduction of the definition to its principles in intellectual light *(intellectus agens)* and in sense whence the phantasms were withdrawn. From that reflective process there proceeds a second inner word, the composition or division by affirmation or negation.

Such is the Thomist structure of intelligence. It can be established beyond any doubt or question from the writings of St Thomas that this is what he meant when he spoke of intellect. He gives, however, a strictly metaphysical account of the psychological process, that apparently does not appeal to data of consciousness.[4]

In the thought of Duns Scotus, of course, there is presented a different

---

2 At this point Lonergan started to draw a diagram on the board. He diagrammed both the Thomist and the Scotist account of intellect.

3 Lonergan added in an aside, 'intellecting, as some people would prefer to say.'

4 When the *verbum* articles were published in book form Lonergan wrote an Introduction, published elsewhere under the revealing title 'Subject and Soul' (*Philippine Studies* 13 [1965] 576–85), setting forth the effort of Thomas Aquinas to fuse Augustine's phenomenology of the subject with Aristotle's psychology of the soul. The positive and the negative are found in this helpful statement: 'But if Aristotle and Aquinas used introspection and did so brilliantly, it remains that they did not thematize their use, did not elevate it into a proper method for psychology, and thereby lay the groundwork for the contemporary distinctions between nature and spirit and between the natural and the human sciences.' For a direct contribution to that side Lonergan turns to Augustine (*Verbum* ix–x).

setup, first from the ontological point of view. Scotus speaks of the intellective power, and he does not wish to determine whether or not it is to be
divided into agent and possible intellect. He also recognizes the existence
of the phantasm and the use of the phantasm by the intellective power to
impress upon intellect — whether agent intellect is really distinct from possible intellect or not is not settled — an intelligible species. But that intelligible species corresponds, not to the Thomist intelligible species, but to the
Thomist simple inner word. Intellect takes a look at that species, and when
it does so it is knowing a concept. It can form several species, take a look at
two at a time, compare them, see whether they are compossible, compatible
or incompatible, or necessarily connected.

Clearly we have here two quite different ontological accounts of the structure of intellect. But there is also a difference in the psychological content.
There is abundant evidence in the writings of St Thomas that the act of
understanding, *intelligere*, regards not only the inner word but also the phantasm. Scotus denies the possibility of that. What understanding would see in
the phantasm either is universal or it is particular. If it is particular, then we
have not understanding, but sense, for sense knows the particular. If it is
universal, then understanding is suffering from an illusion, because there is
no universal in the phantasm. The traditional or regular Thomist answer to
that, of course, is the distinction between the potential and the actual. The
phantasm is potentially intelligible, but the intelligible in act is identical
with the intellect in act.

Another difference is that the Scotist analysis leads to a conceptualized
universe. Scotus saw the need for a further intellectual intuition of the
existing and present *as* existing and present, if one is to know whether or
not this conceptualized network exists. That is not the case with St Thomas.
For St Thomas judgment proceeds from the *reductio ad principia* of reflection.

We have two presentations, then, and the difference between them raises
a question of fact. Does understanding regard phantasms or does it not? In
general, I believe there is no possibility of doubt that understanding does
occur with respect to phantasms. However, it is very difficult to get some
people to admit that this is the case because, if they do, they have to face
epistemological questions that otherwise they could dodge. It is the existence and the dodging of those epistemological questions that, to my mind,
accounts for the fact that what Aristotle and Thomas were talking about
when they spoke about the intelligible in the sensible has been totally disre-

garded for a number of centuries by people proclaiming themselves to be Aristotelians and Thomists.[5]

1.2 Illustrations from Geometry

Imagine a circle. One can ask, What is a circle? One can answer that question, of course, by consulting a dictionary or Euclid's *Elements* and reading off the definition. One can repeat the definition just as a parrot can. Many pupils are taught to do just that, and then they reach no understanding of why that is the definition.

However, one can see that the definition, the inner word, proceeds from an act of understanding with respect to such a phantasm as the following:

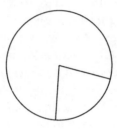

Figure 1

According to the Thomist account of intellectual process, if one asks why this figure is round, one can see that if we pick a central point and draw radii, as many as we please, and all the radii are equal, the curve cannot help being perfectly round; but if any radii are unequal, then there are bound to be bumps and dents on the curve. Everyone can see that, and seeing that in

5 On the epistemological problem that arises from the recognition of insight, see *Understanding and Being* 19, 350–52, 356–59, and note *c* to Discussion 2, p. 425.

   LN 71 has, 'Agreement of Thomistic and Scotist schools in psychology not for these reasons (a) Thomistic not voluntarist (b) potentially and actually visible, seen; intelligible understood

   'Real reason: psychological fact ignored, epistemological problem evaded.'

   Prior to this the notes had indicated another difference between the Thomist and Scotist accounts, which did not find its way into the lecture. The psychological differences include not only the presence and absence of the recognition of insight but also Scotist voluntarism, which 'supposes [an] incomplete intellectual theory.' These latter notes are possibly those with which Lonergan would have begun these lectures, had he chosen to start with cognitional theory rather than with the good. They have the heading 'Fundamental Notions. I. Understanding.' The words 'New Learning' are

the phantasm is understanding necessity and impossibility: it *cannot* be round; it *must* be round. It must be round, if the radii are equal; it cannot be round, if the radii are unequal. One grasps impossibility and necessity in the phantasm, and one does that only by intelligence. One cannot *imagine* the necessary or the impossible. Sense just gives matters of fact: what is there, and imagination merely represents the de facto, the empirical, the given, not the necessary and the impossible. We become aware of our intelligence by grasping impossibilities and necessities in sensible data. In virtue of that grasp we are able to define a circle as a locus of coplanar points equidistant from a center. The definition proceeds from the understanding of the image. That definition cannot arise out of the Scotist comparison of concepts, for there is only one concept of a radius, and we need an infinity of radii to have a grasp of 'necessarily round.'

A second illustration can be found in the first problem in Euclid's *Elements*. The problem is to construct an equilateral triangle on a given base in a given plane. Take base *AB*. Take center *A* and radius *BA*, and draw a circle. Take center *B* and radius *AB*, and draw another circle. Take their point of intersection *C*, and join *CA* and *CB*. Then you have an equilateral triangle.

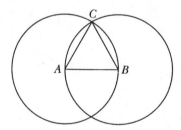

Figure 2

The proof is that radii in the same circle are equal; therefore radius *CA* is equal to radius *BA*, and similarly radius *CB* is equal to radius *AB*. Since things equal to the same thing are equal to one another, if *CA* is equal to *BA*, and *CB* equal to *AB*, *CA* is equal to *CB*. So we have an equilateral triangle.

Now modern mathematicians say that is all very well, the conclusion happens to be true, but Euclid did not prove it. The remark that Euclid did not prove it was made centuries after he had been accepted by everyone, and

---

written by hand next to this heading. And the first item reads, '1. Triple purpose: what is understanding? what is the expression of understanding? outline of the development of expression: pre-classical, classical, contemporary.'

many of you who are not in on the trick will think that his is a perfectly valid proof. However, what Euclid did not prove, and what cannot be proved from his definitions, axioms, and postulates, is that the two circles will intersect at point *C,* and in fact that there will be any intersection at all. Why should we not have two circles, one inside the other, and one outside the other? That's possible. Why must these two intersect? Well, you can see in the diagram that it is necessary. That is, you can have an insight with respect to the figure you are looking at. You can understand that it is necessary that at least those two circles intersect. This insight is what geometers went on for centuries, until somebody said we must be a little more logically rigorous than Euclid was.

Take another example. The former one was a problem, something to be done. Euclid distinguished problems and theorems. The first theorem in which I noticed a fallacy is the one in which you are asked to prove that the external angle *ACD* of a triangle *ABC* is greater than the interior opposite angle *BAC.* Euclid's proof was to bisect *AC* at point *E,* then join *BE,* produce *BE* to *F* so that *EF* is equal to *BE,* and join *FC.*

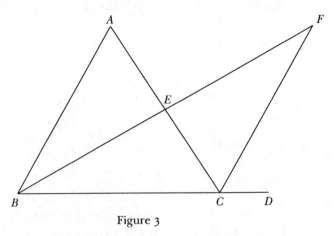

Figure 3

Since opposite angles are equal, and since *AE* is equal to *EC* by construction, and *BE* is equal to *EF* by construction, the two triangles are equal in all respects. Therefore, angle *ECF* is equal to angle *BAE.* But angle *ECF* is only part of the whole *ECD,* and so the exterior angle *ACD* is greater than the interior opposite *BAE.*

That too was accepted for centuries, but the proof is not rigorous. It cannot be proved on the basis of Euclid's definitions, postulates, axioms, and previous problems and theorems, that the line *FC* will fall within the exterior angle *ACD*. If *F* were a point that fell outside the angle, then joining *F* with *C* would not provide any proof that the interior angle is less than the exterior opposite. And how do you prove that *F* falls within that angle? There is no Euclidean method of establishing that proof. But you can grasp it by insight into or understanding of the figure. If you grasp this construction and think of the different lines I have drawn as movable, you can wiggle this triangle around in every way you please, and you will see that *FC* is bound always to stay within. You can perform a thought experiment, and see that *F* must lie within that angle.

I have given three illustrations in the clear-cut area of geometry, on matters that have been familiar for centuries. The illustrations show the existence of an act of understanding grasping necessity and impossibility in sensible data. That fact is *intelligere in phantasmatibus, intelligibile in sensibilibus*. What is known by understanding is form in matter. When Aristotle got hold of this he got hold of hylomorphism: the real world is sensible, but it is not merely sensible; intelligence grasps form in the sensible data, and the form that is grasped is not the same as the concept. What corresponds to form is not concept but understanding.

1.3 Matter, Form, Abstraction

Let us discuss the traditional doctrine a little further. Aristotle in his *Metaphysics* (book 7, chapter 10)[6] distinguishes between parts of the form and parts of the matter. In a circle parts of the matter are, for example, that it is white on black, it is drawn in chalk and not in lead or ink, it is just this big and no bigger or smaller – these are all parts of the matter. The parts of the form are the center, the radii, a plane curve, and the equality of all the radii. The parts of the form, then, are the elements necessary for this to be a circle; they are what intelligence selects out of the merely sensible presentation and puts into the definition.

Now this activity of intelligence selecting out some elements of the data and putting them in the definition, and leaving others behind, is *abstraction*. It follows that abstraction is a matter of intelligence. It is not a matter of metaphysical machinery that operates unconsciously. The account of the illumination of phantasm, of abstraction from sensible data, and of the expression in the concept of what has been abstracted, is not merely meta-

---

6 Lonergan hesitated in identifying the locus in Aristotle: 'in book M – or no, book Z, about chapter 10, but there are a couple of chapters in a row in which he treats the same matter.'

physical talk. It is also psychological description. Once one grasps why this figure must be round, one can see that to express the *must* one can forget about the parts of the matter. It makes no difference how big the circle is, nor what color it is, nor whether it is drawn on a blackboard or on a piece of paper or in the sand. Those are all parts of the matter, and you can drop them and pick out the parts of the form. This picking out is an exercise of intelligence, and because it is an exercise of intelligence we can speak not merely of a metaphysical potency named intellect, but also of the intelligence we all have and experience, either positively when we catch on, or negatively when we simply gape: What on earth is he talking about?[7]

1.4 Implications for Teaching

The notion of insight grasping the intelligible in the sensible has implications for teaching. Because it is a conscious human process, one must not suppose that because a student is a human being, that must be going on, the student must be abstracting intelligible species from phantasm. It is a *conscious* process, and something that people can be helped in. The teacher can help people form the correct phantasm. That is why there are blackboards in schoolrooms. One can use a schematic diagram, where the diagram is drawn to bring out the point. All that is wanted is a diagram that does emphasize the point. It need not be a beautiful drawing. The fewer irrelevant details the better, because that makes it that much easier to grasp the point.[8]

Secondly, St Thomas and perhaps Aristotle speak of the illumination of phantasm. What is that? It is moving into the intellectual pattern of experience. The effort made by the teacher is useless without the proper orientation of consciousness on the part of the student.[9] When one lies on the beach without a care, watching the clouds drift by, one is in a purely empirical pattern of experience. But when one begins to wonder about something — for example, why the clouds are drifting in this direction and not

7 LN 71 has, 'Abstraction: not unconscious automatic process, impression of species intelligibilis on intellectus possibilis; but also conscious, intelligent
        'Initial positive enriching moment: Eureka
        'Subsequent expressive abstractive moment.'
8 LN 71 has, 'Aid them to form correct phantasm
        'Aid and demand accurate expression: pick out what is essential significant relevant important; neglect what makes no difference, accidental, insignificant, irrelevant to insight, negligible.'
9 This sentence is constructed on the basis of LN 71.

that — when one begins to ask why about something, then one has the illumination of phantasm. The flow of consciousness becomes directed by
intelligence. It expresses an orientation of the subject; it exercises a selectivity over what is attended to; one's *Sorge* is engaged; one is asking why.[10] One
is wondering. One has injected into the flow of consciousness a bit of the
wonder that is the beginning of all science and philosophy. Now one cannot
do that for one's pupils; they have to do it for themselves. However, one can
stimulate them by making things puzzling in one way or another (as we tried
to do by saying that no one noticed for centuries that Euclid was illogical.)

   In the third place, if you understand, you can define. But defining also
includes some understanding of language and of the implications of terms.
So a teacher has to help pupils pick out correctly and accurately all the elements necessary for the understanding, and no more than the elements
that are necessary for the understanding. For example, if I define the circle
as a locus of points equidistant from a center, it may sound good, but that
definition can be applied to the outline of Africa on a globe, since every
point on the coast of Africa on a globe is equidistant from the center of the
sphere. Yet the coast of Africa is not a circle. The definition I suggested was
'a circle is a locus of points equidistant from a center,' and in the definition
I omitted the word 'coplanar'; the points have to be all on the same plane as
well as equidistant from the center.

   A teacher, then, can give very direct aid. The teacher helps the pupil
understand in the way the doctor helps the sick person become well. Nature
is the principal cause of a person's recovering health, and the doctor simply
helps, according to St Thomas's illustration.[11] Similarly in learning, the
pupil's own *intellectus agens* is the principal cause; and the *intellectus agens* is
wonder, trying to understand, the desire to understand. You cannot form an
image in the pupil's imagination, but you can suggest to him the image to
be formed. You cannot be sure that the image will be formed in the right
perspective so that intelligence will click and see the point, but you can help
the student get it in the right perspective. You can provide opportunities for
questions and find out what they have got wrong, what they are not seeing.
You can express it in a different way, you can walk around the subject from
all angles, until finally they catch on. In general, there are varying rates of

10 Parts of this sentence are based on LN 71.
11 Thomas Aquinas, *Summa theologiae*, 1, q. 117, a. 1 ad 1m: '... homo docens
    solummodo exterius ministerium adhibet, sicut medicus sanans: sed sicut
    natura interior est principalis causa sanationis, ita et interius lumen intellec-
    tus est principalis causa scientiae.'

comprehension in a classroom. The really bright students find the pedagogy of the teacher rather boring, since they see the point right at the start. Others are just able to grasp it with all the teacher's labors. Some begin to catch on only when they go home and do some homework, others only when there is a review of the material. Finally, there are those that are destined for the wayside, who do not catch on at all. But the teacher can help and stimulate and guide the formation of the phantasm — the transition, the illumination of the phantasm, the formation of a phantasm in the right perspective, the formulation of what is grasped by the act of understanding. But it is the pupil himself becoming habituated to an intellectual pattern of experience that is at once the fundamental condition of the whole process of teaching and at the same time its great fruit. Insofar as you are teaching people geometry, for example, you are using an implement that is magnificently adapted to habituating people to the intellectual pattern of experience. Even though they never bother their heads about geometry for the rest of their lives, at least they have lived at certain moments of their lives in the intellectual pattern of experience. They have some familiarity with the way things go on there, and they have a greater facility of doing that sort of thing on other occasions. Moreover, from the fact that they have been through the experience, there results a shift in the center of gravity in their experiencing. That shift in the center of gravity, that habituation to a differentiated consciousness, is a fruit of education, but an indirect fruit. It is only by doing particular subjects that that fruit results.[12]

1.5 Differences in Expression

We have been dealing with something very fundamental: inquiry, experience and imagination, understanding, and expression. What *differs* from one period to another is not inquiry, not experience, not understanding, but the *expression*; and so attention to these differences in expression is relevant to a differentiation of education at different times and for different cultural levels.[13]

I said that Euclid did not provide the principles for proving that his two

---

12 LN 71 has, 'Hence teacher must also encourage, develop, orientation of consciousness; much more difficult
   'But much more valuable: education is learning particular subjects, but also it is a differentiation of consciousness, development of differentiated consciousness; this will appear as aim and fruit of general, liberal, education.'
13 The material from 'and so' is added on the basis of LN 72.

circles would intersect. Someone might think he has some universal postulate or a priori law in his mind, in virtue of which he knows that in this particular case those two circles must intersect; he thinks he knows the
necessity of that intersection by some implicit deduction, and not by insight
into the phantasm. I will go through the work, then, of formulating the general principle from which that conclusion could be deduced, and you will
see that any knowledge of that principle that enabled one to conclude that
those circles would intersect was in the first instance necessarily a matter of
insight. The general principle itself can be derived only by insight.

If we have two circles, then, one outside the other, and join their centers,
we have a distance R, the radius of the one, and another distance r, the
radius of the other. The distance between their centers we will call S. In that
case (Figure 4) S is greater than R plus r; that is, the distance between the
centers is greater than the sum of the radii. But if they are just touching
(Figure 5), then S is equal to R plus r.

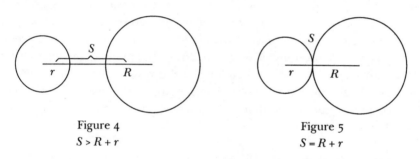

Figure 4   Figure 5
$S > R + r$ $S = R + r$

On the other hand, if one has two circles, one inside the other (Figure 6),
and joins their centers, and produces the line to the outer circumference,
then the whole distance is R, one part is r, and another part, the distance
between the centers, is S. In that case, R minus r is greater than S. But if one
circle just touches the other, then we have an equality: S is equal to R minus
r (Figure 7).

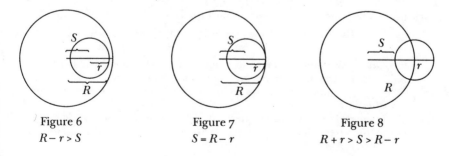

Figure 6   Figure 7   Figure 8
$R - r > S$ $S = R - r$ $R + r > S > R - r$

And if circles are neither outside nor inside one another nor tangential, then they are intersecting (Figure 8). You can see that by an insight. Consequently, our condition for two circles intersecting will be that R plus r is greater than S, which is greater than R minus r. On that condition, and only on that condition, two coplanar circles will intersect. Unless you start from non-Euclidean geometrical principles of betweenness and so on, it is only by insight into sensible data that you can work out that general rule and deduce from it that the two circles that Euclid was using must intersect.

Now that illustrates differences, degrees of explicitness, in conceiving and expressing what one understands. Euclid worked out a rather fine geometry, with little things omitted here and there. People were using their heads without explaining fully what they were understanding, all their use of understanding. The difference between modern geometry and Euclidean geometry is that the conceptualization in modern geometry is much fuller, much more adequate.[14] One of the reasons for the use of symbolic logic is to make sure that there do not occur casual insights, grasp of the intelligible in the sensible that you are not aware of. In that case you are not aware of your premises. Because you are not aware of your premises, you do not know fully what you are doing. When mathematicians treat the sort of material they are handling at the present time, they have to know absolutely everything about what they are doing; they are so far away from anything experiential that they must have the most rigorous methods possible.

1.6 The Greek Achievement

Geometry, then, in its axioms will go beyond Euclid to deal with problems of betweenness, intersection, and so on. On the one hand, then, there is in modern geometry a greater explicitness in conceptualization than is found in classical geometry. On the other hand, let us recall that Aristotle in book 13 of his *Metaphysics* (chapter 4)[15] says that Socrates introduced universal definitions and *logoi epaktikoi* — arguments that lead up. Note that Aristotle attributes to Socrates the achievement of introducing man to universal definitions. Does that mean that everyone who lived before Socrates had no

14 LN 72 has, 'Everyone understands that the two circles must intersect; for two millenia, this was just understood, not explicitly formulated
    'Explicit formulation calls for complete and accurate generality, and this is a further task.'
15 Lonergan did not give the chapter, but said, 'The exact chapter you can get by looking up the indices under the word, proper name, Socrates.' The exact reference is *Metaphysics*, XIII, 4, 1078b 27–29.

understanding at all? Were they all stupid? Not at all. It is one thing to understand, and that occurs with respect to sensible data. It is a distinct thing to arrive at a conceptual definition that is valid *omni et nullo.* That further step is what Socrates was attempting to force the Athenians to take. They all knew by insight, by commonsense understanding, what it was to be wise or silly, intelligent or stupid, brave or cowardly, just or unjust, and so on. But they could not work out universal definitions. They knew and they did not know. They knew insofar as they had a commonsense development of understanding; they did not know insofar as they had not worked out the conceptual expression. And the way up to the conceptual expression is the *logos epaktikos.*[16]

That was the beginning, the Greek beginnings of the intellectual pattern of experience, a differentiated pattern of experience. The Greeks introduced reasoning, the *logos.* According to Jean Piaget, it is only at about the age of twelve or thirteen that children can operate on propositions to settle questions, instead of acting them out and experiencing the consequences.[17] The introduction of a reasoning process, the use of propositions as tools to settle a course of action or to make a judgment, was introduced into Greek culture by the early philosophers. Thus Heraclitus is full of praise of the *logos.* But reasoning is fruitful only if your terms are accurately defined. If the meaning of your terms is not settled, then your reasoning process just bogs down in endless verbal disputes. Thus not only do we have with Socrates, according to the attribution of Aristotle, the introduction of universal definitions, definitions that will hold in every case, but with definitions as a basis of reasoning there is discovered the need of a few basic propositions, and there is introduced the idea of a science as an ordered body of definitions and implications exploring a delimited field of possible human knowledge.[18] Such a formulation of the intellectual pattern of experience was the specific Greek achievement.[19]

The meaning of the Greek discovery of the *logos,* of logic, is that insights

16 LN 72 has, 'Arist., Met. M, Socrates introduced universal definitions and logoi epaktikoi
    'Meaning parallel to problem of equilateral triangle
    'De facto, Socrates of Platonic dialogues, seeks universal definitions of virtues, demands that definition hold omni et nullo, demands that implications of definition should not be paradoxical, moves towards a totality of definitions, which with their implications, constitute a philosophy.'
17 The words from 'instead' are based on LN 72. For more on Piaget and intellectual development, see below, chapter 8.
18 The words from 'as' are taken from LN 72.
19 The break was taken at this point. Nothing seems to have been lost on the tape.

can be expressed in a form that is universally valid, and that on the basis of universal definitions, long chains of rigorous reasoning can be built. The discovery of an ideal of science, conceived in terms of definitions, axioms, postulates, problems, and theorems, was based upon that structure. It was a specific achievement of the human spirit. And it was novel to the Athenians, who did not like it and put Socrates to death.

It is also a distinguishing feature of the West. A student of theology whom I taught in Canada, a Hungarian who had spent three years as a Jesuit scholastic in Japan,[20] told me of the work of a missionary in a small Japanese village who had spent six years convincing the local Buddhist priest of the principle of contradiction. When he finally managed to convince him the whole village became Catholic. The formulation of the principle of contradiction, with the associated notion 'either true or false and if false worthless,' was what was lacking in the Japanese bonze and his people to take them beyond the image of religion as the ascent of the great mountain Fujiyama. For them, there were many ways up the mountain, and all were equally good; different people just chose different ways. Similarly, there were many ways to God, and all were good, for all went up. The Japanese had their religion, and Western Christians had theirs.

The problem of putting religion on the footing of true or false has again become a problem in our own Western culture. Modern methods of education have tended to eliminate it. I have heard of the wife of a convert who was one of the first victims of progressive education; she could not understand in any way the fact that her husband deserted his faith and became a Catholic. She could not grasp the notion of a religion as a matter of something true or false — and if it is false you have to leave it.

The Greek discovery of logic, the classical ideal, received a recent expression in a book entitled *The House of Intellect*[21] by Jacques Barzun, professor at Columbia University, the man who also wrote *Teacher in America.*[22] Although Barzun does not express things in these terms, in effect he is exposing the intellectual culture that derives from the Greeks, and presenting it as something that has to be *re*-achieved due to the influence of progressive education.[23] However, those are asides. The point I wish to draw is to take as it

20 Lonergan is referring to Fr Edmund Nemes. See *Understanding and Being* 425, note *e* to Discussion 2.
21 Jacques Barzun, *The House of Intellect* (New York: Harper & Row, 1959).
22 Jacques Barzun, *Teacher in America* (New York: Doubleday, 1959).
23 LN 72 adds, 'recent study of its [the classical ideal's] emergence, Eric Voegelin, Order and History, Louisiana State, 3 vols.'

were a line of reference in that Greek achievement, the ideal of science as implemented by Euclid, as a controlling influence up to modern times in what intelligence and intellect mean. We call that line of reference the classical ideal. I have already given you an outline of its social and cultural implications. I want to distinguish it from the preclassical and from the postclassical. It is the idea of the postclassical that is the idea of the new learning. It is a new idea of what mathematics is, of what science is, of what philosophy is, going beyond the Athenian achievement.[24] It does not deny this achievement, but there have been further developments in the intellectual field that are fuller refinements of what the Greeks did achieve.

Particularly in our century there has been a great deal of attention given to, and brilliant work done upon, what one might call the preclassical. In depth psychology there has been the work of Freud and Jung. In the study of intersubjectivity, personal relations, there has been the work of Max Scheler. There are the phenomenologists and the existentialists, especially Heidegger, Jaspers, and Marcel. There has been an influence in depth psychology radiating from Heidegger, whose ideas have been used by Ludwig Binswanger as a basis for depth-psychological techniques.[25] Another line of influence from Heidegger is to be found, of course, in the work of Rudolf Bultmann, a great New Testament scholar, who is using Heidegger's philosophy as a fundamental set of notions to be employed in interpreting the New Testament. And Hans Jonas is using Heidegger to interpret the Gnostics. In the history of religions there is the work of Eliade, a name I have already mentioned. There is Voegelin's *Order and History*, and there is the work of Ernst Cassirer.[26] In child psychology there is the work of Piaget, an extremely brilliant man of whom I am going to say more later. All of these are studying forms of experience that are prior to the specialization of intellect that arises with the Greeks.[27]

2   The Postclassical Versatility of Understanding

Now we have to go on to the postclassical versatility of understanding. This

24 LN 72 has, '*Post-classical*: developments in math science; repercussions in philosophy theology.'
25 Lonergan mentioned the book *Existence: A New Dimension in Psychiatry and Psychology*, ed. Rollo May, Ernest Angel, Henri F. Ellenberger (New York: Basic Books: 1958). Binswanger has three chapters in this book.
26 LN 72 adds to the list, 'historicism vs naturalism.'
27 LN 72 adds at the very end of this section, '*Classical*: a good average adapted to teaching, but phil of education has to know about others at least.'

is what brings us to something that is specifically new in the new learning.

2.1   *The Lobatchevskian Experience*[28]

First of all, then, consider the Lobatchevskian experience. Euclidean geometry rests upon the parallel postulate. The parallel postulate is a matter of insight into phantasm. One can easily feel that it is absolutely necessary that there is one and only one case in which lines produced indefinitely in either direction will never meet. The parallel postulate seems necessary, and it seems necessary by the same process as the one we used to define the circle, to see the intersection of the circles, and to prove that the external angle of a triangle is greater than the internal opposite. And there is in fact an insight involved in the parallel postulate. But the fallacy in the apparent necessity of the parallel postulate is that, if you imagine lines produced indefinitely, you are constructing an image. You do not just imagine the lines; you imagine something growing indefinitely; and that indefinite growth occurs according to a certain law. Your imagination extends those lines according to a certain imaginative assumption about space. And that imaginative assumption about space is precisely the parallel postulate. So if you imagine lines produced indefinitely on the imaginative assumption that space is equally roomy all over, that it does not become more or less roomy as you produce these lines indefinitely, then your parallel postulate is true. But it is only a particular case. As you produce the lines indefinitely in your imagination, space may be becoming tighter, less roomy, and then you will have an elliptical space; or it may be becoming more roomy, and then you will have a hyperbolic space. Lobatchevski discovered the hyperbolic space, and Gauss, I think, the elliptical, and these discoveries effected a transformation in the notion of what mathematics is.[29] Prior to the Lobatchevskian experience mathematics was a matter of deducing conclusions from necessary, self-evident truths. But after that experience, first geometry and then mathematics in general became hypothetico-deductive. You selected a number of axioms and postulated them, and mathematics was a matter of working out the implications of your postulates. It was no longer a matter of drawing conclusions from necessary, self-evident truths, but of seeing what

28 The first four subheadings in this section are taken from LN 73. Our section 2.5 was marked off in the notes as a distinct subsection, but without any subheading.
29 LN 73 has, 'Euclidean geometry one of many possible geometries.'

would follow if certain assumptions were made. The question, What is the validity of the assumptions? is the current question of the foundations of mathematics, and there are several different schools on the matter.

2.2   Quest for Rigor

Combining with this change in the conception of mathematics (first of all of geometry, but later of mathematics) there arose the quest for rigor. I have illustrated the reasons for that already. Euclid's proofs are not rigorous. He makes use of casual insights. He always does so when he says that there are three and only three cases. How did he know there are three and only three? He has no way of proving that, but it is evident by insight. But if you are to have the enormous hypothetico-deductive structures that the modern mathematicians construct, then you have to know exactly what you are doing. You cannot tolerate unnoticed insights. You will not know what you are doing, and so you will get lost. Consequently, there arose in mathematics a quest for a logical rigor that surpassed previous thinkers. This applied not only to deduction, but also to the concept of a number, to the concept of an irrational number, and to the concept of the infinitesimal — the notion of the very small that is the basis of the differential calculus — and so on. And so mathematics turned at the beginning of the century to symbolic logic as the tool for providing and securing rigor in the hypothetico-deductive structure that mathematics is. There was a series of attempts to put mathematics on solid foundations. The axiomatic set theory is one type.[30] The foundations of mathematics have split up into a set of schools — we need not go into detail[31] — but what is most interesting for our purposes is that by using symbolic logic mathematicians have been able to work out properties of rigorously deductive systems and to discover the limitations of such systems. Jean Ladrière presented, as the work entitling him to be a member of the Academy of St Thomas in Louvain, a book on the internal limitations of formal structures, what you can and cannot prove. The book is entitled *Les*

30 Lonergan mentioned that 'on that subject' there is a bibliography up to about 1950 in the series by Bochenski. See I.M. Bochenski, *Bibliographische Einführungen in das Studium der Philosophie* (Bern: A. Francke, 1948), Fasc. 3, *Mathematische Logik*. Lonergan referred to Bochenski's 'booklet on mathematics — foundations of mathematics and mathematical logic.'

31 LN 73 has, 'Foundations of maths: axiomatic set theory (Fraenkel); Russell-Whitehead; Hilbert, Goedel; Brouwer; Gonseth; N. Bourbaki' and, handwritten, 'I Bochenski Bibliographische Enführung/J. Ladrière Les limitations internes des formalismes.'

limitations internes de formalisme.[32] The Gödelian type of theorem — Gödel is at the Princeton Institute for Advanced Study now — shows that it is impossible in a finite number of steps to establish the validity of arithmetic, and much less, then, of any more advanced type of mathematics. It has also been shown that by using a transfinite number of steps you *can* establish the validity of arithmetic. In general, the conclusion to be drawn is that you have to think of deduction as occurring on a series of levels. What is occurring in the development of thought is not adding more conclusions on to your deductive structure, but moving from a lower one to a higher one. The significant movement is not deductive, but a movement up through the series of possible deductive structures. Our second point, then, is that mathematics became hypothetico-deductive, extremely rigorous, and has a problem of its foundations.

2.3   Abstraction: What Is Abstracted From

Further, the notion of abstraction becomes generalized. When one abstracts, one grasps the intelligible in the sensible. We used the example of grasping the necessity of the roundness of the curve. In virtue of that grasp of the necessity one could pick out the parts of the form — the elements of the definition — and neglect the parts of the matter. What happens is that one selects from the sensible what is intelligible in the light of a given insight. What is necessary for the insight you call the essential, the relevant, the important, and what is not essential and necessary for the insight you call the incidental, the accidental, the irrelevant, the negligible.

But this process of dropping away the irrelevant and selecting out the relevant has been refined in a variety of ways. The notion of the irrational and the transcendental number is a special case. Newton's first law, that a body continues in a straight line with a constant velocity until some external force acts upon it, is a refined type of abstraction. What Newton is saying is that velocity is not something to be explained; all you have to explain are accelerations. And if all you have to explain are the accelerations, the changes in velocity, then that is the only thing in local motion that is intelligible. All else is material, what intellect abstracts from. Newton was able to work out a magnificently compact theory of movements simply because he did not have to pay any attention to constant velocity; constant velocity no more needs an explanation than does the state of rest. That was a case of deter-

32 Jean Ladrière, *Les limitations internes de formalisme* (Louvain: A. Nauwelaerts, 1957).

mining the level in the sensible of what does not count, and what you attend to when you are understanding. It is a refinement on the notion of abstraction. Newton's first law means that we abstract in our science of movements not only from rest but also from constant velocity.

Einstein's special relativity is a transposition of that Newtonian idea from mechanics to electromagnetics, and from a causal theory to a field theory. What is occurring in special relativity is a new way of determining the level of what one abstracts from.

When I argue that sin is not in itself intelligible, that one is not to look for an explanation of it — and that is the critical answer to the dispute *de auxiliis* — I am introducing again the critical method of saying what one abstracts from. When the theologians introduced the category of the supernatural at the beginning of the thirteenth century, and laid down that the supernatural was something you could not demonstrate and could not understand perfectly, they were introducing a basic methodological principle that created theology as a science; and at the same time they were laying down a level of what you abstract from, because it is beyond the level of your capacity to understand.

You can see from those examples that abstraction is something more versatile than something that can be thought of simply as an automatic process. You can see how there is in modern scientific thinking a versatility in using the relations between intelligence and sensible data, a versatility that is distinctively modern.[33]

2.4 What One Reaches by Abstraction

Let me give a few more determinate illustrations of that, which will be more universally acceptable.

---

33 LN 73: 'Grasp of intelligible: abstract from unintelligible, relatively or absolutely
    'Conditiones materiae: individuality, place, time: nothing accounted for by saying "because it is this instance, at this place, or at this time"; always some property of this instance, something at this place, something at this time
    'Abstracting, an activity of intelligence, not just an empirical fact, but because of a known reason
    'Other instances: *irrationals, transcendentals* (new categories of number); *probability* (Arist., Met E, no science of per accidens; Aquinas nothing per accidens to God; modern, statistical method) *Newton's First Law* (acceleration but not velocity needs explanation) *Special Relativity* (transfer to electromagnetic and field theory) *sin* (de auxiliis); *mystery*, supernatural (method of theology).'

On the traditional view, what intellect abstracts from phantasm is the form and the common matter. In the concept of man, for example, there is abstracted the form (the soul) and the common matter (the bones and flesh), though the common matter is not these particular bones or this particular flesh. That gives the traditional notion of the content of a definition: the definition expresses the form and the common matter.

But an entirely new type of definition was introduced by Hilbert in his formulation of geometry. He called it implicit definition. An implicit definition drops the common matter to express only a relational form. In Hilbert's geometry there is no definition of points by themselves, and no definition of straight lines by themselves, but there is a definition of the relation between points and straight lines: two points determine a straight line; a straight line is determined by two points. The significance of implicit definition is that it does not pin down the meaning of the words 'point' and 'line' to anything. Point, in Hilbert's expression of geometry, can be a Euclidean position without magnitude, and line can be a length without breadth or thickness lying evenly between its extremes. But a point can also be an ordered pair of numbers, where (a, b) is not the Cartesian notation for a Euclidean point, but just that ordered pair. And a straight line can be a first-degree equation: $y = mx + c$ is determined by two ordered pairs, and two ordered pairs will determine a first-degree equation. Hilbert can mean by 'point' and 'line' the imaginable Euclidean point or line, the Cartesian algebraic expression for point and line, or anything else that will satisfy the relation 'two of one determines one of the other,' no matter what they are. The definitions are in terms of relational form, with no attention to any common matter. The relational form selects any common matter that will be thought relevant. Implicit definition is a more abstract type of thinking that omits even the common matter.[34]

Again, Newtonian mechanics is constructed in the same way as was Euclidean geometry. Kepler's discovery that the planet Mars and the planets in general moved in ellipses was for Newton a conclusion to be demonstrated. That was Newton's great achievement. He established, by what seemed to be methods parallel to Euclid's, by rigorous deduction, exactly what Kepler had found by empirical correlations. Newton demonstrated that if there is a central field of force, that is, a force that causes an acceleration according to the law of inverse squares and is concentrated at the cen-

---

34 LN 73 adds 'isomorphic fields' to the other elements of implicit definition treated in the lecture. See below, § 2.5.

ter of a field, then any body moving in that field will move along a conic section, such as an ellipse, a circle, a hyperbola, and so on. You can see that this theorem includes the common matter; there is something that you can imagine, namely, the conic section. And that type of mechanics is determinist; it includes not only the intelligible form, but also an element of the matter. On the other hand, quantum theory deals with what it knows to be processes that cannot be imagined. It is a higher level of abstraction, and getting away from anything that can be imagined is connected with the fact that quantum theory is statistical — it is not the only factor.

So you can see how even the ideas of definition and abstraction have become much more fluid. Scientific thinking is much more versatile, much more attentive to all the possibilities of the fundamental act that is insight into sensible data. I have given a series of illustrations of this.

2.5 Abstraction and Operations: Group Theory

Now let us attempt to line things up. Pierre Boutroux, in his book *L'idéal scientifique des mathématiciens*[35] distinguishes three periods, three scientific ideals of mathematicians. The first ideal is the Greek, where the mathematician is concerned with the object: the circle, the ellipse, the hyperbola, and so on; or the number, the ratio, the irrational number.[36] The second form of the scientific ideal moves from the eternal object of contemplation to the genesis of the object. The chief example in mathematics, of course, is the differential calculus. For the Aristotelians, a movement is understood from its end — *motus intelligitur ex termino* — but the differential calculus and all techniques analogous to it or based upon it are concerned with understanding the motion in itself qua moving.[37] And the third, contemporary stage is called group theory.[38] For abstraction falls upon, not the object, not the process of genesis in the object, but the operations of the subject. In other

---

35 Pierre Boutroux, *L'idéal scientifique des mathématiciens dans l'Antiquité et les Temps modernes*. Nouvelle édition (Paris: Presses Universitaires de France, 1955).
36 LN 73 has, 'Greek: object, its eternal and necessary properties.'
37 LN 73 has, 'Modern: process in which object emerges; differential calculus; motus cognoscitur non solum ex termino sed magis ex via ad terminum si est terminus.'
    'Piaget: constancy of volume, weight, grasped by attending to process: nothing added taken away: 8 and 10 yrs respectively.' On Piaget, see below, chapter 8, § 2.3.
38 LN 73 verso adds the names 'Hamilton, Gibbs, Poincaré' and (handwritten) 'Piaget.'

words, what one abstracts from directly is neither the individual matter nor the individual and common matter of the object, nor the individuality of the movement, but the operations of the subject.

We will take as our illustration of operations adding and subtracting. They are two operations. You can think of what you add or subtract. Thus you can put two blackboard brushes together with a third, and then you have a physical operation. But you can write $2 + 1$, and that is a symbolic operation. But it is a symbolic operation in which you are representing the brushes, and so still specifying what it is that you are performing the operation on. Again, you can operate on the symbols $a + b$ in such a way that you are not saying what a and b are. Operations form a group when their relations with one another are such that you can go anywhere and come back again. So you can subtract all that was added and return to the starting point. Again, what you get by multiplying you can undo by dividing, and what you get by raising to powers you can undo by taking roots. Such operations form a group. The terms are not important; it is the group of operations that must be considered. The terms are whatever is presupposed or generated by the operations. So how do you get the terms? You think of the identity operation, the operation that leaves things as they were. So you define 'zero' as what you add or subtract to get what you already had; with this you have defined one basic term. Similarly, you define 'one' as what you multiply or divide by to get what you already had. And with zero and one you can go on to construct all the numbers. But what comes first are not the numbers, but the operations. A number is whatever you can derive from the operations.[39]

Group theory is a third stage in mathematical reflection, one in which you move back upon the subject from the object. The objects are anything at all that can result from the operations. Let me give you a concrete example to get at the significance of the approach of group theory, one that is of interest not merely mathematically, but also for solving certain problems about the notion of a Catholic philosophy.

One can ask a child to build a square from a heap of marbles. Suppose there are 1764 marbles in all. How many marbles will there be along the side of the square? The child, with a little bit of experimentation, will be able to build the square with the marbles, count the marbles on the side, and find

---

39 LN 73 verso has, 'Operations form group: direct, reverse, null
   'Null operations define basic terms: add zero; multiply by one
   'Terms: anything generated by operations.'

there are forty-two. That is a physical operation upon a set of marbles. A further stage of reflection would deal with the number 1764, instead of with the marbles, and would seek the square root. First of all, mark off the number into pairs of numbers starting from the unit end. The nearest to the square root of 17 is 4. 4 × 4 is 16. Write the 4 on the side and on top. 16 from 17 leaves 1. Bring down the 64. Then multiply the 4 by 2, and you get 8. 8 goes into 16 twice. So write the 2 down on top and beside the 8. Multiply 82 by 2. This equals 164. 164 from 164 equals zero. And so your square root is 42.

$$
\begin{array}{r}
\phantom{\sqrt{1}}42 \\
\sqrt{1764} \\
4\phantom{\sqrt{}}\overline{16} \\
\overline{164} \\
82\phantom{\sqrt{}}164 \\
\overline{0}
\end{array}
$$

But you can go on to a third level and ask, Why does that work? And if you want to know why it works, you have to move into algebra. You know that $(a+b)^2 = a^2 + 2ab + b^2$. Suppose our number has two digits. Call the first digit a, the second b. Then what we really have is $(10a + b)^2$; $(40 + 2)^2$.

$$(10a + b)^2 = 10^2a^2 + 2 \cdot 10ab + b^2.$$

The last part of this can be factorized, giving

$$10^2a^2 + b(2 \cdot 10a + b).$$

First of all, we marked off in twos from the decimal point, and that took care of the 10^2. So when we wrote down the 4, what we were really writing down was 40. We squared it and got 1600. Then we doubled the 40, because of our general formula $2 \cdot 10a$, and we got 80. We then added on the 2, the b, to get (80 + 2), the $(2 \cdot 10a + b)$ in our general formula. Finally we multiplied the whole thing by b and got 2(80 + 2), which when subtracted left no remainder. You can see that the form of the algebraic identity has been used to set up a technique for taking square roots. And what is a technique? A technician is one who knows how to take the square roots but does not understand the algebra that accounts for the method. Similarly, all the applications of science can be worked out into a set of rules like the set of rules for taking square roots. The scientist will know why they work, but the technician need not. All the technician has to do is learn the rules; he does not have to understand. So in a technical society there is a divorce between the people who understand what it is all about and those who, without any understanding, do the material operations, what they have been told to do, what has been dinned into them in a technical education.

We have considered three levels of operations: first, taking the square root by operating on marbles, that is, by arranging the marbles in a square, and counting the number of marbles along the side; second, taking the square root with numbers; and third, taking the square root algebraically and in a way that justifies the technique. The three cases are a rough illustration of what is meant by *isomorphism*. *Isos* means *equal*, *morphê* means *form*. There is a similarity of form in the square made up of marbles, the square with the area 1764, and the square with the sides $a + b$ or $10a + b$. To think of mathematics in terms of group theory is to think of the operations. The operations may be very concrete, as upon the marbles, or intermediate, as upon the numbers, or remote, as upon the symbols. But there is fundamentally a similar form, the same idea, the same insight involved in all three cases. Consequently, a group theory, the notion of a science in terms of a group of operations, enables the science to be indifferently abstract and symbolic, or as concrete as you please, all in virtue of the isomorphism of operations. Symbols can be given a physical interpretation or a spatial interpretation or a numerical interpretation, as they are all generated and controlled by certain operations such as adding, multiplying, and so on. What we have in the algebra is the expression of a pattern of operations: squaring something, adding twice that multiplied by something else, adding the square of the something else: $a^2 + 2ab + b^2$. That is a pattern of operations, and the pattern can appear in a series of quite different instances or realizations. These different realizations will all be isomorphic; they will all have the same intelligibility.

This is an introduction to an entirely different approach to a science, an approach in terms of the operations of the scientist as distinct from the formal object. If you think of science in terms of formal objects, you are thinking of science as the Greeks thought of mathematics. Next, if you move on to think of science as the study of development, you are thinking like the thinkers of the Renaissance and later mathematicians. But if you think of a science as constituted by a group of operations, then the division and unification or integration of the sciences becomes a matter of the division and integration of sets of operations. And human history, the history that is written about, becomes the totality of human operations. Then the problem of synthesis or integration is a problem of putting different sets of operations together. This gives us an alternative approach to the whole problem of integrating the sciences, integrating the different departments of knowledge in the subject, relating the learning of the subject to the history of human life or to the concrete living of the individual. This illustrates again the versatility of postclassical intelligence.

I may note, finally, that my book *Insight* is a study of operations. The fundamental operation examined there is the act of understanding, insight. Everything else is defined in terms of one's experience of insight. Three fundamental levels of experiencing, understanding, and judging are worked out. The universe of proportionate being is found to be isomorphic with the three basic operations of experiencing, understanding, and judging. If the subject will be intelligent and reasonable, if he will perform those operations, he will agree with the conclusions reached in *Insight*; and if he does not wish to agree with those conclusions, he will have to find some way of building a horizon that will close him off from his own intelligence and his own reasonableness. You can see from this how group theory can be used as a presentation of a philosophy.[40]

In the next lecture we will go on to examine the new idea of science that emerges in modernity. Here we have seen that the ideas of mathematical reflection are radically new, and that they head in all sorts of directions. In that sense there really is a new learning, a transformation of older conceptions of the subject itself, not mere additions to previously existing subjects.[41] I have attempted to give an indication of what is meant by the new learning, mainly from mathematics. By the new learning, again, I mean not merely additions to what was known before, but a new structure, a transformation of fundamental concepts regarding what the learning is.

I hope I have succeeded in indicating even to nonmathematicians some notion of the significance of group theory. Mathematics is conceived as a group of operations, with the emphasis on the word 'group': the operations are linked together; they stand, as it were, in equilibrium; you can go and

40 The notes of F. Crowe, written from memory after the discussion of August 8, report a distinction Lonergan made that evening between (1) sciences which are directly about objects: God, angels, men, biology, chemistry, physics, and (2) sciences which reflect on the (method?) of those sciences: logic, methodology, introspective psychology, epistemology, metaphysics, Christian philosophy. The theory of group operations, Lonergan said, handled difficulties of the second type.

41 The fifth lecture actually ended here. What follows formed the introduction to the sixth lecture. We have placed it here since it summarizes the present lecture, and because Lonergan's notes for the fifth lecture contain some of this material.

come back, and so on. The simplest illustration is from the extension of arithmetic into algebra, where there are addition and subtraction, multiplication and division, powers and roots. But that notion has been extended to the whole of mathematics, so that mathematics is fundamentally a group of operations that can be developed by adding or discovering further operations, or by moving from more elementary to more developed operations, as in the transition from algebra to calculus, or by developing the symbols on which one operates, by moving from simple a, b, c, or x, y, z to sets and lattices that take the place of the simple numbers. Finally, there can be extension in the interpretation placed upon the symbols. Pure mathematics places no interpretation on them, but they can be interpreted as a geometry, as a space-time, as a physics, as a chemistry, and so on. In the conception of mathematics in terms of groups of operations, there can be combined the greatest concreteness with a full appreciation of abstraction. The form grasped by insight into phantasm is the form of the group. If you understand what it is to do arithmetic, you can develop from that insight something that stands to doing arithmetic as the definition of the circle stands to the image of the circle. It is something much more rigorous and much more systematic than any image. The group of operations in any particular case is what is represented by a formula, and the formula can be realized simply in the symbols or in a series of isomorphic cases which may be applications or different uses of the symbols. And with this procedure you get new types of definitions, such as implicit definitions that are simply relational forms without the common matter; it is quite possible to add any common matter that one pleases.[42]

42 LN 73 verso contains more on group theory. See below, appendix, § D.

6

Science and the New Learning[1]

I wish today to move on to the notion of science. Science is one of the instruments of education, and educators have to make decisions about the extent to which they propose to use science, and when they are to use it, as an instrument. An important factor in that decision is the question, What precisely is science?

1   Heuristic Structures and Canons

1.1 An Instance

In *Insight* I take as a basic example of scientific insight Galileo's discovery of the law of falling bodies: the distance is proportional to the time squared, or in more modern notation $s = vt + gt^2/2$.[2]

There are two elements in Galileo's conception. His fundamental inspiration was an ideal of system. The system at which he aimed was geometry, an already existing system. That notion of the scientific system was upset when Newton developed his mechanics – something analogous to geometry but not just geometry. The other component, besides the ideal of system, was a movement from sensible data to laws that fitted within the system. It is that movement from sensible data to law that we have to consider. It is the fundamental step in an empirical science.

---

1 Most of the sixth lecture, Monday, August 10, 1959. For the beginning of the sixth lecture, see above, chapter 5, note 41.
2 See Lonergan, *Insight* 57–59.

What Galileo did was select measurable aspects or elements in what he wished to investigate, that is, the free fall of a body. A body falls a certain distance; it does so with a certain weight; it takes a certain amount of time to do so. Galileo eliminated the correlation that bodies fall according to their weight, and he sought a correlation, a connection, between the distance and the time. He measured distances traversed and times elapsed while objects slid down inclined planes. The result was a series of measurements. We get a table with time corresponding to distance. That table represents matters of fact. The idea of obtaining a law is the idea of obtaining a formula that holds for not only those cases but all intermediate cases, and all cases that would be obtained by going beyond the amount of time involved. The simplest way of representing that step is to draw a graph with the times along one axis and the distances along the other, and joining the points with a freehand smooth curve.[3] In that step one has the fundamental idea. What has occurred? One is seeking a regularity that links together all the points. But it is a *possible* regularity; it is not necessary. There is never any way of demonstrating from a discontinuous set of measurements, no matter how great, that one and only one law satisfies those measurements. The mathematicians can always find any number of curves to pass through any number of points. Thus law is always hypothetical, and what is selected is the simplest law. In the example we have chosen, this is the correlation 'distance proportional to time squared.'

The use of the digital computer enormously simplifies the task of finding the curve that goes through the points. Any curve going through a set of points in a space can be represented by a formula such as this: $s = vt + gt^2/2$ – distance is equal to the initial velocity by the time plus the acceleration of gravity by the time squared over 2. Any curve that can be drawn on a graph can also be represented in an algebraic formula; the relation between the two is analytic or coordinate geometry. The digital computer enormously facilitates the process from the sets of measurements to the formula. Shortly before coming here I saw a machine operated in Halifax by a professor of chemistry.[4] He had a series of measurements for the temperatures of molten salt and the electric conductivity through the salt. He would type these measurements out, punch the tape, then put the tape into the machine; the machine retyped them and provided the information. He would press a couple of buttons and the machine calculated in a minute and a quarter the

3 Throughout this exposition Lonergan was illustrating by drawing a graph on the blackboard.
4 Professor James W. Murphy, sj, Saint Mary's University.

best formula of the type $y = a - bx$. And when I say the best, I mean the best fit according to mean root square deviation, the standard deviation. To calculate that would take a considerable amount of time. He pressed two buttons again, and the machine proceeded to calculate the best fit by mean root square deviation where the formula is of the type $y = a + bx + cx^2$. (It goes on to thirteen constants just by pushing the two buttons, though it takes a minute and a quarter for each step. But the amount of labor otherwise required would be fantastic.) He was working with an algebraic formula, but if he does not like the algebraic formula he presses another button that does a transfer, giving formulae of the type, $y = e^{a+bx}$, the exponential function. And after it does that, he presses again and gets $y = e^{a+bx+cx^2}$ and so on to thirteen constants. It works out to at least ten significant figures, which is way beyond what anyone usually would obtain from measurement. (Then it will go on and do $y = \sin x$.) Without the computer, it would take an enormous amount of time for the process of curve fitting. The computer finds not only the best formula, but the best formula according to a certain standard, namely, the standard of mean root square difference.

That procedure selects from data determinate aspects, measures the aspects, correlates the measurements – sets the measurements down in a series of correspondences – and then finds a general formula that covers all cases. One can go on to further tests. One can work out a formula for a discrete series of points, get the curve, and test the curve by trying intermediate points not tried before. One can predict what should be and then perform the experiment to see if that is what happens. That is interpolation: the points one tries are in the field in which the observations were made. But one can also extrapolate as far beyond that field as one pleases and perform another experiment. If the experiment still verifies the formula, one begins to feel fairly certain.

That is the process of verifying a formula. But verifications of formulae are not merely direct as by interpolation and extrapolation; they are also indirect. The formula that is a later expression of Galileo's law has been tested indirectly in all mechanical experiments for over 400 years; and if there were anything wrong with it, if some implication were wrong, in astronomy or any other part of mechanics, that defect would have shown up in time. In other words, the formulas reached by scientists are tested not only by interpolation and extrapolation on the formulas themselves. There is also an enormous indirect verification in all scientific work that uses or presupposes the validity of those formulas.

1.2 Heuristic Structure

We have been considering science as object. But we have to ask a more fundamental question. Mathematics is, so to speak, an expression of developed intelligence. But empirical science provides us with an opportunity to study intelligence as developing. Science is not finished, it is on the way. The mathematician, if he does his mathematics right, is supposed to be right indefinitely. There can occur revisions within mathematics, but the revision is not of the essence, so to speak, as it is in science. There is something intrinsically dynamic to empirical method, and we have to try to understand that. In other words, while a mathematician presents mathematical systems, the scientist is concerned with method; and method is concerned with a movement. What is the fundamental idea in that movement?

We can begin from an example that is nonscientific and then move on to the scientific method. You may remember the sort of problem that comes up in exercises in books on elementary algebra. The clock is at 3:00, and the question is put, How soon after 3:00 is the minute hand exactly over the hour hand? The problem is tricky because when the minute hand moves down, the hour hand also moves; but the minute hand is bound to pass the hour hand before it gets to 4:00; consequently, there is some instant at which the minute hand is exactly over the hour hand.

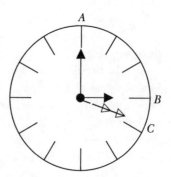

The algebraic procedure is to say, 'Let the number of minutes after 3:00 when the minute hand is exactly over the hour hand be x.' This is a clue to solving algebraic problems: 'Let there be x.' It seems a very useless thing to say, but it is naming the unknown, and not merely giving it a name, x, but saying that x is a number. Any number stands in an enormous pattern of exactly determinate relations with an infinity of other numbers, so you are saying a lot about this x when you say, 'Let the *number* be x,' when you call it a number. If the number of minutes after 3:00 is x, then the hour hand will have moved a certain number of minutes while the minute hand is moving. The hour hand takes twelve hours to make its complete circle; the minute hand takes just one hour, so the minute hand goes twelve times as fast. Consequently, the distance BC is $x/12$ (see the diagram above).

What we have been doing is carrying out the precepts of a teacher of mathematics: draw a diagram; flag the diagram; draw a good large diagram, and mark on it all the things you know and the things you do not know. What is not known, mark x. What you can conclude from naming this x is the name of a further term, $x/12$.

The point to the diagram is to invite an insight. What is the insight we want? It is to see an equation. We see that at 3:00 the difference between the hands is fifteen minutes, so that $x = 15 + x/12$. From then on the solution is routine, a matter of solving an equation: x turns out to be 16 4/11. But the solution is of no import. The moment of insight occurs when you get hold of an equation.

Now we are going to use this as an analogy to understand scientific method. The key step was saying, 'Let x be the required number.' You name your unknown, what you are looking for. What the empirical scientist wants is a law. And so he can write down, 'Let $f(x, y, z, ...) = 0$ be the required law.'[5] In the former case we wrote, 'Let x be the number that is required,' but in this case we simply wrote a general expression for any mathematical function whatever. We do not know what it is, just as we did not know what x was. On the other hand, if you know mathematics, or if mathematics is sufficiently developed for the type of scientific work you are doing, then this function will be some function among the functions whose properties have been studied by the mathematician.

What you are doing is naming the unknown. You fixed upon a certain number of variables; in the case of the free fall, two were picked out, distance and time. As a matter of fact, Galileo's law for a free fall is for a free fall in a vacuum. If something is let fall through air or water or any other medium, then there have to be taken into account velocity and air resistance, and the calculation becomes much more complicated. You need more than one variable, but the scientist has to determine the number of variables he wants. What he is looking for is some function, and he knows that from the start, just as when you start the algebraic problem you know you are looking for x.

5 Lonergan sometimes used 'function' instead of 'equation,' though his meaning is clear enough from the context; see *Insight* 784, note *f* to chapter 2, on the correction he received and accepted on this point.

How does the empirical scientist determine that function? By the method, and the method is twofold. There is a component from above downward, and a component from below upward. It is a scissors action. People with an inadequate notion of science think only of the component from below upward. The movement from below upward is illustrated by the selection of the aspects of the matter that one can measure, by performing the measurements, by their tabulation, by the work of curve fitting that yields the best formula according to mean root square deviation.

But the scientist does not merely work up from the data toward the formula. He also works from above downward. This is an important point, because without grasping that movement from above downward one won't really get into contemporary physics at all. In general, any functions are solutions to a type of equation called the differential equation. And differential equations can be written down simply on inspection. I cannot offer any explanation of that here. But, for example, when a physicist speaks of a wave, what does he mean? He means any function that will satisfy the appropriate differential equation.[6] It can be demonstrated simply from analysis that any wave whatever will satisfy that differential equation; it is so general that the solution to it is simply in terms of this f, the function, any function; Ψ is equal to any function of $x + at$ minus any function of $x - at$, where f does not mean some determinate function such as $a + bx$ or $a + bx + cx^2$. The solution can be any function at all: algebraic, exponential, trigonometric, whatever.

So what the physicist means by a wave is something extremely general. Similarly, there are equally general differential equations that are obtained simply by a priori analysis. And so differential equations are employed by the physicist in a movement from above downward. The possible law is going to be a function that is a solution of certain determinate differential equations.

One obtains a further component in the movement from above downward when one introduces with Einstein a postulate of invariance. This means that certain classes of differential equations are going to be true, and the postulate of invariance in relativity fundamentally means that laws are independent of particular places and times. This is simply the scholastic

6 Lonergan wrote a differential equation on the board. No record of it is found in any notes. However, in *Understanding and Being* (p. 68) we find 'the general formula for a wave motion' in the following equation:

$$\partial^2 y/\partial t^2 = a^2(\partial^2 y/\partial x^2).$$

doctrine of abstraction. But the fundamental thing is to note the existence of that procedure and, moreover, its profound significance. In other words, the physicist will solve problems sufficiently for his purposes without arriving at a determination of their function. He will have a set of differential equations and a set of measurements called boundary conditions, and while he is not able to find out the law, still he is able to solve any one of his concrete problems. So science can be moving along without knowing the law, simply by using these differential equations.

We have considered two cases: first of all a simple algebraic instance and then the general structure of inquiry in the empirical sciences. The general structure is a movement to an unknown that is given a name: the indeterminate function. The goal is reached by determining the indeterminate function, and that is done in two ways: from below upward by measurement and curve fitting, and from above downward by differential equations and by postulating such principles as invariance. Science is in between, and reaching knowledge of the function is not a *sine qua non*. The physicist can do a great deal without knowing what the function is.

Now reflection on that procedure reveals a fundamental assumption, namely, that the scientist is seeking, and that there is to be known, an intelligibility that can be expressed mathematically. We must note the meaning of that assumption. To say that mathematics is the science of quantity is the same as to say that psychology is the science of the body. Mathematics is not the science of quantity, but the science of intelligible groups and relations in quantity, just as psychology is not the science of the body, but the science of an intelligibility grasped in the sensible, in the body, namely, the soul. The first basic assumption is that the purpose of science is the search for an intelligibility that can be expressed mathematically.

Secondly, the mathematician supplies the scientist with a vast range of possible mathematical expressions, and the problem for the scientist is to select out of that range the particular expression that fits the case in hand, that fits all similar cases, and that does so in a manner that is coherent with the laws found in all other cases. The matter has to work. It is not enough for the scientist to have a collection of laws; he needs a system, a systematic collection of laws; he has to be able to use two laws together, or three together, or five at the same time. To be able to use a number of laws simultaneously, he has to know the relations between the laws, and to know the relations between the laws is to have a system. That element of system fundamentally is provided for the scientist by the mathematician.

There is a further property. Not only does the empirical scientist select aspects of data and measure them; he also relates the measurements *to one another.*[7] With that last step science moves totally outside the viewpoint of common sense. When Galileo moved from measuring distances and times to correlating distances and times, he was bringing together two objective, measurable features of objects. He was relating things to one another. Whenever the scientist is seeking to determine some indeterminate function, he is relating things to one another. And that is just what common sense does not do. It understands things in their relations to us. Thus we have Whitehead's two worlds.[8] Eddington[9] said that he had two tables in his room: there was a brown table, made of oak, solid, that had a certain shape, and then there was the scientific table that consisted of electrons bouncing about and so on. Most of it was empty space. Where do the two tables come from? They come from two approaches. Common sense understands the table in its relations to us: a table is something you can lean on, something you do not bump into, something you can use for writing; it has a certain visible appearance, certain tactile qualities, and so on. The table is integrated into the flow, the interests, the *Sorge,* the concern, of the subject. But science relates measurements to one another; and it does not have to go very far along that route to discover that it is introducing an entirely new world. Common sense, like grammar, is egocentric; it concerns the intelligibility of things for *me.* In grammar, time and tense relate to *my* time, *my* present. The meaning of fundamental adverbs like 'here' and 'there' is related to *me.* The first person is the point of reference. If you draw a map of a city, you are expressing a relation of things to one another; and when one looks at a map in a strange city, one can ask, Where am I? How do I correlate my 'here' with this map? Similarly, when you ask, What time is it? you want to correlate your 'now' with the public references obtained from a clock. The scientific procedure of relating things to one another builds up maps and clocks that leave the whole commonsense approach to things out of the picture.

The notion of empirical science that I have just developed is that of classical empirical science, of science as it existed from Galileo to Einstein. Quantum theory introduces a new element that has considerable philo-

7 Considerable editing is involved in this sentence.
8 Alfred North Whitehead, *The Concept of Nature* (Ann Arbor: The University of Michigan Press, 1957). The second chapter is entitled 'Theories of the Bifurcation of Nature.'
9 See Sir Arthur Eddington, *The Nature of the Physical World* (Cambridge: Cambridge University Press, 1928) xi–xv; also *New Pathways in Science* (Cambridge: Cambridge University Press, 1947) 1.

sophic implications. When the scientist ascertains a system of laws, it is possible for him to construct ideal cases. The free fall of a body, or the trajectory of a projectile, and generally all the problems set down in books on mechanics or physics are the construction of ideal cases. It happens that our planetary system corresponds to the construction of an ideal case, and from that fact there follows the view of mechanist determinism that physics is just the correlation of the whole of reality to a set of ideal cases, such as the simple harmonic oscillator. There is a whole series of these ideal cases, and by using them one can proceed to deal with concrete things. If one supposes that the structure of reality is simply the realization of ideal cases, one concludes from one's scientific structure to a determinism. What quantum theory has introduced is the negation of that assumption. There do exist *some* ideal cases, but not everything conforms to ideal cases. Consequently, the scientist has to adopt statistical procedures. Then we have a somewhat different approach. It is not totally different, but to specify the differences here would be to no particular point for our present purposes.

1.3   The Canons of Empirical Method

We can conceive empirical science as a group of operations, and the group may be characterized by what in the third chapter of *Insight* I call the canons of empirical method.

The first canon is the *canon of selection.* It amounts to a definition of what empirical science is. A theory or a hypothesis is scientific in the meaning of empirical science if it has sensible, observable, verifiable consequences. If the theory has no implications as to what you will see at a determinate place and time, or what you can feel or otherwise observe, then it is outside the realm of science. That is the first point in the canon of selection. The second point is that not only must the scientific hypothesis or theory have sensible consequences, but also all the sensible consequences that can be deduced must be verified. If it breaks down at one point, there is something wrong with the theory.

That notion in such a science as physics presupposes the conceptualization of the mathematician. But at least recently people in the human sciences seem to be realizing the necessity of having an elaborate conceptualization for their study similar to that which mathematics provides for physics. This need would seem obvious, but it has been greatly obscured by empiricist tendencies. The whole tendency is to emphasize the movement from the data to the law and to overlook the movement from above downwards, represented in natural science by the movement from differential equations to the set of possible laws. But Talcott Parsons, for example, in his *Social System*,[10] makes it plain from the start that, while there will occur in the book criticisms of other theories and some empirical generalizations, still his concern is to provide sociology with a conceptual system. Unless an empirical science develops for itself a conceptual system similar to what mathematics is for physics, you cannot proceed as in the successful empirical sciences. The canon of selection is the fundamental conception of what an empirical science is and when it is good and when it is to be thrown out. To have that canon of selection you need the conceptual structure provided by a mathematics for physics, and by a conceptual system for human sciences. And that conceptual system must be rich in implications. In other words, its basic terms have to be properly defined and its range of implications clearly determined. Then you can have empirical science and apply a canon of selection which picks out of the conceptual system the elements that can be verified and are verified.[11]

The second canon is the *canon of operations*. If the scientist obtains his hypothesis in the double movement from above downwards and from below upwards – the scissors action – he reaches a formula. That formula is of itself a hypothesis. But he does not just announce, 'I have a hypothesis.' He makes all possible deductions from that hypothesis, either from it alone or from it in combination with other things. From the deductions he proceeds to a process of checking. Does what follows from the hypothesis occur de facto? The fuller that deduction is and the greater the number of checks he makes, the greater the likelihood that he will turn up some facts that his hypothesis does not satisfy. He then moves on to a new insight and a new hypothesis.

So the operations of the scientist form a circle. We spoke of sense, phantasm, agent intellect, possible intellect – where you have *species intelligibilis* – and conception, construction of the hypothesis. A scientist does not merely have an insight that is formulated in a law; he proceeds from the law, the hypothesis, to a deduction, and from the deduction to verification; and the verification very likely yields new significant sensible data that will lead to a

---

10 Talcott Parsons, *The Social System* (Glencoe, IL: Free Press, 1951).
11 In *Insight* Lonergan offered the view that the notion of dialectic developed in the treatment of common sense would be essential in such a conceptual system. At the end of the treatment of common sense he states that 'dialectic stands to generalized method as the differential equation to classical physics, or the operator equation to the more recent physics.' See *Insight* 268–69.

revision of his hypothesis, a new insight, the formulation of a new hypothesis, new deductions, new verifications – and again the matter goes on. That is the dynamic circle of empirical method. There is a new hypothesis or a new law every time there is a really significant insight. When an accumulation of insights implies a revision of all the concepts being used so far, there emerges a new, higher viewpoint. Thus, when Newton discovered something like geometry that was not geometry, namely, mechanics, he shifted the movement of modern science from Galileo's ideal, from 'the system of the world is a geometry' to 'the system of the world is a mechanics.' Again, there is a fundamental revision of the Newtonian idea with Einstein's theory of relativity, and a still more fundamental revision with quantum theory. So it is a circle; after a certain number of turns of the circle, there is an accumulation of insights which yields a new and higher viewpoint. And so the process goes on.

Thirdly, there is a *canon of relevance*. What is it that is scientific in the proper sense? It is the addition by the enriching insight of the intelligibility immanent in the data. Science is knowledge of things by their causes. In empirical science *the* cause is the immanent intelligibility, like the intelligibility expressed in the definition of the circle. If you examine a wheel, you can ask, 'Why is it round?' and then you are asking about its immanent intelligibility. You can ask, 'Who made it?' and 'What kind of tools did he use?' and then you are asking about the agent, the efficient cause. Or you can ask, 'What did he make it for?' and then you are asking about the final cause. You can ask, 'What did he make it out of?' and then you are asking about the material cause. But the formal cause is the immanent intelligibility, and that is what pure science is concerned with. It is applied science that is concerned with agent, end, and material.

Moreover, pure science is concerned *only* with that immanent intelligibility. Hence we come to our fourth canon, the *canon of parsimony*. Newton stated in a debate held after he published his theory of universal gravitation, 'Hypotheses non fingo,' 'I do not fabricate hypotheses.' Now in a sense that is false, but in another sense it expresses a very important truth. It is false, in that Newton's theory of universal gravitation *is* a hypothesis, not something that is absolutely certain. If Einstein's general relativity became more confirmed than it is at present, Newton's universal gravitation would be superseded. The existence of the theory of general relativity raises a question, in that it shows that it is possible to have a theory different from Newton's. For Newton's theory is strictly a hypothesis. On the other hand, there is a world of difference between Newton's theory of universal gravitation and Descartes's theory. Descartes explained the movements of the planets by a theory of vortices. The vortices occurred in an imponderable, invisible matter. The vortices in the invisible, imponderable matter were just what was required to make the planets move exactly as they do. That type of thinking is what Newton rejected when he said, 'I do not fabricate hypotheses.' There is nothing in Descartes's statement that can be tested. He appeals to something that you can't feel, you can't see, you can't weigh, and so on. There is no way of knowing whether statements made about it are true or not.[12] But in general what does the scientist add to the data? He does not add further data. That may happen as an accident or a consequence of his theory, but his fundamental task is to add the immanent intelligibility.

Fifthly, there is a *canon of complete explanation*. Everything is to be explained. Up to Einstein, it was taken for granted that colors were to be reduced to light waves, sound to longitudinal waves in the air, odors to chemistry, weight to mass, heat to temperature. And note that just as weight is not the same as mass, so heat is not the same as temperature. A metal object – this speaker – may feel much colder than a piece of wood – this desk – even when both are at exactly the same temperature. Hence the feeling of hot and cold is not temperature; temperature is something in the scientist's world that is outside the world of common sense. There is a transformation, a movement from what is sensibly given to us to the relations of things to one another. Sensible qualities arise insofar as things are related to us, and they vanish in the relations of things to one another. What Einstein did was to show that what holds for the secondary qualities holds also for the primary qualities.[13] Extensions and durations, just as color, sound, feeling, weight, pressure, and so on, are to be reduced to their immanent intelligibility. The canon of complete explanation demands that the scientific world, which expresses the relations of things to one another, be constructed completely. It is not the world of common sense.

Sixthly, there is a *canon of statistical residues*. In other words, the classical notion of determinism is out.

12 Reading this brief exposition of the canons, one might wonder how canon 4 is distinguished from canon 1, since Lonergan lays down the same relation to what is observable as a requirement for both; but canon 1 deals with the observable as the field of data for scientific study (first cognitional level), while canon 4 deals with the observable as a condition for verification (third cognitional level).
13 LN 74 has, 'drop primary secondary qualities.'

1.4 Teaching Physics

Since I am addressing educators, I would like to add a final note. It's about something I suffered from. Teaching physics without the students knowing the relevant mathematics is not teaching physics. If they know the mathematics, there is nothing difficult about the physics. If they do not know the mathematics, then what they are learning is not physics. That applies to the simplest and most elementary matters. What does a physicist mean by a velocity? He means ds/dt. What does he mean by an acceleration? He means d^2s/dt^2. If you know what is meant by those symbols from the differential calculus, you know exactly what is meant by acceleration and velocity, and if you do not know what those symbols mean, you do not understand acceleration and velocity. It is possible to give students who have not done the mathematics some approximate notion of it, but it will take them a great deal of time to understand that approximate notion, and when they get it, they will be able to do very little with it, because it is not accurate, and its implications do not stand out. If they have a bit of calculus, all these notions can be simplicity itself, and not only the notions, but handling the notions and seeing their implications and movement from one to the other, and so forth. I don't know whether this is universally true, but the teaching of physics without a proper account of the fundamental notions – namely, doing the mathematics, so that the teacher of physics can presuppose the mathematics – gives an illusion of knowledge, a false idea of what the science is. And it clutters the mind.[14]

Again, there are the principles of active method. The principle of active method is that fundamentally any learning is an activity of the subject. It is *his* constructing of *his* world. And if the student knows the mathematics, he can be constructing his world. But if he does not, he is not constructing anything.[15] He really does not know what he is trying to do, and he cannot know it, because that is not what the physicist is doing.[16]

14 LN 74 has, 'set of approximate notions that clutter mind and give distaste of illusion of knowledge.'
15 LN 74 has, 'Active method psychologically sound: but active method is assimilation before accommodation; empirical method of natural sciences adds accommodation to maths.' The terms 'assimilation' and 'accommodation' are taken from Piaget and will be explained in chapter 8.
16 The break was taken at this point. The tape resumes with Lonergan saying that in the time remaining on this day he proposes to discuss the transformation of the notion of science. The opening statement, 'Our topic is the new learning,' is taken from the notes of F. Crowe.

2   The Transformation of the Notion of Science

Our topic is the new learning, and I propose to discuss now the question, What is the transformation of the notion of science that comes out of modern scientific attainment? The Greeks formulated the ideal of science, but the modern Western world has attained science in a manner beyond the wildest anticipations of the Greeks. And we can know what science is more concretely and more exactly from the attainment than from the initial expression of the ideal that man had to lead him into the development of science. The expression of the ideal was a preliminary formulation of what the pure desire to know implies, what the intellectual pattern of experience implies, what is implicit in the wonder that Aristotle thought to be the beginning of all science and all philosophy. Or, as St Thomas puts it, *omnis scientia est nobis naturaliter indita in lumine intellectus agentis,* all science is naturally, virtually given to us in the light of agent intellect, in that light of consciousness that is inquiry.[17]

2.1 *From the Certain to the Probable: Science, Judgment, and Wisdom*

The traditional definition of science is *certa rerum per causas cognitio,* certain knowledge of things by their causes. But the outstanding feature of modern science is that it is not certain. It is increasingly probable. And so we have the question, Why is science not certain? The answer to the question is an account of the act of judgment. I have to do this briefly.[18] I have three chapters in *Insight* on the act of judgment. The general notion is dealt with in chapter 9, the analysis of judgment in chapter 10, and the performance of a strategically significant judgment in chapter 11.

Despite the tremendous brilliance of its creators, despite the endless taking of pains in its formulations, its deductions, its verifications, its combinations of different components, science is not certain. That terrific achievement is not certain for a very fundamental reason, and that is that the human mind affirms absolutely only when there is grasped an unconditioned.

17 An approximate quotation of Thomas Aquinas, *De veritate,* q. 10, a. 6, 'in lumine intellectus agentis nobis est quodammodo omnis scientia originaliter indita.'
18 Lonergan here digresses from his lecture notes, which do not mention judgment and wisdom at this point. The page of typed notes from which he was working is followed by a handwritten page (LN 75) with a few notations on judgment and wisdom.

We have spoken of the level of experience, of the flow of sense data, percepts, and images, and of the level of intellect, of intelligence, of *quid sit,* the questions, How? and What? and Why? And we have spoken of acts of understanding, a flow of insights, and of a flow of formulations of what is grasped in acts of understanding. But we now come to a third level, the level of reflection: Is it so?[19] That question, Is it so? is what makes the difference between alchemy and chemistry, astrology and astronomy, legend and history, opinion and truth. No matter how brilliant, how delightful, how plausible, how complete may be an explanation, we ask, Is it really so? At that point, consciousness takes another leap. On the first level, consciousness is merely empirical; on the second, it becomes intelligent; on the third, it becomes reflective, rational. 'Man is a rational animal' means that man is an animal with that level of consciousness that has the capacity to ask, Is it so?

That question can be answered only if reflective understanding grasps an unconditioned. The words on which Thomism lays so much stress – *est, ens, esse,* it is – express the grasp of the unconditioned, the yes or no of reflective rational consciousness. If one does not grasp the unconditioned, one doubts; one says, 'It might be so,' and talks about possibility and probability and high probability. But one does not simply say, 'It is.'

But what is meant by the unconditioned? The unconditioned is of two types: the formally unconditioned and the virtually unconditioned. The formally unconditioned has no conditions whatever; and there is only one that has no conditions whatever – God. And so, in the tendency of rational consciousness to the unconditioned, insofar as one species of the unconditioned is God, you can see how deeply within the 'light that enlighteneth every man that cometh into this world'[20] is an implicit notion of God.

19 From the notes of F. Crowe it is clear that at this point Lonergan put a diagram on the blackboard, with nine arrows disposed as follows (see also *Understanding and Being* 109):

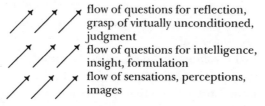

flow of questions for reflection, grasp of virtually unconditioned, judgment
flow of questions for intelligence, insight, formulation
flow of sensations, perceptions, images

20 See John 1.9 – NRSV: 'The true light, which enlightens everyone, was coming into the world.'

There is also the virtually unconditioned, and every human judgment in this life depends, not on the vision of God, but upon the attainment of a virtually unconditioned. A virtually unconditioned is a conditioned whose conditions are fulfilled. Its formal expression is the syllogism. Where A and B stand for one or more propositions, the form is

> If A, then B.
> But A.
> Therefore B.

The major premise is a link between the conditioned and its conditions; the minor expresses the fulfilment of the conditions; the conclusion presents the conditioned as virtually unconditioned. It is a conditioned whose conditions are fulfilled.

On that analysis, then, syllogism is not, as Kant and sceptics generally conceive syllogism, the occasion for an infinite regress: you need two premises to prove the conclusion, two premises to prove the major premise, and two premises to prove the minor. You need four premises, then, and you will need eight to prove them, and so on to infinity. The meaning of syllogism is rather that it expresses in terms of a scheme what is grasped when one has the acts that ground rational judgment. The scheme may be verified in the case where you have two propositions and go to a third, but the scheme can be verified also where the unconditioned and the fulfilment of its conditions are not propositional knowledge. In general, the major premise must express explicitly the link between the conditioned and the conditions: if the series of conditions, then the conditioned. The link is grasped when one grasps that one's insight is invulnerable, that there are no further relevant questions. If A, then B. A link, a nexus between conditions and conditioned, is, in a general case, what is grasped in some insight as a possibility or a necessity. Is that connection correct? We know it is correct when we know that there are no further relevant questions. An insight is corrected insofar as one asks further questions and sees that one needs a further insight that qualifies or corrects, fills out or complements in some fashion, the insight one previously had. When one sees that there are no further relevant questions, one is sure of the link.

Thus, you might wonder, Is the recorder working? If the tape is slipping around, you know you have come to the end of the reel, and there are no further relevant questions about that. If you want to get any further recording, you have to put on a new tape. It is evident that there are no further relevant questions. You are sure of the link. Are the conditions fulfilled? Is the tape slipping around? The fulfilment ultimately is found in either outer or inner experience: the presentations of sense and, as it were, the presentness of the data of consciousness, where 'presentness' refers to the third type of presence that we discussed earlier, where I have to be present to myself for anything else to be present to me.

So much for a schematic account of the nature of judgment. One asks, Is it so? One grasps the unconditioned. What does that mean? The unconditioned means two things: formally, there are no conditions at all, and that is only God (not an analytic proposition, as a reviewer of *Insight* thought);[21] and virtually, there is a conditioned, a link between the conditioned and its conditions, and the fulfilment of the conditions.

Now it is fairly easy to know that the tape will not be recording any more when it is slipping around at the end of the spool. But how do you know in the general case whether or not there are any further relevant questions? To know whether or not, in any given case, there are any further relevant questions depends upon a view of the whole. If you are in a new situation, you do not make many judgments. As the boys were said to do in the Canadian army at least when they came in during the war, you keep your eyes open, your mouth shut, and don't volunteer. You build up gradually in any concrete situation – seeing one thing and another and so on – a familiarity, and gradually acquire all the insights that are relevant to what commonly happens. You get a view of the whole setup. In any particular field one comes gradually to a point where one has a sufficient accumulation of insights; one is at home, one is familiar, one is a master of the trade; one knows whether or not there are any further questions relevant to a particular judgment. That accumulation of insights is what is expressed proverbially in the precept, 'Cobbler, stick to your last.' The cobbler is able to tell whether or not there are any further relevant questions when it is a matter of making shoes. And generally, each one is to be trusted when he speaks on the matters in which he himself has experience of some standing.

The capacity of the cobbler or of the craftsman in any trade or way of life is a particular wisdom and, insofar as it is practical, a particular prudence. But there is also a general wisdom that regards the universe. St Thomas assigns a fundamental position to wisdom; he gives a very clear account of what wisdom is. In the supernatural order, it is one of the gifts of the Holy Ghost: wisdom, understanding, counsel, fortitude, knowledge, piety, and

21 See Jean Langlois, 'Une conception nouvelle de la métaphysique,' *Sciences Ecclésiastiques* 10 (1958) 451–72, at 459.

the fear of the Lord; wisdom is the first of the gifts of the Holy Ghost. In the natural order, wisdom is Aristotle's first philosophy, his metaphysics, and that gives rise to a problem. How does one discover that Aristotle's first philosophy is wisdom? Why not take some other philosopher? Why Aristotle? In particular, how did Thomas know that he had to go beyond Aristotle's metaphysics, beyond hylomorphism, matter and form, to posit essence and existence as the principal elements of his analysis of being? St Thomas himself corrected and amplified Aristotle's first philosophy. Where does this wisdom come from? How does one acquire wisdom?

As you know, there is no rule of thumb for producing men of good judgment. A man of good judgment is a man who has the wisdom to know when there are no further relevant questions, when the matter can be settled, when he can say, 'Yes' or 'No.' Moreover, we know that wisdom is not something we start with, but something we head towards. Children are said to reach the age of reason at the age of seven. They have attained a certain measure of wisdom at the age of seven, but not enough wisdom to be held responsible before the law, to be able to sign legal documents validly, and so on. We wait until they are twenty-one before we suppose they have enough wisdom to do that. Aristotle held that the young did not have enough experience to study ethics profitably; they did not have enough wisdom about human affairs to be able to know whether or not there were any further relevant questions. Because they did not have that experience, because they did not have the necessary wisdom, either they would not ask enough questions and would state things as true when they were false, or they would ask too many questions and keep on doubting.

So wisdom is something that we acquire. With regard to human judgment it is generally acknowledged that we can trust the judgment of a man who is experienced in a given field; he has a certain wisdom there. On the other hand, we do not trust him insofar as he says anything that goes outside his field. Again, we connect degrees of wisdom with age. There is an age of reason about seven, one becomes an adult and ceases to be a minor at twenty-one, and so on.

So wisdom, while it is necessary for good judgment, for knowing whether or not there are any further relevant questions, still is a foundation that lies ahead. It is not the sort of foundation that we have at the start and on which we build; it is the goal towards which we move. And we can always grow in wisdom. Complete wisdom is God's knowledge. God knows his own essence, and in his essence absolutely everything else. He has what is the view of the whole, the total perfect view of the whole. Divine wisdom, consequently, is the absolute achievement of wisdom, and anything short of that is a finite wisdom, an imperfect wisdom. For that reason the gift of wisdom from the Holy Ghost is placed above any wisdom that man naturally can attain. On the traditional view, the philosopher operates in the light of human wisdom, but the theologian's business is to take advantage of the higher wisdom that is the gift of the Holy Ghost and produce judgments that are profounder, truer, fuller, more accurate, more concrete than the philosopher's. How is it, then, that, if perfect wisdom is had by God alone, if it is only with years that one moves toward wisdom – speaking of the development of a culture, we have Hegel's phrase that only with the fall of twilight does the owl of Minerva take wing[22] – how is it that there can be true judgments short of the perfect wisdom that is God, short of the supernatural wisdom that depends directly on the divine wisdom and is mediated to us through the gift, the direction, the inspiration of the Holy Ghost, short of the wisdom of the philosopher who has a view of the whole universe? How do we make true judgments while we are moving towards such a view of the universe? And if we do not make true judgments, how is it that we can be moving towards such a view, not away from it?

The answer is twofold. The first part of the answer is that from the start we have a rudimentary view of the whole. Our inquiry and reflection head to knowledge of *everything*. Inquiry and reflection are not restricted to some particular genus of things; they ask about everything. For St Thomas, all knowledge is virtually given us in the light of agent intellect. And so we have an incipient view of the whole in the very fact of the intellectual pattern of experience, in the very fact of a flow of consciousness that is directed by wonder.

Moreover – and this is still in the first part of the answer[23] – we move to a more detailed knowledge of the whole by a process of dichotomy. Porphyry's tree divides being into material and nonmaterial. Nothing in the universe is left out when there is a division by contradictories. The material divides into the living and the nonliving, the living into the sentient and the nonsentient, and the sentient into the rational and the nonrational. As long as you proceed by dichotomies, you are constructing the whole universe, and your categories are extremely general. In other words, you have a view of the whole that can become more and more articulate, and all along the way that view of the whole is complete insofar as it proceeds by dichotomy.

22 See above, chapter 3, note 79.
23 This clause is added by the editors, in an effort to clarify the structure of Lonergan's response to the question he had just posed.

Consequently, dividing up the whole by dichotomy gives you, as it were, an ever more complete map of the whole.[24]

And so there is a possibility of increasing wisdom. The increase in wisdom is the increase in the view of the whole. But you have it from the start. What you do is gradually block off areas, very large and not at all internally determined areas. It is within that structure of beginning from being and dividing it off by dichotomies that it is possible to make judgments that are true within the context of the view of the whole that one has attained at a given age. Attaining the age of reason means that the divisions of the whole have reached a degree of fulness at which it is possible to make true judgments. Ceasing to be a minor and becoming an adult means that the view of the whole has reached a still further degree of differentiation.

So much for the possibility of a development in wisdom that consists in making true judgments within the context of a given attainment of wisdom. At the same time, that is only one aspect of the genesis of wisdom. The second aspect is the role of the educator. We do not merely find things out for ourselves, we also learn from others. It is above all in the matter of judgment that the child, the boy, the adolescent, the young man needs help and knows he needs it. Children are very docile, and that docility decreases because they have to become themselves; but at the same time, their judgments are insecure, and they know it. So the educator's role in developing wisdom is to develop the view of the whole, to prevent onesidedness, to add differentiations to the virtual whole that is precontained in the pure desire to know.

So much for the notion of judgment. Why is it that the knowledge of the scientist is not certain? It is because the scientist is aiming at a knowledge of our universe, not in its relations to us, but in the relations of things to one another. Considered under that aspect, science, on the one hand, cannot take advantage of what is learned by man in ordinary experience and common sense; and on the other hand, its wisdom, just as all wisdom, lies ahead. The more developed the science becomes, the more it moves to indubitability. Thus, at the present time chemistry has its table of elements, and the

24 Lonergan used the same strategy in the course he had just taught (1958–59) at the Gregorian University, *De intellectu et methodo*: 'Haec divisio entis, per quam progredimur ad sapientiam, semper completa esse potest, si fundetur in principio contradictionis. Sic, per dichotomiam, obtinetur arbor porphyriana, quae praebet completam divisionem, utique adhuc valde schematicam et abstractam, sed semper permanentem ...' (see the notes taken by his students, p. 19).

table explains more than 300,000 compounds, and does so exactly. The fineness of organization of the incredible body of knowledge contained in modern chemistry is so great that the chemist is almost certain; he has differentiated a whole field, and he is finding regularly all along the line that he can put new elements into his periodic table and explain more and more compounds. The number that he accounts for is fantastic. Moreover, he knows that, even if there were to arise some fundamental revision of chemical concepts, such as arose in physics through relativity and quantum mechanics, nonetheless any further new theory would have to contain in equivalent form all the correlations he has already established. So you can see how the science is moving towards a wisdom. It is closing in upon a wisdom in the measure that its differentiation of being becomes ever fuller, ever more exact, and extends an ever wider embrace.

2.2   Things and Causes: Analysis and Synthesis

To return to our fundamental topic,[25] the transformation of the notion of science, we said that science is *certa rerum per causas cognitio*, and the 'certain' we have to put in the future tense. Scientific wisdom is something that is still growing. But we have to add another note. What are the things, and what are the causes in the traditional notion of science, and again in the notion of science one gets from modern scientific attainment?

The things that the Aristotelians were thinking of were the ten categories: substance, quantity, quality, relation, action, passion, time, place, habit, and posture. Those were the things. And what are the causes? They are end, agent, matter, and form.

Now we have to take that notion and transform it. The chemist's causes are not end, agent, matter, and form, but elements, combinations, and such notions. Again, his things are not the ten categories; they are the more than 300,000 compounds. In the Aristotelian notion there is analysis of things into their causes, and there is construction or synthesis of things out of their causes. In chemistry there is the analysis of compounds into elements and the composition of elements into compounds. There is a two-way street that goes from the elements to the compounds and from the compounds to the elements. Similarly, in Aristotelian science, there is the two-way street from the predicaments, the categories, to the causes, and from the causes to the categories. So the double movement of analysis and synthesis remains, but

25 At this point Lonergan returns to the material in his lecture notes.

the chemist has discovered a periodic table to take the place of Aristotle's causes, and he has discovered 300,000 compounds to take the place of Aristotle's things.

There occurs exactly the same shift from the Aristotelian notion in St Thomas's Trinitarian theory. In that theory there is only one thing: God. And the cause is not anything distinct from God. But there is the process of analysis, starting from the divine missions revealed in scripture and moving through the gradual development of theology until one reaches St Thomas and the full analysis. When the full analysis is reached, one begins from the analytic elements and goes back to the starting point synthetically. St Thomas, in his *Pars prima*, question 27, begins from the psychological analogy of the Trinity, and in question 43 arrives at the missions about which the Gospel speaks. Here we have the notion of analysis and synthesis, although there are not things and causes.

2.3 Field Theory

Again, as to the notion of cause, Newton conceived of his forces as efficient causes, and modern mechanics drops the notion of force; it gets along perfectly well without it. It thinks in terms of a field theory, the set of interrelations between any *n* objects. The field theory is a set of intelligible relations linking what is implicitly defined by the relations themselves; it is a set of relational forms.[26] The form of any element is known through its relations to all the other elements. What is a mass? A mass is anything that satisfies the fundamental equations that regard masses. Consequently, when you add a new fundamental equation about mass, as Einstein did when he equated mass with energy, you get a new idea of mass. Field theory is a matter of the immanent intelligibility of the object.

Harry Stack Sullivan has a presentation of the psychiatry of interpersonal relations, *The Interpersonal Theory of Psychiatry*.[27] His method and theory of depth psychology and psychiatry are based on interpersonal relations. He is not explaining things by causes in terms of Freud's libido or anything like that. He is talking about the relation between the patient he is examining and himself, and the relation between that patient and the other people

---

26 There was a brief break in the recording at this point, but from the notes of F. Crowe it appears that nothing of substance was lost.

27 Harry Stack Sullivan, *The Interpersonal Theory of Psychiatry*, ed. Helen Swick Perry and Mary Ladd Gawel (New York: Norton, 1963). Lonergan could not recall the name of the book.

with whom that patient lives. That is psychiatric theory as a field theory: relations between persons. In his essay, 'The Meaning of Anxiety in Psychiatry and in Life,'[28] there is a diagram that is almost exactly parallel to the lines of force of the electromagnetic field. Two people meet, and the one has a psychic block in a particular area. Another person can talk to him from another point and get fine responses, but if he says anything directed to the blocked point, the first person draws right into a shell. This is a field theory, notion: interpersonal relations.

The point I wish to make is that modern science is not simply an addition to what was known before. It is the perfecting of the very notion of science itself, of knowing things by their causes, by analysis and synthesis. What are the causes? The field of intelligible relations that implicitly define the objects. The objects with which a science deals are whatever is defined by its field of intelligible relations, whatever falls into that field. The causes are formal causes; it is only applied science that is concerned with agents and ends.

2.4 From Logical Ideal to Method

The notion of science according to the logical ideal is knowing the essence and deducing the properties. For example: man is a rational animal; because he is both rational and animal, he can laugh. That notion of science is de facto the method that is employed in natural theology when one deduces the divine attributes from a fundamental notion that functions as the divine essence. Again, that notion of science is used by Spinoza. Spinoza can have a syllogistic universe, deducing properties from an essence, because he is a monist. He conceives of properties as modes of the one substance that is.

Insofar as the ideal in terms of properties deduced from an essence is an expression of the logical ideal, it is entirely valid. Any expression of any science will be logical. However, from the viewpoint of a science that develops, we do not know what the essence is from the start. We move towards knowing the essence. We know the essence from the properties, and we find the right properties by applying the trick of empirical method. There is an upward spiral from the data through a series of hypotheses until finally there is reached, as it were, a ceiling, a stopping point in this process of mov-

28 Harry Stack Sullivan, 'The Meaning of Anxiety in Psychiatry and Life,' in Sullivan, *The Fusion of Psychiatry and Social Science* (New York: Norton, 1964) 229–54. Lonergan did not give the name of the essay or of the book.

ing from data to interrelated premises and conclusions that correspond to what may be called essence and property.

2.5 From Analytic Propositions to the Real World

Another notion of science is the deductivist notion. One starts from analytic propositions and proceeds to make deductions from them. The logical empiricists talk a good deal about tautology. Analytic propositions for them are tautologies; they tell one nothing about what really is; they state merely the conventions of grammar. And there do exist tautologies in that sense. Technically, a tautology for the logical empiricist is a set of logical symbols that is true no matter what meaning you give to the symbols. In general, one can say one has an analytic proposition when the syntax of the proposition combined with the definitions of the terms are equivalent to a virtually unconditioned. But the significance of that virtually unconditioned does not take one beyond knowledge of what one chooses to regard as the meaning of the sentence. If I use a certain sentence with a certain meaning, then certain things follow. But there is no reason for supposing that I will ever use this sentence with this meaning. It is simply a tautology, a linguistic phenomenon. If I assert that the necessarily existent being exists necessarily, I am not providing myself with a proof of the existence of God, but am simply stating an analytic proposition that does not contain a reference to a real world.

What is the step, then, from the analytic proposition to the real world? In the *Prima secundae* of the *Summa*, question 66, article 5, ad 4m, St Thomas asks why wisdom is the highest of the intellectual virtues. He distinguishes three speculative virtues of intellect: science, which deduces conclusions from principles; intellect, or intelligence, which from a knowledge of the terms sees the necessity of the principle; and finally wisdom, which selects the right terms. Because wisdom selects the terms that intelligence uses to construct analytic principles, it is superior both to intellect and to science.

What does that mean in language familiar to nonscholastics? It means that there is no knowledge of truth contained on the second level of consciousness, or on the first and second combined. Wisdom's selection of terms is the selection of one meaning of the term 'being' rather than another, and once that selection has been made, the rest is settled. For example, there is Parmenides' notion of being, Plato's, Aristotle's, Avicenna's, Averroes', St Thomas's, Scotus's, and Hegel's. They all differ. There is no first principle that does not attain a different meaning according to the different meaning you give being. How do you pick out which is the correct notion of being? Picking out the correct notion of being is putting in a fundamental determinant in the meaning of all possible principles you may ever appeal to. Why do you prefer Aristotle to Plato and Aquinas to Scotus? That is the function of wisdom. Wisdom governs the selection of basic terms, the selection of basic terms governs first principles, and first principles govern conclusions. Because we move up to wisdom, because wisdom is not a foundation from which we start but towards which we tend, it is by studying different philosophic systems, comparing them, and seeing the different consequences of the different systems that one arrives at the wisdom of one's own that entitles one to prefer one notion of being to another. That preferring one notion of being to another is a strategically very important judgment, and it is a judgment of fact. Which notion of being is the real? To select the notion of being that is the notion of real being as opposed to false conceptions of being is the fundamental wisdom of the philosopher. It is de facto true, and he makes it in a particular judgment in which he grasps a virtually unconditioned. Just what that judgment is, is a further question.

2.6 Conclusion

You can see that there have been transformations in the notion of science due to the attainment of science. I gave the contrast between modern scientific notions and scholastic notions, but I argued as well that there have been transformations within modern science itself. The ideal of Galileo and Newton was law and system; the scientist wanted to know a system of laws. For Galileo, the system was geometry; for Newton, it was something that was not geometry. That ideal of science ran for 300 years, and it has been supplanted by a quite different ideal, in which the ideal is to know states and their probabilities, where the probabilities determine the states. So science in general is a gradual actuation of intelligence with respect to empirical data, and that gradual actuation yields an ever more accurate notion of what exactly science is. Science is a set of operations where the operations are governed by a series of canons that we have mentioned.[29]

---

29 Lonergan did not follow exactly the order of his notes for this entire section on the transformation of the notion of science. He skipped around, introduced the long section on judgment, and omitted several items that appear in the notes. The page of notes for this section is given in its entirety in the appendix, § E.

7

The Theory of
Philosophic Differences[1]

Educators tend to be sceptical of the philosophy of education because there are so many philosophies, and they all differ. But one of the great utilities of a philosophy of education, if the problem of differences can be got round

1 The seventh lecture, Tuesday, August 11, and the first half of the eighth lecture, Wednesday, August 12, 1959. The recording begins with the second sentence. The first sentence is based on the notes of F. Crowe. We have included in this chapter part of the eighth lecture, of Wednesday, August 12, in order to preserve the unity of the content.

Lonergan seems to have been working from two distinct sets of notes in lecturing on the material of this chapter. One set, subsequently numbered pages 65–69, seems to have been composed first. The headings on these pages are 'Being' (65), 'Metaphysics as Theory of a Group of Operations' and 'Epistemology as Theory of Groups of Operations' (66), 'Metaphysics and Epistemology as Group Theory' (67), and 'Epistemology as Group Theory' (68–69). Some of these pages formed the basis of parts of the lectures, but not in the precise order in which the material appears in the notes. The main point of this set of notes as composed is expressed, it seems, on p. 66: 'I think, a clear-headed account of what we are doing today, of what was done in past (though not conceived in this fasion), and of transitions implicit in notion of philosophia perennis, is to be had by *analogous* extension of Group Theory.'

The second set, composed (it seems) later, is on pages subsequently numbered 78–80, each of which is headed 'Theory of Philosophic Differences.' These pages are much more schematic than the earlier set, but the order is for the most part that followed in the lecture. It seems that at certain points in the lecture, Lonergan took his headings and subheadings from this second set, but then referred to the relevant sections of the earlier set for the details of his lecture. (Pages 71–77 contain the notes for the fifth and sixth lectures.)

The notes below that contain references to the lecture notes are referring to the second set, 'Theory of Philosophic Differences.'

somehow, is that it will provide ultimate criteria for judging the truth and estimating the value of what is to be found in the constant, enormous flow of books and articles written for educators.

1   Differences and Problems of Development

The problem of philosophic differences has already been touched upon in different ways. It arises from problems of development, and indeed from three types of problems of development.

First of all, there is development in the sciences: additions to mathematics, to physics, to chemistry, to biology, to psychology, to sociology, and so forth. And these additions may be revolutionary.

Secondly, concomitant with such changes in the sciences themselves, and on a much profounder level, there is development in the notion of a science. We saw that the Greek achievement was first of all the emergence of longer chains of reasoning. Heraclitus appealed to the *logos*; there were the longer chains of reasoning in Parmenides on being; then there was the discovery of the necessity of accurate universal definitions; and there was the combination of definitions with postulates as the basis of a deductive structure, such as is best illustrated in Euclid's *Elements*.

Now the Greek discovery of science does not offer a total explanation for the internal unity of any given science.[2] Why is it that a science is a rounded whole, that it has a completeness? Why does it form an integrated balanced whole? The Greeks did not offer an explanation. Euclid, for example, formed a set of definitions and axioms, but he did not raise or answer the question, Why that set?[3]

That completeness, that element of totality, is de facto found in each science. The simplest explanation of the unity of a science is to appeal to the end, the goal, the aim of the science, the unity of what is to be known. And so sciences are distinguished by their formal objects. They are divided on the basis of their finality, of what is to be known. However, there are difficulties with that view, and the difficulties are threefold.

First of all, there can be the unity and roundedness of a science even though there is no corresponding object that exists. Riemannian geometry has n dimensions for the space of any curvature. One of those spaces can exist, and maybe several of them, but hardly all of them. Why is it that Riemannian geometry is a unity although the totality of Riemannian spaces

2 The words from 'for' are based on LN 78.
3 The last three sentences are based on LN 78.

does not exist? Similarly, the Hilbert space, which is a space in which each point has an infinity of coordinates, is a mathematical construction, but does not seem to be an object that exists.

In the second place, sciences are in process. We saw yesterday that a fundamental difference between the Aristotelian and the modern concept of science is that science heads toward certitude, to ever greater probability and reliability, but it does not claim to be certain from the outset. On the contrary, any scientific theory is regarded simply as probable, as open to revision and improvement. Consequently, science has not yet known its object, and so it is difficult to see how the object accounts for the unity of the science, since that object is not yet attained. Still, though physics, chemistry, biology, and so on, are only probable, yet they develop as unities. How can this be?[4]

However, those are simply minor considerations. The fact is that wherever there is a final cause, there also is an efficient cause, and it is quite legitimate to seek in the efficient cause of the science, that is, in the scientist, the reason why a science forms a unified whole. It is at that point that the significance of group theory comes into view. A science is a unity, and it embraces a totality, because the operations of the scientist, the acts corresponding to his objects, form a unified, interrelated group. The simplest example of this is algebra, where you have the group of operations: addition and subtraction, multiplication and division, powers and roots. The second operation in those three pairs is always the inverse of the first, and the three pairs are interrelated. When the group of operations determines everything that is operated upon, then the unity of the group imposes a unity upon the objects. This is the fundamental significance of group theory, namely, the properties of the whole object of mathematics are determined by the relations among the operations that give rise to the objects dealt with in mathematics, the objects as known. There we have an example of a development in the idea of a science.

Again, one can conceive empirical natural science as a group of operations. It is a dynamic group. That is the conception of the empirical sciences that was worked out yesterday. Inquiry supervenes upon experience and gives rise to insights which are expressed in hypotheses and ground deductions; the deductions are checked against experimental and observational results, which give rise to attention to new data, which in turn give rise to further insights and the expression of further hypotheses. This roll-

4 The last two sentences are based on LN 78.

ing circle of operations, in which the hypotheses are constantly developing, coming into closer contact with the data, and entering into higher unity by their mutual implications and the way in which they give rise to higher viewpoints, defines what is meant by a natural science. So there can be developments within the sciences and developments of the very notion of science.[5]

But there is a third level of development. The subject of a human science is also one of its objects; and a higher viewpoint on the object, a reformulation of the concepts expressing a fuller understanding of the objects, has implications with regard to the subject himself. A transformation of physics or chemistry, a totally new viewpoint in such a science, involves no change in human living. But in a human science such a transformation has implications for the subject himself. There is not merely transformation in the objects, but also conversion of the subject; and unless the conversion of the subject follows or has been prepared, there will be a conflict between object and subject. The subject will feel that the new theory cannot be true. This third type of development is, I believe, the root cause of philosophic differences. The subject is unprepared to be converted, to transform himself in accord with the corresponding transformation of the human object that has resulted from the development of the human science.

2   Developing Objects and the Transformation of the Subject: Illustrations

I will illustrate in a series of instances such changes in the object that imply something like changes in the subject's view of himself. Then I will go on to the general question of philosophic differences.

2.1   Geometry as Intellectual Habit

I have already given some indication of what may be called the dialectic of the concept in considering the question, What is geometry?[6] To the boy in high school, geometry is what is in the book. But the experience of studying and doing geometry gradually forces a transformation of the notion of

5 On the point of the last two paragraphs, LN 78 has the following: 'Besides unity from end, there also is unity from efficient cause; and this unity is explained and as well it is given its criterion by group of operations; ie group forms intelligibly related whole of different operations.'
6 See above, chapter 5, §§ 1.2 and 1.4.

geometry from 'what is in the book' to an intellectual habit that is independent of the book. The transformation is generated by an interaction
between the subject and the book, but its real significance is an intellectual
habit in the subject.

2.2 The Notion of Space

Now let us take another instance, the notion of space. The infant has to
learn to hold its head erect, to control, direct, and coordinate the movements of its arms and legs and trunk. We notice that a baby held in someone's arms will wave its own arms in a helpless sort of fashion. It has no
control over the movements of its arms. Learning the differentiation of the
different members of the body, the distinction between them, the use of
each, the coordination of the movements of all, is the formation of a first
notion of space. It is a kinesthetic-tactile notion or experience of space.
The human body is a spatial entity; it is a part of space that feels, and you
feel differently in moving your arms or feet or in turning your head, and so
on. The differences in those feelings, as interrelated and correlated until
the body is capable of moving in any direction, is a set of felt differences
that provides an orientation in space and a rudimentary notion of space.
Space is a construct of up and down, right and left, forward and backward,
where the differences between up and down, right and left, forward and
backward are felt. They are on the level of feeling movement, feeling what
is touched. That is the first notion we form of space. It is a construct of felt
differences.

The second notion of space is visual. The child has visual experiences
of height and breadth and depth. Those visual experiences are another
approach to space – by turning its head and so on. The visual apprehension of space, the visual organization of objects in space, has to be united
with the kinesthetic-tactile view of space. That visual space admits far
greater development than the kinesthetic-tactile apprehension of space. It
can be extended to include not only the things in the nursery but everything in the house, everything in the town, everything on earth, as well as
the stars, the sun, and the moon. Visual space admits indefinite extension.

When that great extension is given to visual space, where it is all one with
the kinesthetic-tactile space, there can arise such questions as, Is the earth
a sphere? There will follow the gravest difficulties. After all, if the earth is a
sphere the people on the other side would fall off, because there has been

no distinction between visual space and kinesthetic-tactile space. Insofar as one's apprehension of space is built up through one's feelings of movements, up and down are absolute, not relative to the center of the earth. You have to introduce a correction in your apprehension of space so as not to be surprised, not to feel that it is impossible that there should be an antipodes and that the people on the antipodes get along just as well as we do.

However, notice that even when that correction is introduced in the notion of space, when the visual space is made independent of felt differences, one still cannot get along without the felt differences. All one's bodily movements are governed by one's kinesthetic-tactile feeling of space. The notion of space develops enormously through visual space, and the visual space does not have properties that the kinesthetic-tactile space has. One has to retain both: the kinesthetic-tactile space for one's ordinary bodily movements, and at the same time a space that is abstracted from such feelings insofar as they are explained as due to gravity in relation to the center of the earth – a space that is independent of such feelings. This is a first development in the notion of space. Everyone probably goes through a period of wondering how the earth can avoid being flat. How can there be people on the other side? They must be walking about like flies on a ceiling.

The next development in the notion of space is decentering. Visual space has as its center the subject that looks. Piaget has performed experiments with children in which he gave them a three-dimensional design of a mountain range.[7] The child would be looking at this mountain range. Piaget then placed a doll in a different position from the child and asked, Now, how do these mountains look to the doll? The child described the mountain in the same way as it looked to it. It had no notion of the shift of perspective; it was not able to put itself in the doll's place and see the mountains as it would see them if it were there. Now that is a fundamental element in the generalization of one's notion of space: one learns enough of perspective to be able to imagine how things would look if I were in another place. Children are apt to answer yes to the question, When you're walking, does the sun follow you? – even if the question is not put in that leading fashion. The sun follows them when they walk. The visual extension of space gives rise to a series of problems that the child has to solve, and the solution arises when the per-

7 See Jean Piaget and Bärbel Inhelder, *The Child's Conception of Space*, trans. F.J. Langdon and J.L. Lunzer (London: Routledge and Kegan Paul, 1963) 210–13.

son is able to imagine how things would look from any position, not merely from the position in which one is.

That shift, that psychological decentering that enables one to say how things would look from a different angle, has a correspondence in mathematics and physics in the transformation of axes. There is a set of axes K and another set of axes K_1. The physicist or mathematician will present the problem in terms of one set of axes. For example, at the Cape in Florida where they fire off missiles, there will be a set of axes pointing, say, to the north, to the west, and to the North Star. To calculate the trajectory they want a set of axes placed that way. But they will want another set of axes that is independent of the spin of the earth. The missile does not depend upon the spin of the earth indefinitely, and so there is the problem of going from one set of axes to the other. This is the same sort of thing as the child putting himself in the place of the doll and saying what the mountains would look like from that other position.

However, you get a leap when you move into the modern conception of geometry. The modern conception of geometry is that the laws of geometry are what do not change in moving from one set of axes to another; they are invariant under a group of transformations. The transformations are a matter of uniform velocity, or they involve an acceleration, and so on. Transformations can be grouped according to the kind of relative movement of the axes; and what does not change when you go from one to the other is the law of the space itself. Geometry is the study of laws; it is a study of what is independent when you move from one set of axes to the other. That notion of a geometry, where the law is what is independent of changes in spatiotemporal viewpoint, is the basis of Riemannian geometry, and it is the fundamental mathematical presupposition of both of Einstein's works on relativity.

You can see how with that last step one has moved to a purely intellectual view of space as what is independent of the spatiotemporal viewpoint. We have first, then, the kinesthetic-tactile apprehension of space of the infant. It is retained by every one of us insofar as we are able to keep our balance. Next, there is the visual apprehension of space, which is at first perfectly organized with the kinesthetic-tactile, but runs into problems when it is extended to the universe. After all, the universe is not governed by our feelings. There is the celebrated problem of people at the antipodes, and there are the hanging gardens of the ancients. Then there is the problem of shifting perspective, the transformation of axes, and through that problem of shifting perspective and of transforming axes, the movement out of the sensible to the purely intelligible. Geometry is abstract and universal, it is the law, it is what is independent of any particular standpoint in space or time, and consequently it is what does not change when one moves from one set of axes to another. And since you can conceive of a whole series of different types of transformations, you will have a series of geometries: a geometry for a transformation where there is simply a constant velocity; a geometry for a transformation where one set of axes is spinning, and so where there is an acceleration; and a geometry for 'any transformation whatever,' where tensors are a device, a type of mathematical entity defined by the transformation problem. However, we can see that there is a leap when we eliminate any visual space whatever and consider simply the laws that are independent of any visual space or act.

It can be seen from that progress that there is a resistance at each further step. Many people argued for the metaphysical necessity of a flat earth, because they could not separate the kinesthetic-tactile apprehension of space from the visual. There were all sorts of resistance to the development of the geometries of the nineteenth century, and still more to their applications in physics in the twentieth century. But while general relativity is very much a question mark, special relativity has been constantly verified for over fifty years.

2.3 Intersubjectivity and Mythic Consciousness

Let us take another example. There has been a great emphasis upon intersubjectivity, at least since the work of Max Scheler. It appears, for example, in the writings of Martin Buber, who emphasizes the importance of the categories 'I' and 'Thou' in religion. God is Thou, and I address him. That emphasis is of great concrete religious significance. We say, 'Our Father, who art in heaven.' We address God as a person – hence the interpersonal relation. There is also an emphasis upon intersubjectivity in the biblical scholars. They find that it is of far greater help in understanding the Bible than is our Western mentality and everything that derives from the development of Greek thought. There are also epistemologists who take refuge in intersubjectivity. After all, no one ever has any doubts that one is talking to someone else, and consequently there should be no philosophic problem about objectivity. We are urged to become intersubjective, and to forget all these problems in philosophy about objectivity. It is important to know, then, just what intersubjectivity is and just what are its limitations. Consequently, we will consider the phenomenology, so to speak, of a smile.[8]

First of all, a smile has a meaning. It is not simply a combination of movements of the lips, eyes, and facial muscles. We do not go about the street smiling at everyone. We know we would be misunderstood if we did, taken to mean what we do not mean; and if we would be taken to mean what we do not mean, then the smile has to have a meaning. Further, a smile is a smile precisely because of its meaning. It is not the movements of the muscles around the lips or the movements of the eyes. It is the meaning conveyed through those movements. Consequently, there is a great variation in the kinds and combinations of movements that occur in the smile. Because a smile has a meaning, it is enormously perceptible. One can catch the slightest beginnings of a smile on another's face, and one does not do so because one has studied the difference between movements that are smiles and movements that are not. The meaning is, as it were, immanent in the movement. Further, we do not learn to smile. Smiling results from a reflex structure. And we do not learn the meaning of the smile. If one does not know the meaning of the smile, one will never find it out, unless one finds out for oneself. The meaning of the smile is what the Germans call an *Urphänomen* – an original phenomenon not to be reduced to something else. You understand that the smile has a meaning, and what its meaning is, simply from your own smiling and from seeing the smiling of others.

What is the meaning of a smile? It is quite different from the meaning of words. Words tend toward, though they never achieve, a univocity of meaning, a single meaning. De facto, they have a series of more or less univocal meanings, but they are heading to univocity. The smile does not have some single meaning or a tendency toward some single meaning. The smile can express recognition, welcome, friendliness, love, joy, delight, contentment, satisfaction, amusement, irony. A smile can be sardonic, enigmatic, weary, a

8 Lonergan had just treated the same topic in his course *De intellectu et methodo*, where the various meanings of a smile are expressed in Latin by prefixes to 'risus': 'surrisus, irrisus, arrisus' (see p. 31 of the student notes, in the Archives of the Lonergan Research Institute, Toronto). Neither in the course nor in the notes for the education lectures does he give his source; in fact, when he came to treat the topic in *Method in Theology* he remarked that he was quoting his notebook 'from sources I have been unable to trace' (59). Some time later, however, he had found his source and made a notation in his personal copy of *Method*: 'F.J.J. Buytendijk.' A possible source of the idea is Buytendijk's *Phénoménologie de la Rencontre*, translated into French by Jean Knapp (Bruges: Desclée de Brouwer, 1952) 30–31, 49; but if this was Lonergan's source, he elaborated most of the details himself.

smile of resignation. The meaning runs through a whole gamut of human feelings.

Again, a proposition can be true or false, but a smile can be true or mendacious. One can simulate a smile. One can smile at a person although one feels like murdering him. That sort of smile is mendacious. But a smile is true only in the sense that it is opposed to a lie. It is not true in the sense of propositional truth. It is on a prior level. It is the expression, not of the differentiated consciousness that moves into the intellectual pattern of experience and reaches truth and expresses it in propositions, but of the undifferentiated consciousness in which the whole man or the whole woman is expressing himself or herself. It is a total meaning of one person to another, and it is prior to the differentiations of consciousness.

Again – and here we come to our notion of intersubjectivity – a proposition is objective; it is about something. 'This is a cat' – the proposition is about the cat. But when we smile we are performing an intersubjective act. We are not talking about something; we are not meaning in the sense of meaning that arises in discourse. Smiling presupposes a situation – persons are together or coming together. It is a recognition of the existence of the interpersonal situation, and it is a determinant *within* the events of the situation. I go into a room to see someone, and he or she smiles. Well, things ought to run smoothly. If he or she scowls, I will make the visit as short as possible and not raise the more delicate matters I thought I might raise if things went better. So the smile is a determinant in the interpersonal situation; it settles mutual attitudes. If *he* smiles, *I* smile too; if *he* doesn't, well, *I'm* not going to start. The smile betrays, reveals the subject, rather than talking about it, telling us about it. It antedates all distinctions between the sign and what it signifies, between the person that signifies and the sign by which he signifies. The person is, as it were, transparent in the smile.

That is just an example. We could give a whole series of examples of the phenomena of intersubjectivity. I have given a detailed account of the smile, but the phenomena are all of the same type. They have no tendency to univocity; their meaning is immanent in themselves; they are not true or false in the way propositions are true or false. There may be pretense or sincerity, but there is not a question of truth or falsity such as is found in a book. Intersubjective phenomena are not about something; they are determinants within an interpersonal situation. The whole development of consciousness can be of that type. A fundamental part of our knowing, our ordinary living, is on the intersubjective level. The feeling we have with different persons unconsciously determines a great part of our dealings with them.

Now, just as the kinesthetic-tactile notion of space can interfere with its generalization when one moves on to knowledge of the universe, so also an exclusively intersubjective mode of apprehension has its implications. If one tries to apprehend the universe through one's intersubjectivity, one arrives at mythic consciousness. Everything is personified. You apprehend everything through your apparatus for dealing with persons. Animals and all living things are personified. The sky, the sea, the earth, the rivers, the mountains, the valleys – they are the source of all other life, and they too are personified. In primitive consciousness there is that tendency to a universal personification. But that tendency can also function in the modern world. The intensity of passion, for example, connected with the Society for the Prevention of Cruelty to Animals is understood if we realize that they know human beings by their feelings and they know animals the same way. They are not arguing from any Greek notion about the rational animal, for that is not their knowledge of man. They are thinking intersubjectively, and their universal personification is not a figure of speech. Everything is alive, and everything is equally personal, because they do not differentiate sharply between persons and other things. In other words, if one tries to build a philosophy that is simply based upon intersubjectivity, one will have a hard time getting away from mythic consciousness. Some people might think that that is a good thing and find arguments for it, but generally their view would not be accepted.[9]

2.4 Intelligence as Knowing[10]

For a further illustration of how the dialectic of the concept expresses and witnesses to the problem of development, we will consider the discovery that understanding is a part of knowing. There is a spontaneous tendency to think that you know all about everything, and that understanding then adds on mere details. Why is that so?

There has been a brilliant account, even if not altogether perfect, of the development of the child in the work of Piaget, and his thinking fundamentally is in terms of the group of operations. He starts from hereditary sensorimotor schemes and proceeds to their generalization. The child not only sucks to obtain food but also sucks its thumb. Sucking the thumb is a

9 The break was taken at this point. The tape resumes several words into the first sentence of the next section. LN 78 indicates that Lonergan is here treating another example of the problem of development.
10 The subtitle is taken from LN 78.

generalization. The exercise is repeated in different circumstances, and at a later stage the child puts into its mouth everything it can get its hands on. This is a sensorimotor scheme being repeated for its own sake. It is something that infants know how to do. It is repeated on different objects, and so it is generalized. The movements are not the same in the different cases of the generalization, and so there arises a differentiation. The infant begins to recognize these differences because of the difference of the operations.

Then there are other schemes. The infant turns its eyes toward the light and attends to things it sees moving, and there is the development of visual schemes. Similarly, there is the hearing and uttering of sounds, and the grasping of objects – what it does with them, and so on. All these schemes develop in the infant. Not only do they develop singly, but they begin to intersect. At first what the child grabs it will put in its mouth, but later it will look at it; in the reverse operation, what it sees it will grab. There will be the formation of a higher structure out of lower schemes.

According to Piaget, we form our notion of the 'already out there now real' when we get these schemes intersecting. The subject begins to be differentiated from the object. We form that fundamental structure of the psyche, with the differentiation between subject and object, insofar as there are several diverse schemes that are coordinated. The child learns to use any one of them and to move back and forth so as to deal with objects in his environment. From that preliminary learning in infancy and childhood there can be formed a notion of what is real. The real is what satisfies several sensorimotor or perceptual schemes of operations. And there can be a great philosophic block against going beyond that notion of reality. Knowing, operationally, involves what we can deal with, and de facto that is our criterion for a hallucination: if one can only see a thing, but when one gets near it and tries to feel it, one feels nothing, one concludes that one is suffering from an illusion or a hallucination. On the contrary, what meets the requirements of testing from all senses is considered not hallucinatory but real.

Now the notion of reality formed in that manner is of the same elementary order as the kinesthetic-tactile notion of space. And quite clearly, if one holds that that is reality, then the operations of the mathematician and of the natural scientist that arise within the intellectual pattern of experience and form the enormous structures that refer to a world quite different from the world for us, a world rather of things in their relations to one another, give rise to an unreal world. Such knowing is just hypothesis. It becomes knowledge of reality insofar as you can get back to what you can deal with, what you can see with your eyes, handle with your hands, feel to be hot or cold, rough or smooth, wet or dry, heavy or light. Then the real is simply the *aisthêton*, the *sensibile*, what is given to sense. All the rest is instrumental, as Dewey would say. It is immanent, an activity of the subject. It is not knowing reality. It may help you to deal with the reality that is given to sense, but in itself it is not knowing. Activities of understanding help one, they are useful, but they are not knowing. And still less is judgment knowing. Judgment is just putting a rubber stamp upon these activities of understanding. When the scholastics held that the real, *ens*, is *id quod est*, where *est* is said of what you know when you make the judgment 'It is,' they were not talking about reality at all. They were caught up in a verbalism. To throw any doubts upon the convictions about reality formed in infancy is to be an idealist, a Platonist, a Kantian, a relativist, or God knows what. In any case, it is certainly getting out of this real world.

We have here a case in which the notion of the real develops, and we have in patristic literature two brilliant instances of this. For Tertullian, only bodies are real. God has to be a body – not a body such as we see and feel, but still a body. What is not a body is not real. This is an expression of the survival of the infantile view of reality. Similarly, St Augustine, who was a man of extraordinary intelligence, was for years a materialist. He knew he was a materialist, and he said so. But he changed. And then when he wanted to talk about the real, what is really so, what word did he use? *Veritas*. Augustine does not talk about *realitas*, but about *veritas*, about what is true. And the truth is known not without, *non foras*, and not just within, *non intus*, but above us, in a light that he describes as incommutable and eternal. The history of Augustine's thought is the history of the discovery of the limitations of the infantile apprehension of reality and the history of the shift to the true.

2.5 The Notion of Being

Now let us take another instance, one that ties in with the preceding: the notion of being. Parmenides was the first to insist on *to on*. Plato carried the matter further, but Aristotle was the one who really went to work on the issue. He argues out the meaning of the word *ousia* in book 7 of his *Metaphysics*. In the last chapter of that book, after he has considered what *ousia* is from a whole series of different angles, he says, Now let us begin afresh, let us take matters in another way. It is this last study that will, I think, throw a shaft of light upon what Aristotle is talking about.

Aristotle is asking *ti estin ousia*, What is being ('entity,' in Owens's translation)?[11] He says that to ask *what* something is is the same question as to ask *why*. What do you mean when you ask *what?* The difficulty of that question lies not only in the term 'being' but also in what is meant by *what*. Aristotle says *what* has the same meaning as *why*. This can be shown from simple examples. What is an eclipse? You can change that into a *why* question: Why is the moon darkened in this fashion? If you can explain why the moon is darkened in this fashion, you can explain what an eclipse is. The same answer goes for both questions. The moon is darkened in this fashion because the earth comes between the moon and the sun, and so the light from the sun does not reach the moon. What, then, is an eclipse? It is the earth blocking off the light of the sun from the moon. The questions *what* and *why* are the same.

However, Aristotle admitted that not all cases of the question, What is it? can be reduced to questions of *why* in the same simple fashion. In talking about an eclipse of the moon you can ask, Why is the moon thus darkened? The eclipse is the darkening, the covering up, the leaving out. But when you ask, What is a house? or What is a man? how do you change that into a *why* question? There is only one term. Aristotle's answer is to distinguish between the materials and the form. Why are these pieces of timber and lumps of stone a house? Because of the form, because of the way the artificial form orders together all the stones and all the pieces of timber. And why are these materials a man? Because of the form, because of the soul; the intellective soul makes this body a man. So he concludes that when you ask the question, What? you can change it into a question, Why? by asking for the formal cause in the ultimate simple instances. And so when Aristotle in book 7 asks, What is a man? the answer is the *aition tou einai*, the *causa essendi*, the reason why the materials are something. That is the form, the *eidos*, the *morphê*. At the end of book 7, he identifies *ousia* with *eidos*, with form, with the *causa essendi*. Then in book 8 he moves on a step, to discuss material things, and there he says that the *aition*, the 'What is it?' is the essence. In material things this is the combination of form and matter. In immaterial things it is the form alone. So we have the Aristotelian answer to the question of being in terms of matter and form, or, in the immaterial order, of pure form.[12]

Now the Aristotelian answer did not satisfy St Thomas. After all, Aristotle

11 Joseph Owens, *The Doctrine of Being in the Aristotelian Metaphysics* (Toronto: Pontifical Institute of Mediaeval Studies, 3rd ed., 1978) 138–53.
12 For a more detailed discussion of these terms, see *Understanding and Being* 50–51.

is not asking why this man *is*, but why he is a man, not why this house *is*, but why it is a house. St Thomas notes, *ens dicitur ab esse*. 'Being,' the noun, is said from 'to be.'[13] It receives its meaning from the 'to be,' from the 'is.' And the 'is' is something that is not just the same as being *something*.

St Thomas does not drop the Aristotelian notion that *what* means *why*. But he has an answer to the question, What is being? – namely, Why is being what it is? He acknowledges an *ens per essentiam*, a being that in virtue of its own intelligibility *is*. Direct knowledge of that being is the beatific vision. Any other being is a being by participation. To understand an *ens per participationem* is to understand, not being, but a kind of being – the being of a rose, or the being of a monkey, or the being of a man, but not being simply. To know being as being is to have the beatific vision. God knows in his essence himself and everything else that is or could be. Insofar as we participate that divine knowledge in the beatific vision, we have knowledge of what being is. But until we have knowledge of what being is, we know being only by analogy, by knowing some beings and extrapolating to the others.

Now, when St Thomas goes beyond Aristotle on the notion of being, what he is doing is bringing together Augustine and Aristotle. Augustine is the man who first insisted on *veritas*, on truth. The Aristotelian notion of being was, Sense and understanding correspond to matter and form. But in St Thomas, sense, understanding, and judgment correspond to matter, form, and the act of essence: *esse*, existence. St Augustine is the one who developed the notion of judgment as fundamental in knowing, the *veritas*. St Thomas added its metaphysical equivalent, the *esse*, in the composition of the finite being.

However, that movement that begins with Parmenides and passes through Plato, Aristotle, and Augustine to Aquinas is not the only answer to the question, What is being? For Scotus, being is 'not nothing.' It is not a totality that is the whole of reality. You do not need the beatific vision to answer the question, What is being? Being is the concept with the minimum connotation and the maximum denotation. The implications of the Scotist notion of being appear in the order of the philosophic sciences in Christian Wolff, for whom ontology is the study of possible being, and actual being is studied in other departments. Scotus's being is also the being presupposed

---

13 Possibly *Summa contra Gentiles*, 1, c. 25, § 10: 'nomen entis ab esse [imponitur],' or *Summa theologiae*, 1, q. 104, a. 4, ad 3m:'sic enim ens dicitur, quia eo aliquid est.'

by Hegel. The being that is not found in anything, that is just 'not nothing,' is the sort of being that never exists. Nothing is merely 'not nothing,' and consequently Hegel's dialectic of the concept goes from being to nothing, the 'not-nothing' being. 'Not nothing' is the minimum connotation with the maximum denotation, and there is nothing that exists corresponding to that; and if there is nothing that exists corresponding to the concept, the concept is a concept of nothing. And so Hegel goes from being to nothing and reconciles both in becoming.

Now, if we try to put together all the elements in the notion of being, we can distinguish five points: (1) the intention of being; (2) the concept of being; (3) knowing a being; (4) knowing the notion of being; and (5) knowing being, or knowing the idea of being.[14]

The intention of being is the light of intellect, the origin of wonder, the origin of all questions asking Why? How? What? and again, Is it so? It is the ground of human intelligence. It is not knowing anything or conceiving anything; it is consciously discontented ignorance. One wants to understand, one wants to know, one asks. The asking in words is an expression of that fundamental dynamism, the origin of all science and philosophy. It is in virtue of the intention of being that St Thomas concludes to a natural desire to know God. When we know the existence of God, we ask, What is God? To ask what something is is to want to know it by its essence, and the only knowledge of God by his essence is the beatific vision. Consequently, when we ask, What is God? we are expressing, not any acquired or infused habit, but something that is natural to man, namely, to ask, What is it? with regard to anything he meets with or knows about. The pure desire to know is the root of the intellectual pattern of experience and is to be contrasted with Heidegger's *Sorge*, concern, which is man as he ordinarily is. Man's flow of consciousness is not simply an expression of the pure desire to know, but is modified by concerns of all types.

One moves from the intention of being to the concept of being with a further step. One has the *intellectus agens*, sense, phantasm, possible intellect, *species intelligibilis*, the act of understanding, and its expression in a concept,

14 Lonergan kept clarifying his expressions for quite distinct usages of the word 'being.' In *Insight* (665) he had distinguished '(1) the pure notion of being, (2) the heuristic notion of being, (3) restricted acts of understanding, conceiving, and affirming being, and (4) the unrestricted act of understanding being.' On further clarifications, some years after the present lectures, see note *b* to chapter 19 of *Insight*, p. 804.

a definition. The act of understanding grasps in the phantasm the reason why the circle must be round. The sensible presentation is of a figure; understanding grasps in it why it must be round; and the combination of the sensible presentation and understanding can be expressed in a concept. When it is expressed in a concept, the content is of those two and nothing more. We arrive at simply the quiddity, the abstract: circularity as distinct from circle, humanity as distinct from man.

But this inquiry that uses the phantasm as an instrument to impress the *species intelligibilis* and leads to the act of understanding expressed in the definition has an ulterior intention. Its aim is not simply to know what things are but also whether they are; it is heading for the judgment. It is this heading for the judgment, combined with the abstract essence, that gives you the concept of being, thinking of a being. In other words, it is at this point that there arises the distinction between the concept of the *ens quod* and the concept of the *ens quo*. It is at this point that there arises the question of the subsistent. The *ens quo* is simply a component in a being, such as the essence, the combination of intelligibility and matter. But insofar as the conjunction of intelligibility and matter is part of a knowing that heads towards knowing something that is, one can consider that part in itself and speak of the *ens quo*; or one can consider the whole that one intends, and then one is aiming at the *ens quod*.

On the level of conception, one is thinking of being, and one thinks of being insofar as the intention takes us beyond the mere combination of intelligibility in sensible matter to something that is. One knows a being when one adds the judgment. It is on this level of reflection, it is when one judges, that one knows.

Knowing the notion of being, our fourth consideration, results from a series of reflections upon the other three: intention, concept, knowing a being. The notion of being, then, is something that underpins the *intentio entis*. It uses the phantasm as an instrument towards knowing a being, and so it underpins the sensitive order; it selects and directs the sensible flow so that things fall into the perspective in which one gets an insight. It combines in the concept what is grasped by understanding and what is presented to sense, and it adds on to that its ultimate intention, to get the thinking of being. You are not knowing being yet, but you are thinking of it. Finally, when you make the judgment, you are knowing a being.

Finally, the idea of being is the act of understanding that understands being, and that act of understanding is infinite; it is God. And so the idea of being is the same as the divine essence. God in his essence knows himself and everything else that can be or is. The divine essence is the idea of being, and knowing God by his essence is the consummation of intellectual activity.

2.6 The Notion of Objectivity

Let us now take another notion that develops, the notion of objectivity. Presumably, at a first approximation everyone assumes that we know just what is meant by objectivity. You tell people they are not being objective, and usually all you mean, of course, is that you do not agree with them. But if you ask them what they mean by objectivity, or if you ask yourself, What do I mean by objectivity? the first spontaneous answer is that the objective is what is out there; and being objective is seeing what is out there, seeing all of it, and not seeing anything that is not out there. That is what objectivity is. If one follows out logically that notion of objectivity, one agrees with the empiricists, the positivists, the pragmatists, the sensists, the modernists.

One moves to a second notion of objectivity when one thinks of impartiality, detachment. We say a person is guided by his passions; his thinking is wishful; he is not thinking in the intellectual pattern of experience; he does not have the detachment necessary for serious scientific inquiry; he is speaking on behalf of his native town or country, his political party, or his religion; he is a hired thinker. With that notion of objectivity one moves into a different field.

There is a third component in the notion of objectivity, and that is when one reaches the absolute, the unconditioned. One is objective when what one says is true, and one is not objective when what one says is false. The dividing line between objectivity and nonobjectivity or subjectivity lies in truth and falsity. If one holds that the objective is what is already out there, then it makes an enormous difference, it is a fundamental question, whether one is seeing what is out there, whether one is grasping what is imposed by the data, or whether one is projecting into the data one's subjective ideas, reading things into the data. That is the fundamental criterion if objectivity means the already out there now. But if objectivity is a matter of truth and falsity, then it makes no difference whether one is reading into the data or not. What counts is whether what one reads truly is – and that alone counts. And how do you know whether it truly is or not? You know when you have reached the unconditioned.

There is a fourth stage of the notion of objectivity that combines elements from the other three and brings us back to the starting point equipped with what we have learnt on the way. Consider the set of true judgments: A is, B is, C is, D is. Again, A is not B nor C nor D; B is not C nor D, and so forth. And finally, I am *A*. In all cases, one is knowing by the true. The truth is the medium in which one knows being. *Verum est medium in quo cognoscitur ens.* And if *A* is, *A* is a being; if *B* is, it is a being; if *C* is, it is a being. *A* is not *B* nor *C*. There is a series of real distinctions between *A*, *B*, *C*, and *D*, and they are known through comparative negative propositions. *A* is not *B*. Saying 'I am *A*' is the same as saying 'I am a knower.' I am the one who makes these judgments, and I have been named *A*. If that set of judgments is true, what is an object? An object is a being that is. There are two, three, four objects if there is a corresponding number of relevant negative comparative propositions (*A* is not *B*, and so on). There is a subject really distinct from objects if I am one of the objects that is really distinct from the others. They are all on the level of truth and being. One is knowing a universe of objects and the subject as one of the objects in the universe. That is the statement, based upon being and truth, of what is true in the statement when you say that the objective is what is out there. If what is out there is, it is an object; if what is out there is rationally affirmed, it is a reality, and my knowledge of it is rational. But if I consider it real simply in virtue of my infantile notion of reality, then I am subscribing implicitly to quite a different philosophy from a philosophy which insists upon truth and being. If I insist on retaining as absolutely valid the notion of reality that I formed in infancy, then I am contracting the universe apprehended by Aquinas within the horizon of my earliest steps in seeking knowledge.

So you see that this problem of development is intimately connected with a proper apprehension of traditional doctrine, and that the subject has to grow up to the level of Aquinas. People are naturally realists because naturally they experience and understand and judge. But people are not naturally realists in the sense that naturally they distinguish the three and know that it is judgment and truth, and truth alone, that is the criterion. And if one has difficulty in making the adjustments necessary to move on the Thomist level of thought, then that too is an advantage. One will understand then why people think scholasticism is foolishness, why they think it is verbalism, why they think it is out of date. One will experience in oneself the difficulties that prevent others from regarding scholasticism as anything but an antiquarian blunder.

3   The Theory of Philosophic Differences

3.1   The Basic Group of Operations

We have our basic group of operations in human knowledge. They are experience, understanding, and judging. The group forms an interrelated whole. You can define experience as what is presupposed by the inquiry that leads up to understanding; as the materials in which one understands; as that from which one abstracts the essential, what is necessary to the act of understanding. One can grasp that understanding, of itself, is not knowing; it does not involve a distinction between legend and history, alchemy and chemistry, astrology and astronomy. To make those distinctions one has to appeal to judgment, and that gives us the third level, the attainment of the unconditioned. All of human knowing is a matter of performing those three operations.

Those operations, as a group, determine an object. There is an object proportionate to such operations. The object will be compounded of act, form, and potency, where act is the component in the reality corresponding to the *is* of judgment, form is the component in the reality corresponding to the intelligibility grasped by understanding, and potency is the component in the reality corresponding to what is abstracted from in all science, a purely empirical residue. Hence scientific knowledge, in the process and in the attainment of its ideal – an explanation of all phenomena – will be the set of theories (form) verified (act) in instances (potency).[15]

The basic group of operations yields the structure of material being in scholastic philosophy. We can go beyond material being by excluding potency. This leaves two possibilities: (1) form and act, and (2) act. These pertain, respectively, to angels and to God. And from this basic group of operations we can go on to discuss the differences among philosophers, and so to offer a theory of philosophic differences.

The importance of the theory of philosophic differences is that, if one gets a sufficient grasp of it, one can read fruitfully all sorts of material without losing one's way. If one is limited in one's reading and inspiration exclusively to the works written by Catholics that have been approved as

15 The next paragraph is based on the notes of F. Crowe. It concludes the seventh lecture. The eighth lecture (Wednesday, August 12) begins with Lonergan indicating that he intends in the remaining lectures (1) to complete the discussion of philosophic differences, (2) to say something about Piaget's theory of psychological development and its connection with the idea of a general education, (3) to treat sign, language, and art as an aspect of the new learning, and (4) to say something about the idea of history, which, he said, 'brings us back to our starting point.' We have chosen to incorporate (1) in this chapter and to limit our next chapter to (2), which constitutes the remainder of the eighth lecture.

safe, one is cutting down enormously one's field of study, one's sources. Also, for many, such limitations are not possible; they have to be in the field just like anybody else. But some grasp of the theory of philosophic differences can be extremely helpful. If you are able to spot a Kantian or a certain type of existentialist, for example, and to know just what are going to be the problems with which the thinker is dealing and where he is liable to go wrong, you will not only not be misled, but also you may very easily obtain a great amount of help and a number of insights; for there is a great deal of intelligence and hard work represented in the writings of these thinkers.

Let us begin with the three basic levels of conscious operations: the experiential, the intellectual, and the rational or reflective. The three basic types of philosophy are organized, respectively, about the level of experience, about the level of intelligence, and about the level of rational reflection.

De facto, in artistic and literary work the experiential level is most prominent, in mathematical and scientific work the intellectual is most prominent, and in philosophical work the rational and reflective is most prominent. Because rational reflection leads to saying A is, A is B, or A is not C, philosophy can be very jejune. And that is no harm. But that is the controlling level of the other two. Acts of understanding are much rarer than acts of experiencing, and acts of judging are much rarer than acts of understanding. We need a flow of experiences to have a single insight, and a flow of insights to have a single judgment. But rational reflection is the key level, and this is the level that comes to the fore in philosophy: not that it prescinds from the other two, but just as the scientist does not care what example you get the insight from so long as you get the insight, and so any experience or example will do, so the philosopher does not care what your insights are – any insights will do – so long as you understand what an insight is. You can deal with insights that are all X's, but the philosopher's emphasis is on the 'is' or 'is not.'

However, men in their living can be organized more on the level of experience, or more on the level of intelligence, or more on the level of rational reflection; and so there arise three basic classes of philosophy. The tendency to organize on the experiential level is manifest in the materialist, the empiricist, the sensist, the positivist, the pragmatist, the modernist. These same types of philosophy recur throughout the whole history of philosophy. There are differences in the experiential philosophies due to different objects of intellectual interest, but they are all of that basic type. On the second level, there are the philosophies of the Platonist, idealist, relativist, essentialist varieties. On the third level, there are the realists, where what is meant by the real is what is known when one truly affirms, 'It is.' As St Thomas said, for example, we know the existence of God when we know the truth of the proposition *Deus est,* God is.[16]

Now these philosophic differences will radiate through the whole of life. Earlier, we considered three levels of the good: the particular good (the level of satisfactions), the good of order, and value. We distinguished aesthetic, ethical, and religious values, where the aesthetic value is apprehended by insight into the concrete, the ethical value is the individual demanding correspondence between *his* rationality and *his* activity, and the religious value is the rational individual using truth to know being, orientating himself before God within the world and history. The distinction of the aesthetic, the ethical, and the religious comes, of course, from Kierkegaard. He used the three categories in speaking of three spheres of existential subjectivity. A person moves from one sphere to another only by a leap. In other words, when a person is within a given sphere of existential subjectivity, as Kierkegaard would put it, or within a given horizon, to use the terminology that we developed earlier, then it is not by arguing from that sphere that one will bring him to another sphere. That sphere becomes a closed system, and a person has to be dynamited out of it. We then related to this distinction of operations Sorokin's analysis of Western culture in terms of three types of cultures or civilizations. There are the sensate, corresponding to the experiential; the idealistic, corresponding to the intellectual; and the ideational, corresponding to the reflective, the 'It is.' Consequently, meeting those fundamental types is the approach implied in *Insight* in the distinction between positions and counterpositions. Fundamentally, positions are philosophic, ethical, artistic, practical views that are in harmony with the full implications of the three levels. Counterpositions are views, whether philosophic, ethical, practical, or artistic, that involve a blind spot, a limited horizon, where the limitation is either to the intellectual level or to the experiential level. The systematic formulation of the difference between positions and counterpositions is given in epistemological terms: if the real is what you know by understanding correctly, you have a

16 Thomas Aquinas, *Summa theologiae,* 1, q. 3, a. 4, ad 2m: 'Scimus enim quod haec propositio quam formamus de Deo, cum dicimus, "Deus est," vera est.'

position; if the real is anything but that, or if no real at all is acknowledged, you have a counterposition.[17]

3.2 Variations on the Basic Philosophic Differences [18]

What I have said thus far is very general, and now we may illustrate it. I begin with the empiricist movement.

Galileo did not merely discover the idea of the natural law in the instance of the law of free fall. His real inspiration was the idea of a *system* of laws, and his concept of that system was a ready-made system, namely, Euclidean geometry. For Galileo the object of science was a geometrization of the world. In proposing this he had to meet the objection that it is obvious to everybody that the real world is far more than is treated in geometry. To meet that objection he drew a distinction between primary and secondary qualities. Primary qualities are qualities inherent in things themselves. The things themselves have length and breadth; they move; they have weight

17 LN 78 has more under the heading 'The Basic Group' than was given in the lecture. The notes read:
'C. The Basic Group
  Experience understanding judging
  Potency form act as constituents of proportionate being
  Metaphysics as basic semantics
  Metaphysics as integration of sciences and common sense
  Metaphysics as basis for ascent to transcendent being
  Basic group as basis of criticism of philosophies proceeding from poly-
    morphic consciousness of man
  empiricist idealist realist
  aesthetic ethical religious
  satisfaction order value
  sensate idealistic ideational
  Positions & counter-positions.'
18 Lonergan skipped a section in the notes headed 'Variations on the Basic Group.' This section (LN 79) reads:
'D. Variations on the Basic Group
Rationalist, the basic group as exclusive
truth is exclusively what one can know by one's own (any human) understanding and by grasp of unconditioned
revealed mysteries cannot be true

Potentially Catholic Philosophy
The Basic Group, as not exclusive, as open to a higher wisdom
to truth from a higher source as a theoretical possibility

Actually Catholic Philosophy
The Basic Group as completed by light of faith
God could and in Christ, Head and Members, God has provided man with a
  participation in Divine Truth Love Life.'

and mass. These are all measurable qualities in the things themselves. But there are also secondary qualities: color, sound, odor, taste, the feeling of hot, cold, wet, dry, rough, smooth, heavy, light. The characteristic of all of these is that they are not in the thing but in the subject. They are like tickling. A local motion produces tickling in the animal, and the sensation that we call being tickled is not a property of the local motion of the finger that produces the tickling. Colors, sounds, odors, tastes, hot, cold, wet, dry are all like tickling. They are secondary qualities. They result from an interaction between the real thing, which is just geometrical, and the animal.

Now this was a doctrine invented by Galileo to sell his theory of science. And, while his theory of science underwent subsequent revisions, the distinction between primary and secondary qualities continued to have a great influence in philosophy. Nor is this incidental. For it was the real concern of philosophers to arrive at a theory of knowledge that would ground the scientific methodology and justify how science is able to produce such results. And that aim has been attained to a great extent. But as you can see, the position of Galileo that what is really out there is the geometrical object, and the rest of it is just in the subject, is a theory about what is real. It rests upon an epistemological assumption that most people find self-evident, namely, that knowing is a matter of taking a look, that a real distinction between subject and object, and a confrontation of the object to the subject, are of the very essence of knowledge, so that Aristotle was completely wrong when he asserted that sense in act is the sensible in act, that intellect in act is the intelligible in act, and that in things that are without matter the one that understands and what is understood are identical. The fundamental Aristotelian axiom is that knowing is by identity.

Following Aristotle's lead, St Thomas held that the truth of God's self-knowledge is a matter not of an *adaequatio*, of a similarity, but of an absence of dissimilarity. If you presuppose that knowing involves a duality, you deny the simplicity of God. This implication of the dualist position on knowledge has recently been resurrected in another form by Sartre, who holds that if you think of God as conscious, your view of God is contradictory. For the *en-soi* cannot be the *pour-soi*, and vice versa. If you posit God as reality, as *en-soi*, then God cannot be conscious, since knowing involves a duality. The view of knowledge as involving a duality is the position that is self-evident to common sense. That is, the first and most rudimentary attempt of common sense to say what knowledge is usually comes forth in those terms. This is what Husserl would refer to as *Selbstverständlichkeit*, and Marcel as the *tout naturel*. 'It goes without saying' that this is what knowledge is. What Husserl and Heidegger and Marcel are attacking is the large circle of things that 'go without saying,' the circle resulting in the conventional mind. And the conventional mind is our situation.

The dualism comes to the fore in Descartes. Descartes is usually described as a dualist. On the one hand, his position is rational, an appeal to reason. *Cogito, ergo sum*: he affirms his own reality because of a reason, and he knows his reality by the affirmation. Thus one side of Descartes is upon the third level, the level of rational reflection and judgment. But on the other hand, Descartes also identifies material substance with extension, and there he is on the experiential level. He has two views of reality. Material substance is extension. And what is extension? It is what is out there; we all see that; there is no problem about that.

In subsequent philosophy, the rationalist side of Descartes was developed by Malebranche, Spinoza, Leibniz, and Wolff, and the empiricist side was brought to the fore in the English philosophers – Hobbes, Locke, Berkeley, Hume – and finally in Kant. Once the two sides are split, the problem is to put them together again. There is basically the same fundamental theme running through Berkeley, Hume, and Kant, and it all turns on the fundamental assumption that when you know, you are knowing something out there. There are difficulties raised by these philosophers against that view, but their arguments do not proceed a priori from Aristotle's assertion that sense in act is the sensible in act, intellect in act is the intelligible in act, and in the case of the immaterial substances[19] what understands and what is understood form an identity. The arguments are rather from concrete instances.

Thus Berkeley argues that the primary qualities are just as much in the subject as the secondary qualities, and in fact even more so. If color, sound, taste, touch, hot and cold, and so on, are all like tickling, and so are simply effects produced in the subject, then the primary qualities, spatial qualities, must be still more in the subject, because you know these spatial qualities, these geometrical qualities, only *in* the colors, the sounds, and so on. If, then, all sensible presentations are in the subject, how is it that our sensitive experience comes to us, not in the fragmentary and arbitrary fashion of our dreams, but in an orderly manner? What makes experience ordered? Berkeley explained the orderliness of experience by appealing to God. Hume put himself the same problem, and he explained the nexus, the con-

19 At this point Lonergan quotes the Greek from memory, correcting himself as he goes. It is difficult to follow his Greek, but it is close to *De anima*, III, 4, 430a 3: 'to auto esti to nooun kai to nooumenon.'

nections, the causal relations, the unifications in our knowledge as due to custom and habit, and so as purely subjective factors. This explanation disturbed Kant very deeply. After all, Newtonian mechanics was a magnificent creation. How is such a science as Newtonian mechanics possible? To account for it, to explain the order of experience that it manifests, Kant appealed not to God, nor to habit and custom, which would invalidate all science and make it worthless, but to a priori structures.[20]

Newton had affirmed the existence of an absolute space and an absolute time. What is the absolute space of Newton? Suppose I drop a piece of chalk. Strictly speaking, if I dropped it with a perfect release, it would fall in a straight line, perpendicular to the floor. But if the floor were the floor of a moving train or airplane, then it would not fall in a straight line. It would fall in a parabola relative to the earth, and in a straight line relative to the train or airplane. If I take into account the fact that the earth is spinning on its axis and it does one turn every twenty-four hours, I get a more complicated curve. And if I take into account the fact that the earth is moving around the sun, then the curve becomes still more complicated. If I think of it relative to the receding nebulae, the trajectory of the falling piece of chalk becomes even more complicated yet. But then I can ask the ultimate question, Are the earth and the sun and the nebulae themselves all moving relative to space itself? Is there a set of immovable, eternal places that we call space? Newton thought he could prove that there was such a set, and that set is his absolute space. His absolute time is a similar construction. De facto there is no evidence whatever for either absolute space or absolute time; Newton's arguments for the existence of absolute space and time are fallacious. Kant believed in this absolute space and time, but he attributed them to a priori forms of the sensibility. Why do you think there could be a movement of everything relative to space itself, that is, relative to eternal places? Kant reduced that to an a priori form of the sensibility of the subject; and he employed a similar procedure to explain absolute time.

Moreover, besides the a priori forms of the sensibility which grounded geometry as a universal and necessary science – Kant had made Euclidean geometry a universal and necessary science because our apprehension of spatial objects contained an a priori element imposed upon the material of the sensation, and that is why geometry can be universal and necessary – Kant deduced as well a list of a priori categories of the understanding from

20 LN 79 has, 'Kant: order is due to a priori, to fixed modes of construction of sensible impressions, Empfindungen.'

a list of twelve different types of propositions.[21] Finally, to these he added
the ideals of reason, to which he conceded a regulative, normative value –
always ask more questions, investigate things more thoroughly, and so on –
but denied any constitutive value.[22]

That, very roughly, is the Kantian position. Kant dropped much of the
rational level. Simply to say, 'It is,' is just to talk; it is not knowledge of anything. The pure desire to know is transcendental illusion, because it moves
you beyond the level of possible experience. The Kantian criterion, the ultimate criterion that is constantly operative in the *Critique of Pure Reason*, is the
idea of possible experience. Knowledge is possible insofar as we construct
experience. When we start talking about angels and God, we are not constructing any experience, and consequently our sets of a priori forms are
irrelevant. It is a fundamental Kantian assumption that what makes knowledge knowledge is experience, not a grasp of the unconditioned, not something that occurs in the judgment.

The Kantian position is not easily transcended. If one reflects upon one's
capacity to reflect, one can see that there is a demand for the unconditioned, and this demand makes one say that science is only probable, that it

21 LN 79 adds at this point: 'integrated through schematism of imagination.'
22 The lecture departs a bit from the notes (LN 79) at this point, which read as
    follows:
    'Truth in Empiricism
    a) pure reason as deduction from analytic propositions is empty
        wisdom has to validate basic terms I-II 66 5 4m
    b) understanding develops through interaction with data of sense; there is a
        fact of insight; one must attend to data
    c) understanding goes beyond sense, not less than sense, a mere impoverish-
        ment of sense: in this sense, a priori true
    Error of empiricism
    a) knowing is basically looking, or some equivalent to looking
    b) knowing is basically experiencing or some equivalent to exp
        experience is just one component out of three
        judging is not just going back to experience, essentially it is going on to
            unconditioned, to what is independent of any particular subject and so
            public
    c) Kantian a priori an outworn rigidity
        space and time, Riemannian manifold, whichever verified
        insights, endless variety, accumulations to ever higher viewpoints
        real is not filling of empty form of time
        substance is not permanence of the real in time
        real is ens, id quod est; substance, type of ens
    d) pure desire to know, unlimited
        no reason for asserting its transcendental use to be illegitimate: Kant's
            view of legitimate as restricted to possible experience is mere empiricist
            prejudice.'

has not yet reached the unconditioned. This demand for the unconditioned and obtaining of the unconditioned is something that constitutes a
third level in our knowing. But if one simply speaks vaguely about evidence,
it is not self-evident that one has to go beyond experience and understanding to posit a third level in which the unconditioned is reached; one ignores
that reflectivity and thinks simply of the fulfilment of the conditions, of verification in the materialist sense of having the requisite sensation. One does
not think of having the requisite sensation as the fulfilment of the conditions that, combined with the link between the conditions and the conditioned, introduces something new, namely, a satisfaction of the demand of
rational reflection for the unconditioned, a satisfaction that through the
attainment of the unconditioned gets beyond the subject. If the unconditioned is attained, then there is attained something independent of the subject, something in an absolute order, that something that we name truth.
Truth is absolute, and it is the means through which we know the real.

In other words, in all that development there is the naive assumption that
knowing is taking a look. I say the assumption is naive, but it has been held
by very profound philosophers. Why are there subsistent universals in
Plato? Well, you know the universal, and knowing is taking a look of some
sort, or at least remembering a look, and therefore there has to be the universal. Why is it that in Plotinus the first, the One, does not know, is beyond
knowledge? Because knowledge involves an imperfection. The first knower
is had in the Intelligence, the Nous, that emanates from the One; but the
One is beyond being and beyond knowing, because being and knowing
imply a duality.

That is an example. There are many other criticisms that can be made of
Kant, but the fundamental objection is that the issue is not placed on the
rational level. His a priori is validated insofar as it is a necessary condition of
possible experience. His ultimate is experience, not truth, not the unconditioned; and that is where he differs from being. Moreover, because he does
not reach the unconditioned, his doctrine is an immanentist doctrine. One
gets out of merely experiencing and understanding, to reality, through an
absolute, through the unconditioned. In Kant there is not that unconditioned. It is implicit, of course, in that he does acknowledge simple fact –
you can prove a position by introducing a virtually unconditioned; but he
does not have the unconditioned as a systematic structural element in his
philosophy, and he cannot introduce it into his philosophy without destroying that philosophy. As long as the unconditioned is not recognized, implicitly or explicitly, the philosophy is an immanentist philosophy. You have the

experiences, you perform acts of understanding, but you cannot use true propositions as the means through which you know reality.

If one makes the same mistake as Galileo, as Descartes in one side of his thinking, namely, when he asserts that material substance is extension, as Hobbes, Berkeley, Hume, and Kant – namely, if one assumes that knowing is somehow taking a look, even if a constructed look as in Kant – then one cannot answer Kant by appealing to the unconditioned, because that means nothing to oneself. One will not think of answering Kant by appealing to the 'is' as unconditioned, as attaining an absolute, as reaching something independent of the subject, as reaching *ens*. One would not think of knowing objects as knowing several *entia* and knowing their real distinctions or of knowing subject and object by knowing the subject as an *ens*, as something that is affirmed. All that would be meaningless. One really would be in the same boat as Kant. How, then, would one meet him? One denies the existence of any a priori; one says that knowing really is taking a look at what is out there, and that is all there is to it. But of course that answer does not impress anyone in the Kantian stream of thought, because such a one would know that Berkeley and Hume made a mess of that position.

3.3 More Recent Variations [23]

We will now investigate another stream of thought that will put us in touch with a great deal of contemporary writing. Kant wrote a critique not only of pure reason but also of practical reason. And it is an implication of the work of Bergson that Kant's pure reason is transformed into a merely practical reason. According to Bergson, reality is the *élan vital*; it is dynamic, a flow; and any intellectual activity involves a falsification of the flow, an imposition of abstract, rigid categories upon the flow, so that all that can be known of reality by intellect is simply a series of cross-sections that cannot do justice to the reality. On that view, Kantian pure reason cannot be pure reason; it is simply something that is useful. The Kantian categories of a priori forms and ideals of reason and so on have become simply a set of useful directives that lead to the construction and development of science. This science has great utility, but it is not a matter of pure reason, of pure intellect knowing

23 LN 80 opens this section with the following, not treated in the lecture.
  'a) Idealists: to reassert pure reason in a new manner
     to provide philosophy as instrument in man's making of man; historicism
     differs from earlier problem of method.
     Fail to reach notion of virtually unconditioned; hence no facts.'

reality, and it cannot be. This is not the whole of Bergson's view of science, but the general drift of Bergsonian influence was to break down the Kantian distinction between pure and practical reason. Kant's pure reason, in the last analysis, is merely practical.

The same implication or assertion is found in the Italian idealist, Benedetto Croce. Croce distinguished three human activities: intuition, perception, and action. By intuition, which pertains to art, he means the vital balance between an image and a retinue of emotions and feelings. That is the essence of art. Perception for him is judgment. Judgment gives history (in the sense of what you *think* happened in the past) and philosophy. Every age finds a new meaning, a new interpretation of the past, because it has a new viewpoint. So history is always in the present, and that history is also philosophy. Finally, there is action, and the directive of action, the basis of human action, is found in mathematics and science. So for Croce mathematics and science belong simply to the practical side of human nature, doing things.

Again, the fundamental element in mathematics is group theory. Note that I say 'fundamental.' Bourbaki distinguished three basic sources of mathematics: first, the group; second, the order (the series of natural numbers, the correspondences, functions, what is operated on); and finally, the interpretation of the symbols, of which the fundamental one is topology, the most general type of geometry. So group theory does not exhaust the whole of mathematics – I mustn't give that impression – though it is the most fundamental of the three sources. Group theory, as a group of operations, again suggests that mathematical and scientific knowledge is merely practical. It is not knowing the real essences of things, the reality of things; it is knowing how to operate upon things. Finally, pragmatism reaches the same conclusion in a much less elaborate fashion.[24] The pragmatist simply asks, 'What difference does it make?' and if you cannot point to a difference, 'Well, so what?'

Now you can see why the existentialists are very little concerned with science. Whereas physical science, in the form of Newtonian mechanics, may be regarded as a fundamental element in the inspiration of Kant, in the twentieth century it has passed out of the picture, it has become simply a part of practical reason, something that is of interest to people who do things, but not of any concern to the philosopher or the humanist. Now to deal with this problem we have to go back to the meaning and significance

24 LN 80 has, 'Pragmatism: same conclusion from more primitive source.'

of the distinction between pure and practical reason in Kant, or more fundamentally, speculative and practical intellect in the scholastic position. As I noted already, if one thinks psychologically in the concrete, one thinks about the flow of consciousness. One notes that consciousness flows in different patterns. It can flow in the artistic pattern, in the dramatic pattern of ordinary living in which I am dealing with other people, in the practical pattern of people who do things, who get things done, in the intellectual pattern of people like Thales tumbling into the well when he was studying the stars, in the mystical pattern of people who withdraw entirely from the imaginative world. Consciousness, then, flows in many patterns. What is meant fundamentally by pure reason, in terms of the patterns of the flow of consciousness, is consciousness within the intellectual pattern of experience, consciousness as dominated by the desire to understand and by the reflectiveness that follows from understanding. The whole of consciousness in the intellectual pattern is orientated upon these objectives. If consciousness is within the intellectual pattern, then whether or not what is so attained has practical results is immaterial. If through the intellectual pattern of experience one arrives at the unconditioned, one arrives at truth and being, and that is all that can be demanded. That is the formulation, concretely, of what is meant by speculative intellect or pure reason. If your attainments in the intellectual pattern of experience are the sort of thing that you can live out, then you are being an intelligent and rational man. You are living concretely up to the level of what you know. This is the basis of the autonomy of spirit. It is the ideal of the ethical man. Religion simply places the ethical man within the broader context of God, his creator and judge, and of human history as the field within which he exercises his autonomy. So I do not believe there is anything more than an apparent argument from group theory or from the tendencies of people like Bergson, or from idealists like Croce, to belittle science and consider it as merely practical.

There is also in contemporary thought a survival of subjectivism. There is very little difficulty understanding the naturalists, and the naturalists are, of course, the dominant figures in the English-speaking world, though differently in England from North America. However, the German thinkers belong to a historicist tradition. They are both more illuminating and more dangerous, because more obscure.

In both Heidegger and Jaspers, one is in the field in which the unconditioned, truth, and truth as the medium through which being is known have not been reached. Heidegger speaks a great deal of *das Seiende* and of *Sein*. He aims at an ontology, but he is quite clear that he has not got there yet, and he does not see how one can. He deals with the ontic in the hope of being able to arrive at an ontology. (Ontology means an account of being; ontic is just being.) What does Heidegger mean by *das Seiende*? He means the given as merely given, as stripped of all intelligibility, which, after all, comes from the intelligence of the subject. To know *das Seiende* one needs a breakdown of consciousness, because consciousness intellectualizes, makes intelligible the whole flow of experience. You need a breakdown of consciousness to know what *das Seiende* is.

Sartre, in his *La nausée* – the passage is repeated in an appendix to de Waelhens' book on Heidegger[25] – describes a man sitting in a rather dusty, slummy sort of park and seeing the roots of a tree, and *merely* seeing the roots of the tree. There is no intelligibility to them at all; they are just there. Artistic apprehension can make a thing like that stand right out. And for there to be absolutely no meaning, no significance to it, normal consciousness has to have a breakdown. You are confronted with what is, with the universe apart from man. Man is the source of all intelligibility in the universe. It is by human inquiry and understanding and activity that intelligibility accrues to the universe. *Das Seiende* is the merely given without any intelligible embellishment attributed to it by human consciousness. And *Sein* is the contribution of human intelligence, what is added to *das Seiende* by insight.

Heidegger's concern is with the subject. What kind of intelligibility, what kind of insights are given to *das Seiende* by the subject? There is his insignificant subject, *das Man*, the cipher, the average someone, the primitive as far as intellectual development goes. He is a conformist, a drifter, in the modern mechanized world. Heidegger has a devastating description of his *das Man*, somebody, anybody.

What does Heidegger's philosophy lead to? He talks a great deal about the development of the subject, the subject's being in the truth, but he does not get very far, at least in any perceptible fashion. It is insofar as the subject is in the truth that he will add to the mere data an intelligibility that is, so to speak, artistically satisfying. You can see from that position, of course, that there is no question of getting on to any ontology, which is to attain to rational affirmation: 'It is.' Heidegger's philosophy is a concrete phenomenological description of man living on the levels of *das Seiende* and *Sein*, and

25 Jean-Paul Sartre, *La nausée* (Paris: Gallimard, 1938); in English, *Nausea*, trans. Robert Baldick (Harmondsworh: Penguin, 1965); Alphonse de Waelhens, *La philosophie de Martin Heidegger* (Louvain: Publications Universitaires de Louvain, 1942) 367–69. Lonergan mentioned that the latter book had gone through four or five editions.

knowing that anything he understands is his addition to a nonintelligible world. You can see in that Heidegger's desire to get behind Plato and Aristotle to the early nature philosophers of Greece. His philosophy is of an artistic tendency, and in that way it is quite fine. It is also a useful philosophy; he has great capacities for analysis and description, and his philosophy is probably of real use to depth psychology and psychiatry.

We turn now for a moment to Jaspers. He was a professor of psychology in a German university. As a young man, he wanted to be a philosopher, but he thought that no one intended to be a philosopher any more than anyone intended to be a poet; you had to get a profession and do something; and so he became a psychologist, and his early works were in this field. Gradually he moved to philosophy. Jaspers's concern is also with the subject. He has a first-hand acquaintance with science because of his professional studies. His idea of science is empiricist and pragmatist. He can give you magnificent descriptions and analyses of the experiencing, intelligent, rational subject. His philosophy is mostly worked out by explanations of the meanings of German words, but it is brilliant in its nuances.

Jaspers's two fundamental concepts are *Existenz* and *Transzendenz*, existence and transcendence. As he states in his *Philosophie*,[26] these words mean what is expressed by mythical consciousness with the names 'soul' and 'God.' Why is it that Jaspers uses these two terms and says that their meaning is equivalent to what the mythmaker named soul and God? It is because he sees no answer to Kant. He is in line with Kant's *Critique of Practical Reason*, the moral side of Kant, as well as with Nietzsche and Kierkegaard, and he made them much more profound and far-reaching. He has no idea of rational consciousness reaching the unconditioned and using truth as a medium through which reality is known. Because he does not have that idea, the only knowledge he can have is of two kinds: the knowledge you can have from pragmatic science – it works – and the experience one can have of oneself as experiencing, intelligent, reasonable, free, and responsible. In one's experiencing oneself, above all as free and responsible, one has an *experience* of soul. But one must not speak of soul as though one were knowing a reality through that experience. For him, there is no way of breaking the Kantian immanence. If you could break the Kantian immanence, then you could use the word 'soul' and be talking about a reality; but you cannot break it, and so to talk about soul as though it were a reality is myth. In this experi-

---

26 Karl Jaspers, *Philosophie* (Berlin: Springer-Verlag, 1932); in English, *Philosophy*, 3 vols., trans. E.B. Ashton (Chicago: University of Chicago Press, 1969, 1970, 1971).

ence his philosophy is aimed at an illumination of *Existenz*. It is a matter of self-appropriation. Self-appropriation is, of course, *essential* to Jaspers, because he has no way of saying anything that is true, that corresponds to reality. That is blocked off by his Kantian assumptions, his failure to get beyond Kant. His philosophy aims at an illumination of *Existenz*, and in self-awareness, in the illumination that self can have in experiencing itself, there emerges an awareness of *Transzendenz* in the exercise of freedom, especially in the exercise of freedom in limiting situations, situations involving guilt, struggle, suffering, and death.

The universe for Jaspers is a set of ciphers. One can interpret the ciphers and use them as means heading to transcendence. (We can think here of Bonaventure's ascent of the soul to God.) But to think we are knowing anything in that, rather than[27] merely giving an artistic interpretation to the world, would be metaphysics; and metaphysics is myth.

Now the people who write about Jaspers usually are very rich thinkers on the spiritual side of their lives. About half of the essays in the volume of the Library of Living Philosophers devoted to Karl Jaspers are by Americans; and if you want to pick out a group of contemporary American philosophers who think and write in a very spiritual fashion, you should read those essays. I call attention especially to the one by Kaufmann (though he disagrees with Jaspers.)[28] People moving in that circle are spiritually akin to us, but they do not have the philosophic apparatus to talk the way we do. They want to talk about the soul and God; that is their chief interest, and the whole meaning of life for them. But they do not know about the unconditioned, nor about reaching being.

Finally, there is a series of books by a French Catholic priest by the name of Henry Duméry.[29] He attempted to develop a philosophy and theology simply in terms of the subject, simply in terms of what Jaspers was talking about, without bothering about the object. Bothering about the object is *chosisme*, thingism. There is a great deal of this sort of thing in France at the present time. It is a reaction against the superficial interpretation of scho-

27 We are editing here; Lonergan said 'that you are merely giving an artistic interpretation ...'
28 Fritz Kaufmann, 'Karl Jaspers and a Philosophy of Communication,' in Paul Arthur Schilpp, ed., *The Philosophy of Karl Jaspers* (New York: Tudor, 1957) 210–95.
29 Lonergan does not mention specific titles. A list of many of Duméry's books appears opposite the title page of his *La foi n'est pas un cri* (Paris: Editions du Seuil, 1959). Lonergan mentioned in an aside that Duméry's books were 'put on the Index this last year.'

lasticism. There is in Duméry's work a great deal of inspiration from Plotinus, who is reinterpreted as a subjectivist.

I have given a general scheme of the three levels of consciousness and the three general types of philosophy, and on this basis I have given very brief indications of how one can use that fundamental orientation to understand, and at the same time see the limitations of, fundamental philosophic terms. The utility of that is that, insofar as one can really be at home in it, one can read without danger and with fruit a great deal of work done by non-Catholics.

8

Piaget and the Idea of
a General Education[1]

I have mentioned Piaget several times, and I would now like to relate his work to my idea of a general education,[2] as opposed to vocational training, technical education, and professional education. What is the idea of a general education?

1   General Background

Piaget began his scientific career as a biologist. He then moved into child psychology, and spent thirty years at it, with the aim of working out a genetic epistemology. During these thirty years he was connected with the faculty of science at Geneva, and also no doubt with the Institut Jean-Jacques Rousseau, a pedagogical institute in Geneva. He has two volumes on children from the ages of zero to two: *La naissance de l'intelligence chez l'enfant*,[3] and *La construction du réel chez l'enfant*.[4] In these two volumes there figure largely his

---

1 Second part of the eighth lecture, Wednesday, August 12, 1959.
2 The tape begins with Lonergan saying, 'and take advantage of that occasion to say something on the idea of a general education, as opposed ...' The notes of F. Crowe indicate that Lonergan's meaning is captured in our recasting of this first sentence.
3 Jean Piaget, *La naissance de l'intelligence chez l'enfant* (Neuchâtel, Paris: Delacheux et Niestlé, 1936); in English, *The Origins of Intelligence in Children*, trans. Margaret Cook (New York: International Universities Press, 1952).
4 Jean Piaget, *La construction du réel chez l'enfant* (Neuchâtel, Paris: Delacheux et Niestlé, 1937); in English, *The Constitution of Reality in the Child*, trans. Margaret

three children Jacqueline, Lucienne, and Laurent. He describes the tests he used to try out his ideas on them. He also has written on the representation of the world in the child's mind,[5] on the language and thought of the child,[6] on judgment and reasoning in the child,[7] and on moral judgment in the child.[8] I have already mentioned this last study in talking of the way children play marbles. He has studies on physical causality,[9] chance,[10] and space,[11] and on spontaneous geometry.[12] The spontaneous geometry of the child is not Euclidean. It is topology. Topology is a matter of proximity. If twisting a piece of sponge rubber does not effect any geometrical change, you are in topology. Every piece of the rubber that was next to another piece remains next to it, even though the rubber is twisted. This is the most fundamental type of geometry. You can move into more specific fields, either into projective types of geometry or into metrical types.

Cook (New York: Basic Books, 1954). Lonergan gave these first two titles in an English translation of his own, indicating that he did not know which of Piaget's books had been translated into English. His notes reveal extensive reading of the French works. They also contain a full-page bibliography of Piaget's works (LN 82).

5 Jean Piaget, *La représentation du monde chez l'enfant* (Paris: Alcan, 1926); in English, *The Child's Conception of the World*, trans. Joan and Andrew Tomlinson (New York: Harcourt, Brace and World, 1929).

6 Jean Piaget, *Le langage et la pensée chez l'enfant* (Neuchâtel, Paris: Delacheux et Niestlé, 1923); in English, *The Language and Thought of the Child*, trans. M. Gabain (New York: Meridian, 1955).

7 Jean Piaget, *Le jugement et le raisonnement chez l'enfant* (Neuchâtel, Paris: Delacheux et Niestlé, 1924); in English, *Judgment and Reasoning in the Child*, trans. Marjorie Worden (New York: Harcourt, Brace and World, 1928).

8 Jean Piaget, *Le jugement moral chez l'enfant* (Paris: Alcan, 1932); in English, *The Moral Judgment of the Child*, trans. Marjorie Gabain (London: Routledge and Kegan Paul, 1932).

9 Jean Piaget, *La causalité physique chez l'enfant* (Paris: Alcan, 1927); in English, *The Child's Conception of Physical Causality*, trans. Marjorie Worden (New York: Harcourt, Brace and World, 1932).

10 Jean Piaget and Bärbel Inhelder, *La genèse de l'idée de hasard chez l'enfant* (Paris: Presses Universitaires de France, 1951); in English, *The Origin of the Idea of Chance in Children*, trans. Lowell Leake, Jr., Paul Burrell, and Harold D. Fishbein (London: Routledge and Kegan Paul, 1975).

11 Jean Piaget and Bärbel Inhelder, *La représentation de l'espace chez l'enfant* (Paris: Presses Universitaires de France, 1948); in English, *The Child's Conception of Space*, trans. F.J. Langdon and J.L. Lunzer (London: Routledge and Kegan Paul, 1963).

12 Jean Piaget, Bärbel Inhelder, and Alina Szeminska, *La géometrie spontanée de l'enfant* (Paris: Presses Universitaires de France, 1948); in English, *The Child's Conception of Geometry*, trans. G.A. Lunzer (London: Routledge and Kegan Paul, and New York: Basic Books, 1960).

He also has studies of the child's ideas on number and quantity,[13] and a series of monographs on the formation of symbols in the child's mind, *La formation du symbole chez l'enfant*.[14] He has written a book on each of these topics, some of them in collaboration with others, some by himself alone.

These monographs started appearing in the 1920s. At the end of the 1940s, Piaget started putting out theoretical works. He has presented a summary of his notion of intelligence in *La psychologie de l'intelligence*.[15] It gives all his notions on the psychology of intelligence, but you have to do a considerable amount of reading in the other works to grasp what he is talking about here. He has another work, *Classes, Relations, and Numbers*,[16] and a treatise on logic, *Traité de logique*,[17] which attempts to reduce symbolic logic to group theory.

In 1950 the Presses Universitaires de France published a three-volume work, *Introduction à l'épistemologie génétique*,[18] in which Piaget sets forth what he had been aiming at in all the previous studies. In the first volume he treats mathematics, in the second physics, and in the third biology, psychology, and sociology. He has attracted the attention of the Rockefeller Foundation and of the Sorbonne, where he is part-time professor in addition to his teaching in Geneva. The Rockefeller Foundation enabled him to bring to Geneva every year three or four top people in some specialized field. He works with them, and at the end of the year invites a dozen others to discuss the results of the work done during the year, which they then publish. In col-

13 Jean Piaget and Alina Szeminska, *La genèse du nombre chez l'enfant* (Neuchâtel, Paris: Delacheux et Niestlé, 1941); in English, *The Child's Conception of Number*, trans. C. Cattegno and F.M. Hodgson (London: Routledge and Kegan Paul, and New York: Humanities Press, 1952). Jean Piaget and Bärbel Inhelder, *Le développement des quantités chez l'enfant. Conservation et atomisme* (Neuchâtel, Paris: Delacheux et Niestlé, 1941). 2nd expanded ed., *Le développement des quantités physiques chez l'enfant. Conservation et atomisme* (Neuchâtel, Paris: Delacheux et Niestlé, 1962).

14 Jean Piaget, *La formation du symbole chez l'enfant: Imitation, jeu et rêve. Image et représentation* (Neuchâtel, Paris: Delacheux et Niestlé, 1945); in English, *Play, Dreams and Imitation in Childhood*, trans. C. Cattegno and F.M. Hodgson (New York: W.W. Norton, 1951).

15 Jean Piaget, *La psychologie de l'intelligence* (Paris: A. Colin, 1947); in English, *The Psychology of Intelligence*, trans. M. Piercey and D.E. Berlyne (London: Routledge and Kegan Paul, 1950).

16 Jean Piaget, *Classes, relations et nombres: essai sur les 'groupements' de la logistique et la réversibilité de la pensée* (Paris: Vrin, 1942).

17 Jean Piaget, *Traité de logique* (Paris: A. Colin, 1949).

18 Jean Piaget, *Introduction à l'épistémologie génétique*, 3 vols. (Paris: Presses Universitaires de France, 1950).

laboration he published four volumes in 1957 and at least two more in 1958. The general title of this series is *Studies in Genetic Epistemology*.[19]

2   Assimilation and Adjustment

2.1   The Fundamental Idea

Piaget's fundamental idea is that a development is a sum of adaptations, and that an adaptation has two poles, two elements that are at least notionally distinct and can become really distinct. Those two elements are assimilation and adjustment.[20]

An adaptation is an assimilation insofar as the activity involved in it proceeds from a preexisting scheme of operations. But it is an adjustment insofar as the preexisting scheme is modified because the objects, the circumstances, or the end differ from those of previous uses of the scheme. A child has a sensorimotor structure that enables it spontaneously to feed at the breast, and feeding in a number of instances makes the child much more efficient at the operation. The sensorimotor scheme involves elements from both the biological and the psychic levels. The scheme fundamentally is hereditary, but it develops with practice, and it can be differentiated. When the child gains sufficient control over its arm, it is able to stick its thumb in its mouth and suck again. It is performing the same scheme but on a different object, and performing it on a different object involves a certain amount of adjustment. There is an adaptation insofar as the preexisting scheme is functioning in a modified way upon a different object.

It was in biology that Piaget had formed this notion of adaptation as assimilation plus adjustment, preexisting scheme of activity shifted in some manner to deal with a new object or under new circumstances. He then applied it throughout the development of the child, and he applied it to the mathematical scientist. Insofar as the mathematical scientist draws upon his knowledge of mathematics, he is assimilating preexisting schemes of oper-

19 Lonergan added humorously, 'So you can see he's a big-time operator.'
20 Lonergan indicated that 'adjustment' was his own English word for Piaget's French *accommodation*. On the distinctions, notional and real, between assimilation and adjustment, LN 84 reads, 'Adaptation involves two elements, notionally distinct, and only in varying degrees really distinct inasmuch as the development stresses one aspect rather than another for a time.'

ations; and insofar as he carries out experiments and observations and fits his mathematics onto the results obtained by the experiments and observations, he is adjusting.[21]

So you can see that the notion of assimilation and adjustment is a notion that is *functional*. In other words, it involves no denial of the differences among merely organic development, psychic development in the child, and intellectual development in the scientist discovering a new theory. The three can be functionally analogous and yet differ in content. Piaget does not reduce everything to nothing but biology or nothing but sensitive psychology. He acknowledges differences where they exist, and his theory can be applied analogously to different levels — to the biological, to the sensitive psyche, and to intellectual activity.

As a psychological theory his position explicitly differs from the associationist position, which is in terms of images and the similarity between images. It differs, too, from a psychology of needs. Piaget has no doubt of needs, but he considers a need as simply an introspective aspect of the scheme. Again, his theory differs from the theory of the conditioned reflex. The conditioned reflex is simply an accidental elaboration of a scheme, one that lasts just as long as it gives satisfactory results. According to Piaget, conditioned reflexes do not produce permanent differences. Finally, his position differs from Gestalt theory. They are similar insofar as in each case the scheme has a structure, a form. But the structure for Piaget is an operational structure, whereas the structure in Gestalt theory is within the percept.[22]

Again, Piaget's position grounds active methods. Development proceeds from the activities of the subject, from what the subject already can do. There has to be something to work on, and what there is to work on is what the subject already can do. Consequently, habits for Piaget are not impressed passivities, but acquired modes of activity developed out of previous modes of activity. His general analysis accounts for the fact of repetition. (Chesterton has a marvelous passage on the child saying, Do it again, Do it

21 LN 84 has, '... in the mathematical scientist (hypotheses from maths are assimilative element; process of verification, adjustment).'
22 LN 84 has, 'As a psychological theory, it differs from: associationist: conjunction of images, percepts, via similarity
        'need: the need is an introspective aspect of the scheme, not the whole story
        'conditioned reflex: cr continues to function only so long as condition is fulfilled, the functioning meets with success
        'Gestalt: there is a form but it is a form of operation or the form of a group of operations.'

again.)[23] The child is always willing to repeat. Piaget's view accounts for this repetition. Just as the organ develops by functioning and atrophies from lack of functioning, so the sensorimotor and perceptual schemes of activity develop by functioning. The child, by feeding at the breast, learns to feed at the breast, learns to do it better. Repetition, then, has a utility; it is a means of development, and so there is a real reason for it. Finally, Piaget says that his analysis explains the mode of development, why new schemes of activity result from the differentiation and combination of previous schemes.

Piaget's volumes are enormously detailed. He does not talk in generalities, but to back up what he says he presents scientifically collected cases of instances and calls on collaborators. So he presents an enormously detailed and at the same time a brilliantly organized account of how the child develops, what the child can and cannot do at any stage, why there are different stages, and why the child can or cannot do these different things at these different stages. As an explanation of the course of development, what he offers is, from a certain viewpoint at least, a complete theoretical structure that organizes an enormous mass of details.

2.2   Generalization and Differentiation

Piaget distinguishes cumulative repetition of a mode of activity, such as grabbing something, from generalization and differentiation. When the child learns to close its fingers, it will grab anything it can get its hands on, and it will do this again and again. This is cumulative repetition, the repetition of the operation for the sake of the operation — looking for the sake of looking, sucking for the sake of sucking, grabbing for the sake of grabbing, talking for the sake of talking. But there occur as well a generalization and a differentiation of the scheme. There is a generalization insofar as the scheme that has been developed by repetition is used on new objects, and a differentiation insofar as new activities are added because of these differences in the object. When the scheme becomes differentiated, there occurs a recognition of differences in the object. That is a first level of development.[24]

23 Gilbert Keith Chesterton, *Orthodoxy* (London: The Bodley Head, 1908, reprinted 1949) 92–93, in 'The Ethics of Elfland.' Lonergan had a long-standing affection for and admiration of Chesterton, and had written short articles on him years earlier (1931 and 1943).
24 LN 84: 'Generalizing and differentiating: using the developed scheme on new objects in new ways; adjustments of the original scheme; basis of recognizing differences.'

But any single scheme develops, and as Piaget says, every scheme tends to embrace the whole universe. When the child puts everything in its mouth, it is developing an oral space prior to a space based upon the body. Group theory appears in his analysis as soon as different developed generalized schemes start combining with one another. Looking is combined with grabbing, so that the child does not put into its mouth what it grabs, but looks at it; conversely what it sees it grabs. We have here the construction of a larger whole out of two prior schemes. This combining of different schemes is a building up of a group of operations. What is lacking in this stage of development is the completeness of the group. For example, consider displacement in space, movement. You walk a certain distance with a child and come back. But for the child this is not coming back; rather, there have occurred two displacements, and they have not been synthesized into going and coming back. Piaget is able to establish that at a certain stage the operations of displacement have not yet been grouped. His stages are groups of operations on a certain level.

One group of operations gives the mastery of the movements of the child's own body. This mastery enables it to deal with objects in nearby space, to be master in the nursery, where it can go and get and handle anything it wants.

Next, there is the insertion of language and symbols into these operations. Here there are operations of a different kind, operations with words, moving toward a group of operations with words. Children from two to six cannot carry on a conversation. If two children of this age are together, they will both be talking, but they are not talking to one another. Nor can they give an explanation or tell a story. They have not mastered talking as a group of operations. Piaget is satisfied that, with concrete operations, the grouping will brusquely emerge by the time the child is seven or eight years of age. But before that, the operations are easily blocked. He provides all sorts of illustrations of this. At the age of eleven or twelve, there emerges the grouping of operations that are not concrete, operations that use propositions or statements as an intermediary. Then there emerges the capacity to argue and reason.

2.3 Group Theory

Some knowledge of group theory is necessary if one is to understand what Piaget is doing. He is using the idea of the group of operations. When the group or rounded whole is attained, there occurs what Piaget calls a stage in development. Moving up to the group, the child is able to perform a number of the operations, but not the whole system. Consequently, there will be points where he will be blocked, where he will not be able to do things or figure things out. Piaget is able to discern where the group of operations will be lacking. He gives the child things to do and finds that the group has not yet been attained. The child reaches an equilibrium, a capacity to act on a given level, when the group is attained. Development is occurring along a certain line, and the development is attained when the group is attained. From the notion of the group Piaget derives a theoretical structure that defines when development is still occurring and the group has not yet been attained, and again when development is attained. So his theoretical structure gives a precise meaning to stages and to the 'not yet attained' of stages.

Piaget thinks up very implausible types of experiments. For example, he will have two large bottles full of water, and he will pour the water from one into a series of smaller bottles. He will then put the empty bottle aside and ask the children, Is there more water in the big bottle or in the series of little ones? Now the children just look; they will not know. It is only at a certain stage, when, instead of comparing the end results, they think of the process and realize that no more water was added and none was spilt, that they will know there is the same amount of water in the series of smaller bottles as in the larger bottle. And only two years later will they be able to apply the same sort of thing to another problem — if we cut something up, does the whole weigh more than the sum of the parts? Again, it is a matter of thinking of and understanding the process, not of comparing the end results. Piaget constructs endless experiments and gives surprising tests to children, but his fundamental inspiration is the idea of the group. And, of course, the notion of the group of operations is used here in a sense that is merely analogous to the use in mathematics. He is not talking about mathematical operations, but about the operations of the child in looking, grabbing, and so on.[25]

25 The lecture contains much that is not in Lonergan's notes, but LN 85 has a few items not mentioned in the lecture: 'Difficulties in process of development explained by fact that grouping not yet attained: analogous problems recur on successive levels
    'Meaning: activities within functioning scheme related to one another; what does not come within the scope of any scheme is vague, neglected, marginal, cause of ill ease; (at the horizon).'

2.4 Language

Piaget has illuminating things to say about language. The child's difficulty does not consist merely in learning words. The child has to learn a universe of meanings, as well as a set of words that are not his own invention. The child would like to have a language of its own, its own grammar, which is much more logical than the one learned. Moreover, the universe of meanings of words does not consist in the meanings that the child has developed. This is the basic stage of the socialization of the child's mind.

2.5 Symbolic Play and Imitation

Piaget's volume on the symbol is brilliant. Symbolic play, 'Let's pretend,' the make-believe, is assimilation on its own. The child is living in a world that simply does not exist; everything is make-believe; and it is at this from morning till night, with the greatest intensity. I take a daily walk through the Borghese Gardens while the children are playing. Some of them have expensive toys, and others have just a stick. They are playing cops and robbers, or some such game, and the stick is just as good as the expensive toy; the child with the stick is having just as good a time as the others. It is all make-believe. This is a case of assimilation, of constructing the sensorimotor and perceptual schemes of activity without bothering whether they fit into any real world or not. As a matter of fact they do not, but nonetheless this is an important aspect of the child's development.

During the same period of development, there is also imitation of what others do. That imitation is acting out the percept. Before consciousness is differentiated, a perception is incomplete until it is acted out. Imitation is the element of adjustment at this period. Though adaptation is a combination of assimilation and adjustment, in this period of symbolic play the two are developing apart. The child learns adjustment by imitation, and it develops its powers of assimilation by the instrument of symbolic play. Piaget gives the following example of assimilation. During the day his daughter had seen a cat run along a wall, hop onto a tree, and climb the tree to the top. That night she was playing in the house with a pebble and a cardboard box, and she started moving the pebble along the top of the cardboard box, saying, 'Cat.' Then she brought the pebble to her breast and said, 'Tree.' Finally, she put the pebble on her head and said, 'Top.' Those were about the words she could handle at the time. This symbolic play is the child's means of developing assimilation. The whole period of symbolic play is one in which the assimilative side is developed. Though development is both assimilation and adjustment, at a certain period the two develop independently, just as in growth, which can be longitudinal and then out another way, in a certain rhythm — one doesn't grow in all directions at the same speed, one grows more in one way than in the other at different times.

Piaget's book on the symbol is so filled with details that one really has to read it to appreciate what he is saying. It presents some brilliant criticisms of Freudianism. When he speaks about the formation of unconscious symbols, Piaget points out that anatomical symbols are not restricted to the sexual organs, as the Freudians would lead us to believe. Rather, these symbols form quite a general phenomenon of experiences of the kinesthetic or tactile order being expressed on the visual plane. For example, if a person goes to sleep with cotton batting between two teeth, he is apt to dream of two big rocks with moss between them. The feeling of the cotton between the teeth has been translated; the feeling is thrown onto the visual plane.

2.6 Subject and World

There is another fundamental point in Piaget's idea of development. As the group of operations is developed, there occurs a concomitant development. There is a development, on the one side, of the world, and, on the other side, of the self-conscious subject. It is as though there were two circles, the world and the subject. Experience before the development, leading up to the group of operations, is, as it were, at the tangential point, where there is a minimum of objectivity and subjectivity. When development moves to the level of the group of operations, the group orders all the objects. That is the general idea of group theory. The fact that the operations are a group gives a dominance over the objects that come under the group. The objects become an organized whole on a certain level — on the level of the nursery, on the level of elementary childish talking, and so on. So as sensorimotor schemes multiply, become coordinated, and are extended to ever greater ranges of objects, the world becomes a spatially and causally integrated set of objects. Assimilation and adjustment become ever more differentiated. The specialization of adjustment in imitation and of assimilation in symbolic play is an illustration of their separation. The subject is distinct from his world; and insofar as the subject becomes capable of decentering, of seeing things from a different viewpoint, in different perspectives, he becomes just another object in his own world.

Piaget writes that 'the essential epistemological significance of the hypothesis of assimilation amounts to the supposition that objectivity is constructed through the coordination of operations or actions, and does not result simply from the play of perceptions and associations.'[26] The child constructs an objective world by grouping operations. Just as the mathematician, with different types of operations, has complete dominance over his objects because his operations form a group, similarly the child – insofar as different sensorimotor schemes multiply and become differentiated and coordinated, so that he is able to perform the reversible operations, to go back to the starting point in any sense of the word – will be able to link all the operations together, to use any one of them at will, and to combine them all into a complete circle at any time. The command of the operations becomes a command of the objects of the operations. And insofar as the totality of objects of the operations is commanded, the child has an ordered universe, a world, a horizon. One's horizon corresponds to the group of operations one has mastered.

2.7 Evaluation

I asked Georges Cruchon, professor of pedagogical psychology at the Gregorian University, what he thought of Piaget. He answered, 'C'est un mathématicien.' There is in Piaget's work, undoubtedly, a brilliant theoretical structure that puts things together. Of itself it is not a distorting structure. It leaves him open to recognize differences among the organic, the sensitive, and the intellectual. There is a tendency, of course, simply to emphasize the elements in the development that correspond to his conceptual tools, and in that sense there is a bias in terms of the grouping of operations.[27] But in his account of the child's world, Piaget is not working with the most accurate notions of the primitive mind. He speaks, for example, of stages, of elements of animism in the process of the development of the child's mind. But his statements in that area can, I believe, be made entirely acceptable if they are reformulated in a more satisfactory context. Development as knowledge is a matter of differentiating *ens*, being. It is a matter of knowing that *A* is, that *B* is, and that *A* is not *B*, and a matter of knowing that making those judgments is significant – *that* is the big catch. The major question is, Does this really count? Does it mean something to make

26 Quoted from LN 85, which gives as the source *Lecture de l'expérience* (1958) 59.
27 LN 86 has, 'Tendency to think of development as intellectual, and of intellectual development as moving to level of logico-mathematical operations.'

such judgments? If this is really what our knowledge ultimately is, then there will be a period when the universal is not distinguished from the particular. There will be a primitive stage of mentality characterized by mythic consciousness.[28]

The reality of that primitive stage of mentality has been illustrated rather beautifully by Christopher Ryan, in his account of his visit to a leprosarium in the Belgian Congo.[29] There were large numbers of people with a primitive mentality working there. They were doing what they could to communicate ideas of civilization, and one of them was holding courts to settle disputes. But one of the anomalies of these courts was that a large percentage of the disputes that came before them involved accusations of the use of magic. The people thought that way; they had a primitive apprehension of causality that could not be gotten out of their heads, and so that had to be given legal recognition.

I do not think Piaget is to be criticized because he talks of the real world as something that is constructed. I do not think that 'construction' is a word that makes one an idealist or a subjectivist. It does, of course, for people who think that knowing is taking a good look at what is already out there now. But with that idea of knowing one cannot give an adequate response to any unsatisfactory philosophy from Plato to the present day. And that idea is certainly not Aristotelian or Thomist. But Piaget, though his study is scientific and objective, has to be completed by adding a fuller appreciation of the subject, of what has meaning for the subject.[30]

At the present time Piaget is trying to use games theory to account for the process of development from one group of operations to a larger group. Games theory is the latest thing in mathematics. There is an elementary introduction to it by John D. Williams, *The Compleat Strategyst*,[31] which shows

28 LN 86 has, 'More accurate account of mythological features in childish thinking, if grasp that goal is being, that it is reached by drawing distinctions, that until distinctions are drawn explicitly and, especially, until the significance of distinctions (A is not B) is grasped and appreciated, mythic consciousness follows.'

29 We have not been able to locate this reference. It may be that Lonergan was referring, not to a publication, but to some other medium of communication.

30 LN 86 has, 'I have no difficulty with his notion of construction of reality, world, etc.: subjectivity does not mean that knowing is an activity that goes on in me; it does mean that I do not perform that operation with sufficient detachment, that I do not arrive at truth, that I do not think that the real is being
    'To be completed by going on to basic group theory experience −
understanding − judgment.'

31 John Davis Williams, *The Compleat Strategyst, Being a Primer on the Theory of Games of Strategy* (New York: McGraw-Hill, 1954). A revised edition appeared in 1966.

that games theory is a higher-level use of probability. The military is extremely interested in it because it is a way of outwitting the enemy, no matter what he does.

3   General Education as Development in Assimilation

What is Piaget's significance? One way in which his work possesses significance is that his idea of the gradual differentiation between assimilation and adjustment provides a formulation for the idea of a general education. In his terms, general education is development in assimilation, and leaves the problems of adjustment to a later age and a different situation. If the child can develop by symbolic play, then he can develop by studies and activities that increase his assimilative powers but that as yet do not raise questions of the adjustments that have to be made to deal with the real world. In other words, one is educating, in the sense of developing assimilative power, by the teaching of language, by teaching people to read, so that they are able to read not merely the comic books and the captions under the pictures in *Life*, but anything. If people spend long hours reading Thucydides and Plato, they do not find much that has been written since heavy going.[32] They are in training, so that when they sit down with a book they are not overcome with an irresistible urge to go to sleep or to get out somewhere and move around. There is a development in assimilative power in the study of languages and literature. That study does not commit one to any judgments of fact, but it is developing in you a power to assimilate on the most general level, because everything ultimately is communicated through language.[33]

Similarly, the study of mathematics rather than natural science, and of philosophy and history[34] rather than the human sciences, are cases in

32 LN 86 has, 'Learning to read: ie acquiring the ability of sitting down and reading through and understanding and criticizing intelligently any book on any subject no matter how abstruse, difficult, complicated.' The notes also add, 'Learning to write: to marshal one's thoughts, put them in order, enter into the minds of others, hold their attention, reveal to them the reasons that guide one to one's opinions or convictions.'

33 LN 86 adds, 'If insistence on adjustment, then the only learning is of the type of the empirical sciences; one learns what is so, and anything else is just eye wash — Learning what is so is learning particular subjects, multiplication of subjects, overloaded curriculum.'
    Again, 'Element of adjustment, of attention to simple matters of fact in their endless multiplicity not to be overlooked; in principle it is to be instilled; but its detail is not the concern of general education.'

34 LN 86 mentions art and literature, and adds by hand philosophy and history.

206 Topics in Education

which the assimilative power of the student is developing, enabling him to do whatever he may choose in any particular field. Piaget himself was able to move from biology into child psychology, into discussions of symbolic logic and the use of games theory. He had at the start a great development of assimilative powers. He was able to start in biology, get an idea there, and then move into child psychology with the aim of working out, thirty years later, a genetic epistemology.

General education, then, aims primarily at the development of assimilative powers. If one learns to know man through the reading of literature and the study of history, one will have a basis for stepping into the human sciences that is much more useful perhaps than the study of those sciences.[35] If one spent all that time studying the human sciences, what would he know? He would learn what his professor knew of what the bigger men in the field had figured out five, ten, fifteen, twenty, thirty years ago. By the time he set about working in the field, he would have all he could do just to keep abreast. And ten years later everything he knew might be out of date. And would he have the capacity to judge the new, to move with it or stand against it? If he has undergone a more general development of assimilative powers, if he has received a more intimate communication of what it is really to be a man, if he has developed the human touch that comes through the traditional classical or literary education as opposed to the scientific education, then he will have a basis within himself that enables him to judge about human beings and not become a crackpot. It is easy to produce crackpots by premature specialization.

Insofar, then, as Piaget's notion of the differentiation or separability of assimilation and adjustment is correct, there is a validity to the notion of a general education that studies language, art, literature, history, and philosophy rather than the human sciences, and mathematics rather than the natural sciences. Give the student a preparation, a development of his assimilative powers, his ability to move about. The big men today are not specialists; they move about. The outstanding statistical economist, at least in England, is Colin Clark, a professor at Oxford. He started out as a specialist in chemistry. Talcott Parsons has moved around. Albright, at Johns Hopkins, is first in the world in two or three disciplines, fourth or fifth in about seven or eight, and among the first twenty in about twenty disciplines in his more general field of Near Eastern Studies. What general education pro-

35 LN 86 has, 'understand man and one will be able to judge the human scientists.'

vides is a common background for all educated men and women. It provides a sound background for all specialization, making sure that people
have the human touch along with that specialization. It is a basis from which
the educated man can proceed in his leisure, during his time as a student
and later, to the pursuit of any specialized knowledge that interests him.
That, briefly, expresses in a general form what the idea of a general education is.

9

Art [1]

1   From Differentiated Consciousness to Ordinary Living

We have been considering products of differentiated consciousness: mathematics, natural science, philosophy, and pedagogical psychology. In these cases, we have been considering both specialized groups of operations that regard particular fields such as mathematics, natural science, and psychology, and a general group of operations, namely, experiencing, understanding, and judging, precisely as a group. Philosophy considers the total field, seen through the basic group as a group, through its character as a basic group, its structure, and its implications.

We now have to turn back to the operations that are grouped, to ordinary living in its concrete potentialities. Neither mathematics nor natural science nor philosophy nor psychology is the same as life. I propose to seek an apprehension of concrete living in its concrete potentialities, through art today, and through history tomorrow.

I have already had occasion to mention Bergson's doctrine that intellect is not equal to reality, that it is simply an insertion, seeing reality through a screen, taking cross-sections and missing the flow that *is* the reality. There is a similar but inverse doctrine in Aristotle. For Aristotle, reality, insofar as it is movement, insofar as it is dynamic, is not yet equal to intellect. He is saying

---

1 The ninth lecture, Thursday, August 13, 1959. The session began with a belated word of welcome to the participants from the President of Xavier University, Fr Paul O'Connor, SJ. The tape continues with the beginning of Lonergan's lecture.

the same thing as Bergson, but in a different way, from a different viewpoint. Bergson finds that reality is movement, and says that intellect is not equal to knowing it; and Aristotle says that movement is not real enough, not good enough, to be known by intellect. Aristotle conceives movement, not as in any of the categories, but as the coming to be of being in a place. When you are moving, you are not in a place but on your way to a place. When the qualities of a thing are changing, the thing is not black or white, heavy or light, but on its way to being white or heavier, on its way to being of a determinate quality. It is similar with regard to quantity. How big is something that is growing? It is on its way to being a certain size; but the movement itself escapes the category. Movement is the *actus imperfecti inquantum huiusmodi*, or the *actus exsistentis in potentia inquantum huiusmodi*.

One can put this point in a different manner and by putting it in a different manner see how the problems of apprehending the concrete can be turned to some extent by thinking about art and history. Any type of differentiated intellectual consciousness, such as mathematics, science, and philosophy, can express more or less adequately precisely what it is. But any such type of differentiated consciousness is simply a withdrawal for a return. Just as development occurs now in one direction, now in another, and then in a third, and it is only at the end of the whole spiraling process that one has the finished product, so differentiated consciousness is, as it were, a stage in the development. It is a withdrawal from total activity, total actuation, for the sake of a fuller actuation when one returns. What one returns to is the concrete functioning of the whole. In that concrete functioning there is an organic interrelation and interdependence of the parts of the subject with respect to the whole, and of the individual subject with respect to the historically changing group.[2] Art mirrors that organic functioning of sense and feeling, of intellect not as abstract formulation but as concrete insight, of judgment that is not just judgment, but that is moving into decision, free choice, responsible action.[3]

Let us recall by way of a preface to what I am going to attempt to say about art what we said about the good as the developing subject. We must pass from the logical essence of man, something that is common to heroes and scoundrels, mewling infants and saints, something that is verified in everyone equally, to man as concrete potentiality and concrete duty; from man as substance to man as conscious subject; from thinking of a set of faculties

2 The words 'historically changing' are taken from LN 4.
3 LN 4 has, 'of judgment solidified into decision, free choice, responsible action.'

and their actuation to thinking of a concrete flow of consciousness, and to thinking of that concrete flow in terms of the subject and his concern that defines the horizon of his world. The subject is not only in his world, but by his intersubjectivity, which we indicated by the phenomenology of the smile, he has a *Mitwelt*, a world-with-him of other persons with whom he is aware of living. Again, he has a world about him of tools, artifacts, buildings, and so on — an *Umwelt*.[4] That flow of consciousness is captured by Ludwig Binswanger, who used Heidegger's thought to give a new angle to depth psychology.[5] Binswanger wrote a little essay entitled 'Traum und Existenz.'[6] There is a French translation of this essay, *Le rêve et l'existence*,[7] the advantage of which is that Binswanger's rather short essay is prefaced by a long introductory essay by the translator that runs to about 130 pages and helps one get the point. Binswanger distinguishes between the dreams of night and the dreams of morning. The dream of night is influenced organically, for example by the state of one's digestion, and is of no great significance. But the dream of morning is the *Dasein*, the existential subject beginning to posit himself in his world. He is doing so symbolically, but it is the first movement towards being awake. The subject with his concern will be in his world; the world and the subject are simultaneous. The reason Heidegger speaks of *Dasein* is that he does not want any split between subject and object. *Dasein* means the subject and his world; both are simultaneous and correlative. If we think of ourselves that way, we realize that if we know anything about anything it is through meaning, through the intentional order. The stuff of our lives is intentional insofar as we have any consciousness of it at all. Consciousness is not the whole of reality; there are such sciences as biology and neurology, physics and chemistry; but anything that we are above the biological level, and anything that we know, is contained within a field of intentionality, a field that includes the sensitive, intellectual, judicial, and voluntary. These transitions from logical essence to concrete potentiality, from substance to subject, and from faculty psychology to the flow of consciousness are a helpful background to what I want to say about art. And

4 The expression 'an *Umwelt*' is based on LN 4.
5 Part of this sentence is supplied by the editors, in an effort to capture the continuity of thought in the lecture at this point.
6 Ludwig Binswanger, 'Traum und Existenz,' in Binswanger, *Ausgewählte Vorträge und Aufsätze* (Bern: A. Francke, 1947), vol. 1, pp. 74–97; in English, 'Dream and Existence,' in *Being-in-the-World: Selected Papers of Ludwig Binswanger*, trans. Jacob Needleman (New York: Harper Torchbooks, 1963) 222–48.
7 Ludwig Binswanger, *Le rêve et l'existence*, with introduction and notes by Michel Foucault (Paris: Desclée, 1954).

Binswanger's distinction will soon prove helpful in speaking about experiential patterns.[8]

2   A Definition of Art

I propose to reflect on a definition of art that I thought was helpful. It was worked out by Susanne Langer in her book, *Feeling and Form*.[9] She conceives art as an objectification of a purely experiential pattern. If we consider the words one by one, we will have some apprehension of what art is, and through art an apprehension of concrete living.

2.1 Pattern

First we will meditate on the word 'pattern.' Art is the objectification of a purely experiential *pattern*. One can think of an abstract pattern, such as a musical score. It contains all the notes, but it is not the music. It has all the pattern of the music, but the pattern as in the musical score is existing differently from the way it exists when the music is being played. The pattern is being realized concretely only when the music is being played. Again, we can think of the pattern of indentations in a gramophone record. The pattern is there, but the pattern is in the world of sound only when the record is playing. That pattern when the record is playing or the score is played is in the concrete, in these tones; or, with painting, it is in these colors, with sculpture in these volumes, with the dance in these movements. The pattern is the set of internal relations between these tones, or between these colors, or between these volumes, or between these movements. Music is not a note simply by itself. In music a note is related to the other notes with which it is united in the work of art. What we have to attend to are the internal relations. There may be as well an external relation; the work of art may be representative; but that is not the point to attend to. What is to be attended to are the internal relations of the pattern. They are there whether or not the art is representative.

8 The last two sentences are supplied by the editors.
9 Susanne K. Langer, *Feeling and Form: A Theory of Art* (New York: Charles Scribner's Sons, 1953). In fact, this definition does not appear in Langer's book; it seems to be a definition that Lonergan worked out from reading Langer. Langer gives her definition of art on p. 40: 'Art is the creation of forms symbolic of human feeling.'

2.2 Experiential

I have been illustrating the notion of a concrete pattern of internal relations in a work of art. But first we want to think of an *experiential* pattern. The coming to consciousness in the dream of the morning is patterned. The difference between the dream of morning and the dream of night that is under the influence of digestive functions and organic disturbances is that there is more pattern to the dream of morning. Consciousness is a selecting, an organizing.[10] And being awake is more organized than the dream of the morning. Patterning is essential to consciousness. If one hears a tune or a melody, one can repeat it; but if one hears a series of street noises, one cannot reproduce them. The pattern in the tune or melody makes it more perceptible, something that consciousness can pick out and be conscious of, so to speak.

Similarly, verse makes words memorable. One can remember 'Thirty days has September, April, June, and November,' because there is a jingle in it, a pattern to it. And decoration makes a surface visible. We can see curtains better than we can the wall between them because there is a pattern on the curtains. So decoration makes a surface visible because it imposes on it a pattern. Spontaneous patterns, moreover, are organic; decorations and motifs are modeled on roots, trunks, branches, leaves, flowers; the curlicues in carpets have an organic swing to them.[11]

What we experience is patterned because to be conscious of something involves a patterning of what is perceived and a pattern of the feelings that flow out of and are connected with the perceiving. The perceiving is not by itself, not without a pattern. Consciousness, basically and commonly, is undifferentiated, not in some specialized pattern such as the intellectual. But on the sensitive level it is patterned.

2.3 Pure Pattern

Now we have to add a further term. Art is the objectification of a *purely* experiential pattern. We have considered the word 'pattern' and the word 'expe-

---

10 LN 5 adds, 'sensibile in actu est sensus in actu — pattern of perceived is pattern of perceiving.'
11 LN 5 has, 'Logic of Gestalt: organic analogy: root, trunk, branches, leaves, flowers, repeat with variations, growing complexity → organized whole → perceptible.'

riential,' and now we have to attend to the word 'purely.' We do so in two ways: first, insofar as it modifies the term 'pattern,' and second, insofar as it modifies the term 'experiential.' We can say that it modifies both by a process of condensation.

When we speak of a *pure pattern* we mean the exclusion of alien patterns that instrumentalize experience.

First, our senses can be an apparatus for receiving and transmitting signals. At a red light the brake goes on, and at the green the car starts again. Then our senses are just an apparatus for connecting the lights with the movements of the car. Our sensitive living, in such a case, has become simply a sensory apparatus in a mechanical process. The pattern is not *purely* experiential; it is not the subject coming to life in his dream and in his awakening. It is not the sort of pattern that arises out of the subject. It is rather an instrumentalization of man's sensory power.[12]

Secondly, one's senses can be at the service of scientific intelligence. Sensory experience will be patterned by conceptual classification, by genera and series of *differentiae*. A man who knows nothing of botany does not see a flower in the same way as a botanist does. Nor in looking at a bug does the ordinary person see all that the entomologist sees. The scientist will see all kinds of things that ordinary people will miss; and he will see them because he is able to take the whole lot successively into view. The person who has no special knowledge of the flower or the bug does not have the categories in which to organize his sensitive experience. He may attend to various features; the scientist may point them out to him one by one, and he may see them all; but he soon will not know whether they are all different, and he will not be able to repeat the series. His capacities for experiencing have not been developed in the specialized way that makes sense an instrument of scientific intelligence. Again, the geometer will geometrize his experience. Any type of subordination, of putting one's spontaneous consciousness at the disposal of intellect or of a mechanical society, is an instrumentalization of experience. I do not say that there is anything wrong with such instrumentalization, but just that this is not what we want to think about when we think about art.[13]

Thirdly, one's sensitive experience can be reshaped by a psychological or epistemological theory. One can have a notion of sense data and a notion of

12 LN 5 adds, 'automatic behaviour of *ready-made* subject in a *ready-made world.*'
13 LN 5 has, 'what fits into schema (geometrized): what might confirm, oppose judgement: evidence for a proposition.'

objectivity which can make one try to apprehend according to the dictates of the theory. In that fashion one can instrumentalize the experiences one would have, eliminate the spontaneous experiences one would have, or reshape them according to the dictates of the theory. For example, if someone holds that impressions are objective and the patterning of the impressions is subjective, one is introducing a philosophic motif and devaluating the pattern. But if one thinks that one knows when one arrives at truth, then the difference between subjectivity and objectivity does not arise on the level of experience.

Fourthly, experience can be patterned by one's motives, and then one will not have a pure pattern. If during the whole of one's life or a large part of it one is thinking with regard to everything one senses simply of 'what I can get out of it,' then one is putting one's sensitive living at the disposal of a utilitarian motive. There are many ways, then, in which one's sensitive living may be instrumentalized. And when one speaks of a pure pattern of experience one intends to exclude that instrumentalization.[14]

2.4 Purely Experiential

Further, the pattern is purely *experiential.* It is of the seen as seen, of the heard as heard, of the felt as felt. It is accompanied by a retinue of associations, affects, emotions, incipient tendencies that are part of one, that arise spontaneously and naturally from the person. It *can* be didactic, a lesson can arise out of it, but the lesson must not be imposed from outside in the manner of didacticism, moralism, or social realism.[15] The Russian art that attempts to inculcate communist doctrine is not purely experiential.

Moreover, besides the retinue of associations, affects, emotions, tendencies, there is also in the purely experiential pattern what in *Insight* I referred to as the operator. Just as on the intellectual level the operator is wonder, the pure desire to know, so on the sensitive level there is a corresponding operator. With it are associated feelings of awe, fascination, the uncanny. It is an openness to the world, to adventure, to greatness, to goodness, to majesty.[16]

14 On these points LN 5 has, 'reshaped by an a priori theory of experience: *physics, physiology, psychology* of sense; *epistemology*: impressions objective, pattern subjective; *utilitarian*: what can I get out of it; do not experience but move onto other.'
15 The terms 'moralism' and 'social realism' are added from LN 5.
16 See Lonergan, *Insight* 555.

2.5 Release

So far I have been describing largely in terms of exclusion an experience that is purely patterned and purely experiential. More positively, we must note that it is also a release. This in fact is the point to be noted. When experience is in a purely experiential pattern, it is not curtailed, not fitted upon some Procrustean bed. It is allowed its full complement of feelings. Experience falls into its own proper pattern and takes its own line of expansion, development, organization, fulfilment. It is not dictated to by the world of science, the world of inquiry, the world of information, the world of theories about what experience should be, or by utilitarian motives. It *is*. It has its proper rhythm, just as breathing has. In breathing, exhaling occurs, and when it reaches its peak, it sets going the opposite movement of inhaling. A rhythm is a succession of opposite movements where each movement calls forth and makes necessary the other movement. Inhaling builds up tensions that are resolved by exhaling; and exhaling builds up tensions that are resolved by inhaling. Such rhythms can involve increasing variations and complexity. That increase in variation and complexity, like the build-up of a symphony, will be enclosed within a unity. There is what is called the inevitability of form. If you sing a single note, there are no implications as to what the next note must be; but if you sing four or five, the inevitability of form is taking over; there is only a limited number of notes you can go on to. The surprise that the master musician or composer causes is to go on always to further notes that would not occur to you, and yet retain the inevitability of form.[17]

2.6 Elemental Meaning

Now the purely experiential pattern that is also a release has a meaning, but the meaning is elemental. What do I mean by an elemental meaning?

According to the Aristotelian axiom, sense in act is the sensible in act, and intellect in act is the intelligible in act. But a full theory of knowledge cannot be formulated simply on that basis. According to Aristotle, knowledge is rooted in an identity, an identity of the sensible and the sense in act, and of the intellect and the intelligible in act. But if knowledge is merely identity, you are never knowing anything. You have to go beyond that initial identity

---

17 LN 5 verso adds, 'cf. organism: differentiating organs and using them as it grows.'

to reach a knowledge that is *of* something, to reach a meaning that means some 'meant.' This occurs through the pattern of true judgments.[18]

But we are not doing epistemology now. My point now is that meaning has an initial stage, which is the Aristotelian identity, and a second stage when it moves on to a meant, and by elemental meaning I mean that first stage. When meaning is fully developed, we have distinctions between objects; but prior to the fuller development there is an elemental meaning. When meaning involves one in an ontology, it is about objects. But prior to the ontology there is the ontic of which Heidegger speaks; and that is another way of indicating what is meant by elemental meaning.[19]

Let us try to say something more about elemental meaning. It is, first of all, a transformation of one's world. When experience slips into a purely experiential pattern, one is out of the ready-made world of one's everyday living. One's experience is not being instrumentalized to one's functions in society, to one's job, to one's task, to all the things one has to do. It is on its own. One's experience is a component in one's apprehension of reality. And this quite different type of experience that corresponds to the release of the purely experiential pattern is a transformation of the world. To put it another way, it is an opening of the horizon. Some people will say that art is an illusion, others that art reveals a fuller, profounder reality. But the artistic experience itself does not involve a discussion of the issue. What we can say is that it is opening a new horizon, it is presenting something that is other, different, novel, strange, new, remote, intimate — all the adjectives that are employed when one attempts to communicate the artistic experience.

When experience slips into a pattern that is purely experiential, one is transported, for example, from the space in which one stands and moves and looks, and into the space represented in the picture. The space represented in the picture is not just two-dimensional; you cannot move about in it, but it is the space into which consciousness has moved. Again, one moves from the time of sleeping and waking, working and resting, into the time of the music. One moves from the pressures and determinisms of home and office, economics and politics, to a more elementary apprehension of aspiration and limitation, of help from outside and hope.[20] One moves from

18 LN 5 verso has, 'when fully developed, meaning → meant, goes out to universe, world → functional within that world (metaphysics, science, common sense).'

19 LN 5 verso adds, 'subject in actu, object in actu, are still one.'

20 Thus the lecture. LN 5 verso has, 'from pressures, determinisms of home, office, economics, politics to powers depicted in dance.'

the language of conversation, the newspaper, television, from the technical use of words in a science or in philosophy, to the vocal tools that focus and mold and grow with one's consciousness.

Next, slipping into the purely experiential pattern is a transformation not only on the side of the object, but also on the side of the subject. The subject in act is the object in act on the level of elemental meaning. The subject is liberated from being a replaceable part adjusted to and integrated in a ready-made world. He is liberated from being a responsible inquirer in search of exact knowledge of some aspect of the universe. He is just himself – subject in act, emergent, ecstatic, standing out. He is his own originating freedom.

Now this elemental meaning, with the transformation it involves of the world and the subject, can be set within a conceptual field. It can be described and explained. But words and thoughts will not reproduce it, just as thermodynamic equations do not make us feel warmer or cooler. Art is another case of withdrawal for return. The mathematician goes off into his speculations, but returns to concrete reality, to the natural sciences. Similarly, the artist withdraws from the ready-made world, but that withdrawal has its significance. It is a withdrawal from practical living to explore possibilities of fuller living in a richer world. Just as the mathematician explores the possibilities of what physics can be, so the artist explores possibilities of what life, ordinary living, can be. There is an artistic element in all consciousness, in all living. Our settled modes have become humdrum, and we may think of all our life simply in terms of utilitarian categories. But in fact the life we are living is a product of artistic creation. We ourselves are products of artistic creation in our concrete living, and art is an exploration of potentiality.

2.7 Objectification

Art has been defined as the objectification of a purely experiential pattern. We have been speaking of the purely experiential pattern. But art is the *expression*, the *objectification*, of such a pattern. The purely experiential pattern is a mode of experience, but it is merely experience. It is within the cognitional order, an awareness; it is intentional, but it has not reached the full stage of intending. It is elemental meaning. That experience not only is unknown to other people, it is not fully known even to the one who does experience it. Within the one who is experiencing, the pattern of his experience in its complexity, its many-sidedness, is only implicit, folded up, veiled, unrevealed, unobjectified. The subject is aware of it, but has yet to get hold of it. He would behold, inspect, dissect, enjoy, repeat it; and to do that he has to objectify, unfold, make explicit,[21] unveil, reveal.

This process of objectifying is analogous to the process from the act of understanding to the definition. The definition is the inner word, an expresion, an unfolding of what one has got hold of in the insight. Similarly, the purely experiential pattern becomes objectified, expressed, in a work of art.

The process of objectifying introduces, so to speak, a psychic distance. No longer is one simply experiencing. Objectification involves a separation, a distinction, a detachment, between oneself and one's experience. One can experience emotions and feelings, but at that moment one is not artistic. Poetry, according to Wordsworth, is emotion recollected in tranquility. The phrase 'recollection in tranquility' expresses the psychic distance between the subject and his experience. And that separation is needed for the subject to express his experience.

Again, one can distinguish between art and symptomatic expression. When one feels intensely, one will reveal it in one's gestures, facial movements, tone of voice, pauses, and silences. All that revelation of experience is not art, but simply the symptoms of the experience itself. One moves to art when the actor, understanding how a person would feel, puts forth deliberately those symptoms. The necessity of the psychic distance explains why the artist, when he is perturbed, cannot work. Mozart complained that he could not compose when he was being troubled and harassed in various ways. Art is not simply spontaneous manifestation of feeling.

The process of expression or objectification involves not only psychic distance but also an idealization of the purely experiential pattern. Art is not autobiography; it is not going to confession or telling one's tale to a psychiatrist. It is grasping what is or seems significant, of moment, of concern, of import to man in the experience. In a sense, it is truer than the experience, leaner, more effective, more to the point. It grasps the central moment of the experience and unfolds ideally its proper implications, apart from the distortions, the interferences, the accidental intrusions that would arise in the concrete experience itself.[22]

Art is the abstraction of a form, where the form becomes idealized by the

---

21 The word 'explicit' is supplied from LN 6.
22 Relevant to this point LN 6 adds, 'Expression supposes an insight into pattern of the experience — basic insight — commanding form that has to be expanded worked out developed; process of working out — completing adjusting correcting initial insight.'

abstraction. And the form is not conceptual.[23] It is the pattern of internal relations that will be immanent in the colors, in the tones, in the spaces. The expression, the work, the what-is-done is isomorphic with the idealized pattern of experience. It may also be isomorphic with something else, and in that case the art is representative. If I draw a house, the work represents a house, but it also corresponds to a dynamic image in me. Otherwise I would not have been able to draw it. There is here a double correspondence: there is a similarity between the house I draw and something further, namely, the house itself, but there is also a similarity between the house I draw and the image in me that led to the drawing. If there is a similarity to something else, the art is representative. But whether or not there is the further similarity is not the point. The immediate point is the similarity between the pattern in the work and the pattern of the free experience. The pattern, then, is not a conceptual pattern, and it cannot be conceptualized. It is intelligibility in a more concrete form than is got hold of on the conceptual level — just as, for example, the intelligibility of the simple harmonic oscillator of the planetary system is an intelligibility of a more concrete type than the intelligibility of a scientific synthesis. There are material conditions that must be fulfilled to have this concrete type of intelligibility. By contrast, the scientific synthesis will be true regardless of whether determinate material conditions are fulfilled or not.

Moreover, the conceptual is also reflective. The conceptual answers the questions, or is prepared to answer the questions, What do you mean? What is the evidence for what you mean? It is prepared to determine whether one is certain that the meaning is correct or only probable, and whether that probability is of importance or negligible. Anything that is conceptual is also at least incipiently reflective. But the expression of the artistic meaning not only is on a more concrete level than the conceptual, but also it is without the reflexivity of conceptual meaning. The symbolic meaning of the work of art is immediate. The work is an invitation to participate, to try it, to see it for oneself. It has its own criteria, but they are immanent to it, and they do not admit formulation. We have already seen an example of this in the inevitability of form.

2.8 Symbolic Meaning

With symbolic meaning we reach a fundamental point of importance in

---

23 LN 6 has, 'it is the abstraction of a form, not conceptually, but by doing, poiê-
    sis.'

many ways. The symbolic is an objectifying, revealing, communicating consciousness. But it is not reflective, critical consciousness. Critical consciousness deals with classes, with univocal terms, with proofs; it follows the principles of excluded middle and of noncontradiction. But the symbol is concerned, not with the class but with the representative figure, not with univocity but with multiple meanings. The artist does not care how many different meanings one gives to his work or finds in it. The symbol does not give proofs, but reinforces its statement by repetition, variation, and all the arts of rhetoric. It is not a matter of excluded middle, but is rather overdetermined, as are dreams. Freud speaks of the overdetermination of the dream, of all sorts of reasons for one and the same symbol. The symbol has no means of saying 'is not,' of negating, and so it is not a matter of contradiction in the logical sense;[24] rather it piles up positives which it overcomes. So St Paul says, Neither height nor depth nor principality nor power.[25] He gives a long series of negations. Why does he negate all these things? Because he is on an immediate level of symbolic communication. He posits all these terms and then brushes them aside to communicate the completeness of his devotion to Christ. The symbolic does not move on some single level or track, dealing with one thing at a time. There is a condensation, an overexuberance, in the symbol. We see this in a particularly striking way in Shakespeare, where images come crowding in from all sides to express the same point.

Finally, if one apprehends what is meant by the symbolic and the artistic, one has an apprehension of the reality behind the abstraction 'figures of speech.' 'Figures of speech' is a reflective construction of grammarians who did not quite understand why people live and talk in the apparently irrational way that grammarians find that they do. But the real meaning of simile, metaphor, synecdoche, and the rest is the normal flow of symbolic consciousness. If you try to understand St Paul in terms of logical categories, you are constantly being baffled. But think of St Paul in terms of representative figures which are constantly returning, such as sin and death, life and resurrection – not in terms of univocity. How many different meanings, how the meanings constantly change! There are many meanings of *zôê* and *thanatos* in St Paul. His use of the symbolic is not a proof but a reinforce-

---

24 The material from 'and so' is based on LN 6.
25 See Romans 8.38–39. NRSV: 'For I am convinced that neither death, nor life, nor angels, nor rulers, nor things present, nor things to come, nor powers, nor height, nor depth, nor anything else in all creation, will be able to separate us from the love of God in Christ Jesus our Lord.'

ment. St Thomas asks the question, Is theology argumentative? and quotes St Paul, If one man rose from the dead, then we also rise.[26] But it is very difficult to find such syllogisms in St Paul. It is anything but the general rule. Normally he is using reinforcement; the properties of the normal artistry of everyday life come out in the symbol.[27]

2.9 Ulterior Significance

So far we have been considering art analytically, and on the level of its proper nature and in a manner consonant with the theory of knowledge and the philosophy we have presented. We are concerned with the subject coming to be himself. What makes the difference between dreaming and being awake? When awake you are more yourself, you have more control over the patterning of your experience. The dream is a negation of the patterning of your experience. But that patterning is proper to experience, and the patterns imposed upon experience that instrumentalize it also falsify it. Just as to think that we have to be looking at an object instead of thinking of the identity in act of seeing and seen falsifies the experience, so instrumentalizing experience in various ways can remove us from the primal mode of being that is proper to man and that is the normal level of human living apart from the differentiations of consciousness.

Mircea Eliade, in a small book entitled *Images et symboles*,[28] points out that rationalism drew man's attention away from his symbols and the importance of symbols in his life. But, though man's attention was drawn away from symbols, and though man tried to live under the influence of rationalism as though he were a pure spirit, a pure reason, this did not eliminate the symbols or their concrete efficacy in human living, but simply led to a degradation and a vulgarization of the symbol. Hera and Artemis and Aphrodite were replaced by the pinup girl, and 'Paradise Lost' by 'South Pacific.' But symbols remain necessary and constant in human experience whether we attend to them or not. Their importance in the whole of human living is exemplified, for example, by the saying, Let me write a nation's songs, and I care not who writes her laws. This points to the fundamental fact that it is on the artistic, symbolic level that we live.

26 Thomas Aquinas, *Summa theologiae*, 1, q. 1, a. 8 c.
27 The break was taken at this point. The tape resumes with the word 'analytically' in the next sentence. The sentence is reconstructed from the notes of F. Crowe.
28 Mircea Eliade, *Images et symboles: Essai sur le symbolisme magico-religieux* (Paris: Gallimard, 1952); in English, *Images and Symbols: Studies in Religious Symbolism*, trans. Philip Mairet (New York: Sheed & Ward, 1961).

Now questions are raised about art: Is what I said all there is to it, is that all it is? That question can be put in several ways. Part of the indictment against Socrates in Athens was that he held the moon to be just earth and the clouds just water. To think of the moon as just earth and the clouds as just water, of the mountains as thrown up by contractions in the earth's surface and of rivers as just part of the earth's circulatory system is to drop something away from reality, away from man's world of experience. Art, whether by an illusion or a fiction or a contrivance, *presents*[29] the beauty, the splendor, the glory, the majesty, the 'plus' that is in things and that drops out when you say that the moon is just earth and the clouds are just water. It draws attention to the fact that the splendor of the world is a cipher, a revelation, an unveiling, the presence of one who is not seen, touched, grasped, put in a genus, distinguished by a difference, yet is *present*.[30] St Augustine says in his *Confessions* that he sought in the stars, and it was not the stars; in the sun and the moon, and it was not the sun and the moon; in the earth, the trees, the shrubs, the mountains, the valleys, and it was none of these.[31] Art can be viewing this world and looking for the something more that this world reveals, and reveals, so to speak, in silent speech, reveals by a presence that cannot be defined or got hold of.[32] In other words, there is to art an interpretative significance as a possibility. Not all art has it, but when art is without this ulterior significance, which is not formulated but lived,[33] it becomes play, it is separating objects from the ready-made world by way of exuberance, like the exuberance of a child, or by way of a distraction. Or it becomes aestheticism, just the enjoyment of the pattern. Works of art then supply the materials for exercises in one's skill of appreciation. Or art becomes technique. The compelling form is there, but there is no sense of that ulterior *presence*.[34]

To make what we have said a little more concrete, and also to tie it in with the basic point that I wish to make, namely, that art is an exploration of potentialities for human living, I will now attempt to summarize some points from Susanne Langer on different art forms.

29 The emphasis is not apparent in the lecture itself, but the word 'presents' is underlined twice on LN 7.
30 Again, the double underlining on LN 7.
31 See Augustine, *Confessions*, trans. F.J. Sheed (London and New York: Sheed & Ward, 6th impression, 1951) book 10, chapter 6, pp. 170–71; *PL* 10, 6, vol. 32, p. 783.
32 LN 7 adds, 'Insight: the dual operator.'
33 The 'which' clause is based on LN 7.
34 The word 'presence' is underlined once on LN 7.

3   Art and Space

Earlier, we spoke geometrically of kinesthetic-tactile space, of visual space, and of decentered space. We then went on to discuss the geometries of physical theories. Art, too, is concerned with space: in the picture, the statue, the work of architecture.[35]

3.1   The Picture[36]

The space of the picture omits all of the kinesthetic elements — balance, sense of direction, what you can reach into, move through, touch. Again, it eliminates the knowledge of space that comes through hearing as sounds approach and recede. But the picture, as distinct from the photograph, compensates in its presentation of space for these omissions. The photograph simply gives you the visual reproduction of what is there to be seen, the reproduction according to perspective, the geometry of what is there to be seen. The picture 'puts there' to be seen, in such a way that the space will be visible despite the absence of the kinesthetic and auditory indications of space. It gives you a merely visual space.

The space of the picture is not the actual space in which we move and into which we ordinarily look. We ordinarily look into a space in which we could move forward and bump into things. In this real order, the space of the picture is just two-dimensional, a flat canvas with pigments on it; but the virtual space of the picture is the space that emerges for sight. The space that is seen in the picture is, if you wish, an illusion, but because it is illusionary, or at least separate, surrounded with a frame that sets it apart from the rest of space, it pulls the subject out of his ready-made world, and presents him with another space that is only for sight. You cannot move through this space, and consequently it is irrelevant for all the practical or theoretical instrumentalizations of experience. It imposes the purely experiential pattern, because it is merely a virtual space.

That being pulled out of one's ready-made world is a moment of withdrawal, of pause. Such moments are moments in which one can start afresh,

---

35 LN 8 has, 'Geometry relations in what already is spatial — if only the relations, analytic — *what* is *the related*? Art answers by representative figure, instance: Picture, Statue, Architecture.'

36 LN 8 has, '*Decoration*: makes surface visible; *Picture*: makes space visible.'

release a new movement to the realization of one's own idea of being human, to the appreciation of what it is to be a Christian, a new movement towards this ideal.[37] That interruption, the pulling out from the ready-made world, is a release of potentiality.

The virtual space to which one is invited by the picture — and if one accepts, one is pulled out of one's ready-made world — is a space to be seen. To be seen, it has to be filled, and it is filled with form. Langer suggests that one think of the space of the picture as a pool of water into which vessels are sunk at various distances to make the space visible. The forms may be representative, and if they are, they are not there in their actual size. They are there according to a proportion, and the proportion varies according to the laws of perspective.[38] Moreover, the forms that are there according to a varying proportion are composed, and the composition is the pattern. It is a pattern of contrasts and balances, of tensions and their resolutions. It all ties together into a single view, a unity of vision, and there is that unity of vision because of the pattern. The composition has a logic of its own, but it is not the logic of discourse, not the logic of the machine, but the vital logic of the pattern of experience, the pattern in seeing.

Sense in act is the sensible in act; intelligence in act is the intelligible in act; and perceiving the picture is the identity in act of the perceptive capacity of the subject and the what-is-there-to-be-seen. It is an event that occurs in the subject. And there can be an insight into that perceiving,[39] a grasp of the pattern, the import, the meaning of the picture. Artists talk constantly about the picture's being 'alive' — even things that have no life at all, like a stone. It's all alive. Why? Because what is alive is the perceiving. You say that something is 'alive,' but it is because *you* are coming to life. Our understanding of this process is helped by reading Keats's 'Ode on a Grecian Urn,' in which an artist expresses artistically his appreciation of looking at the urn. There is a certain advantage in having an artist rather than an analyst or a theoretician talk about a work of art.[40]

But the fundamental meaning important to us in art is that, just as the pure desire to know heads on to the beatific vision, so too the break from

---

37 Lonergan's expression in the lecture was elliptical. LN 8 has, 'such experience opens the door to becoming oneself, to becoming one's own idea of a man, a Christian, to knowing, appreciating, loving other selves.'
38 LN 8: 'and the proportion varies to yield perspective, reveal space.'
39 LN 8 adds, 'insight into perceptible is also insight into perceiving.'
40 LN 8 adds, 'communication of artist's visual experience; communion with him and other viewers – Celebration of that communion.'

the ready-made world heads on to God. Man is nature's priest, and nature is God's silent communing with man. The artistic moment simply breaks away from ordinary living and is, as it were, an opening, a moment of new potentiality.

3.2 The Statue

The meaning of the statue may be illuminated by recent work on the part of phenomenologists, and in particular Merleau-Ponty. In his book on perception,[41] Merleau-Ponty emphasizes that we are spatial beings. What is my body? It is a piece of space, and it is a piece of space that feels. We think of bodies as something to be felt, but the fact about our bodies is that they are feelers, feeling in the active sense.

The body, then, is feeling space; it is feeling distributed through space. And the statue is the visual presentation of the space that feels. My hands are space that grasp; my head is space that looks and listens; every organism is a spatial entity. Different organs have their different places. As object, the organism is something to be seen and felt. But as subject, in the organs and by the organs, I feel. And prior to the objectified axes of reference — north and south, east and west, up and down — there is the organization of space that arises as the baby learns to control the movements of its different members and to coordinate them.[42] It is a kinesthetic space in the subject and on the side of the subject. It is not the space out there that is organized, but the space that I am. It is the set of differences, not in the felt, but in feeling.

The statue makes that subject visible. It makes visible the presence that is not the presence of the chairs in the room, or the presence of you to me as object, but the prior presence of me to myself that is required for anything to be present to me. It is presenting-consciousness.[43] It is the presence that needs a place. And so the statue needs a place. You cannot put a statue just anywhere. If one were to put a large statue in a small room, there would be an enormous incongruity. There are statues that need a whole public

41 Maurice Merleau-Ponty, *The Phenomenology of Perception*, trans. Colin Smith (London: Routledge and Kegan Paul, 1966). Lonergan refers as well to Alphonse de Waelhens, *Une philosophie de l'ambiguïté: L'existentialisme de Maurice Merleau-Ponty* (Louvain: Publications Universitaires de Louvain, 1951).

42 LN 8 verso: 'Prior to objectified axes ..., there are the subject's sense of balance, direction, gravity.'

43 We have used a hyphen here, to indicate that 'presenting' adjectivally modifies 'consciousness,' and is not part of the verb.

square for their position. And there we have the presence of the person ready to meet others.[44]

3.3 Architecture

Architecture is the objectified space. There are objective axes of reference.[45] For Heidegger, the world, or space, consists of ways and places. That is the ordinary apprehension of the objective space: places, and ways to get there and come back again. Architecture is the expression of the center of one's world, of the world of one's group. It draws a line that settles an orientation in objective space, a basic line about which all objects in space are organized. The song has it, 'There's no place like home,' because home is the first objective orientation in space about which all other objects are organized. Of course, that is less so today, as families keep moving about from one place to another. But the old-time home constantly recurs in our dreams and provides an organizing background for anything. Orientation in space[46] is also given by the circle of stones, the dolmen, the totem pole, the temple, the church, the cathedral – the home of the gods, the center of the earth where the gods are; or by the tomb, the pyramid, the mausoleum, the *campo santo*, the Whispering Glades – the home of the dead; or by the capital, the palace, the public buildings – the home of the king, of the people's head; or by a fortress, by city and walls, by a castle, by a market, a shop, a factory, the stock exchange, banks,[47] and so on.

Architecture is functional, and it has to be. It has concrete, useful purposes in human living. But it is also an expression of the people's orientation in this world. When architecture is dominated by stock exchanges, banks, and office buildings, it expresses the life that the people have, the orientation which, by being there, they impose upon consciousness, just as the castle or the cathedral can be the basic orientation within this world, the

44 The meaning is perhaps clearer on LN 8 verso: 'Presence (1) chairs to room (2) me to you (3) you to yourselves: if asleep, nothing present to you. Statue makes objective and visible the presence (3) and so demands a place, where presence (3) meets presence (2).'
45 LN 8 verso, 'besides kinesthetic, perceiving axes, there are objective axes, organization of world, ways and places - organization needs origin and orientation.'
46 This sentence and the first sentence in the next paragraph are missing on the tape, because of accidents in the taping. The materials are supplied from the notes of F. Crowe and from Lonergan's lecture notes.
47 The words 'stock exchange, banks' are supplied from LN 8 verso.

orientation that is distinct from that provided by the subject who can control the movements of his own limbs.

The orientation in space need not be a fixed place. There is an organization, an orientation in space corresponding to the orientation of the subject, just as much in a gypsy camp, or in the encampment of an army, or in life on board a ship. Architecture expresses that orientation in space. It places a wall between man and raw nature, a field in which mutual operations and relations intersect, a base from which a people reaches to heaven or is closed in under a sullen dome. (We can think in this connection of Wordsworth's 'The world is too much with us.')

4   Art and Time

Art is concerned with time as well as with space. Our thinking about time usually reduces time to space. We measure time spatially. In Aristotle's definition *numerus et mensura motus secundum prius et posterius*,[48] the *prius et posterius* is not temporal but spatial. It refers to the parts of space that you cover first in the motion, and the parts that you cover later. Again, mathematical thought about time is usually a reduction of time by thinking of it on the analogy of space.

Fundamental thought about time in St Thomas is in terms of the *nunc.* Eternity is the 'now' that has no change, the 'now' of a being that does not change; and time is the 'now' of a being that does change.

4.1   Music

The basic time that is the 'now' of a being has a nonspatial objectification in music. Music is the image of experienced time. It is not a movement in any spatial sense. It is not the movement of the hands that strike the keys or move the bow. It is not the movement of the propagation of sound waves. Music is the movement within the music itself, the movement from one note to another. Physically, the higher note will be a more rapid vibration. But in the music, if the previous notes are brief and the next higher note is long, the higher note will be a point of rest. Music is a movement that is simply over time. It is a movement that ties in very closely with what Bergson meant by the *durée pure*, or, again, with the Thomist notion of time as the 'now' of a being that changes.[49]

---

48 Aristotle, *Physics*, IV, 11, 219b 1.
49 LN 9 has, 'Virtual movement has *pattern*: melody a non-spatial shape, that is not at instant but only *over time*: present to enduring subject, to *durée pure*.'

The *durée pure*, the *nunc*, the 'now' of a being that changes is not a single dimension. Measured time is unidimensional, but the time that is the 'now' of the subject is a time in which many things are going forward at once. The music expresses this by taking one theme, and then another, and blending them. There are oppositions, tensions, resolutions. The life of feeling that is in that 'now,' in its rhythms and turmoil and peace, is expressed in the music.[50] The time of the music is a nonspatial movement and has a non-spatial shape. And this nonspatial shape corresponds to the way in which feelings multiply and change.[51]

I am drawing attention to elementary aspects of our consciousness. Since I have to speak in general, and very rapidly, of pictures, statues, architecture, and music, I can do no more than this. Besides, anything more would have to get its specification from works of art themselves, and not from talk about works of art.[52]

5   Poetry

Let us try to say something briefly about poetry. We speak of people calling a spade a spade. Shakespeare remarks that a rose by any other name would smell as sweet. But it is also true that one can say something, and someone

50 LN 9 has, 'crescendo diminuendo - development, differentiation, integration — turmoil, peace.'
51 LN 9 has, 'Time of the music, virtual movements of music, isomorphic with the life of feeling of the subject — an objectification in which subject can see how to live.'
52 There is on LN 9 a section on dance that did not find its way into the lecture. It reads:

'Dance: art of stone age – principal exercise of speculative intellect in primitive
   intersubjectivity: smile, countenance, voice, hands, movements
objectification *induces, heightens* intersubjectivity: intoxicating, enthralling, ecstatic
useless purposeless: liberation of man: acrobatic liberation from gravity/ Shelley's skylark
movements of intersubjectivity: request, hesitation, reluctance, agreement, demand, refusal, dispute, consent; command resistance struggle submission
movement of intersubjective group: its experience and memory, power and limitations, desires and fears, intentions and prayers, sacrament and magic, *liturgy*
war dance, rain dance, harvest dance
swirling dervish, holy rollers (big appeal to Xtian Ojibways).'

else will remark, 'It sounds so horrible (or dreadful, or wonderful) when you put it that way.' There is a way of putting things that can be horrible or wonderful. Making a spade a spade may be all very well, but it may be very horrible. Why is that so? Why can there be ways of saying things that are wonderful and horrible, when words are just tools for conveying meaning?

The fact is that words have not only their proper meanings, but also a resonance in our consciousness. They have a retinue of associations, and the associations may be visual, vocal, auditory, tactile, kinesthetic, affective or evocative of attitudes, tendencies, and evaluations. This resonance of words pertains to the very genesis, structure, and molding of our consciousness through childhood and the whole process of our education. It pertains to the dynamic situation in consciousness that the words provoke.[53]

In contrasting scientific and literary writing, we may recall Carlyle's phrase that economics is the dismal science. In a sense, all scientific writing is dismal. Scientific words simply have meaning; they have no resonance. They are products of the intellectual pattern of experience, and this pattern is detached, concerned with things not in their relations to us, but in their relations to one another. The intellectual pattern is concerned with judgments that are valid for everyone, with propositions whose implications can be worked out automatically by logical calculations. On the other hand, poetry and fiction — the two words have the same meaning, one with a Greek, the other with a Latin root — introduce us to the world of human potentiality. They reveal the many dimensions of experience as experienced by the subject. They exhibit the concrete manner in which men apprehend their history, their destiny, and the meaning of their lives.

5.1 Narrative

Poetry, then, can be conceived as the living memory of the group. A group can carry on current affairs, deal with common opportunities, hopes, dangers, fears, only insofar as it possesses a common vehicle of meaning. That common vehicle resides in a common language, in common customs, values, ways of understanding and doing things. It results from the past, and is transmitted through popular tradition and traditional history. Popular tradition or traditional history informs, explains, delights, instructs, through the medium of narrative and story. It is at once factual, explanatory, aes-

---

53 LN 10 has, 'They [these associations] are the dynamic situation that speech releases.'

thetic, pedagogical, and moral. It is said of traditional historians that they are guardians of tradition, priests of the cult of nationalism, prophets of social reform, exponents and defenders of national virtue and glory.[54] In any case, the thing to be apprehended is that there has to be a tradition for a people to live together and work together. That tradition is above all the possibility and the vehicle of meaning. A language is not simply a set of words, but also a set of meanings. It is not a set of abstract meanings by which one can communicate scientifically, but a set of meanings that has a resonance that brings to life the potentialities of the individual.

Now popular tradition not only selects its facts but also simplifies them and[55] groups them about a few striking figures. It provides explanatory links that often are not true. 'Why are things like this? So and so did it.' And so on. It loves anecdotes and picturesque stories. And always there has to be a moral. Such popular tradition, whether it be poetry, fiction, or acceptable history, is something essential to human living. It is what an existentialist would call an existential category. It is a constitutive component of the group as human. It is an aesthetic apprehension of the group's origin. The aesthetic apprehension of the group's origin and story becomes operative whenever the group debates, judges, evaluates, decides, or acts — and especially in a crisis. The Soviets during the war had to revive the memory of national heroes who had been anathema to doctrinaire communism. They had to talk to the people, and to talk to the people effectively they had to talk to them through their memory. Those memories constitute the fund of common meaning, the common psychic, intellectual, moral, religious, human resources of the group as a group. They contain the structure, spirit, ethos, the potential of elementary common consciousness that, in England for example, responded to Churchill's speeches in 1940, and in the United States responded to the Depression and Pearl Harbor.[56]

That common historical consciousness is not to be confused with scientific history. Scientific history does not aim to please, and it does not always uplift. It is a product of the intellectual pattern of experience. It uses traditional histories as mere materials; and it criticizes traditional history to arrive at sources and data for finding out what things really were, what really

---

54 LN 10 refers to 'Bagby, *Culture and History*, Longmans 1958.' See Philip Bagby, *Culture and History: Prolegomena to the Comparative Study of Civilizations* (Reprint, Westport, CT: Greenwood Press, 1976) 50.

55 The wording here is based on LN 10. In the lecture Lonergan said, 'Now popular tradition not only simplifies and selects its facts, but also groups them ...'

56 Reference to the Depression is added from LN 10 verso.

happened. It pierces through what may be the myth of traditional history. But scientific history is not alive, whereas that traditional, popular history, that common fund of ways of thinking and judging, is alive. It makes the group the group that it is. The memory of the group — it may be and usually is, at least originally, the product of poetry, the creation of the poet, in the sense in which the Homeric hymns provided the education of Greece — may be myth, aberration. But you cannot use scientific history to set it right. Scientific history cannot fulfil that function, for it is not an existential.[57] What is constituted by the vital tradition is a group potentiality on the aesthetic level. Its need to be purified, corrected, deepened, and enriched has to be met on its own level. If it is not met on its own level, it keeps on as it was, because it is essential for human life. On the other hand, to treat this traditional memory as though it were a set of logical premises from which deductions are to be made is to misunderstand it.[58]

5.2 Drama

As fiction or poetry, as narrative, is the expression, the creation, the formulation of the living memory of the people, which is the link that makes the people into a group, so poetry as drama is the image of destiny. There is an initial situation from which the drama proceeds through the decisions of the participants. The decisions of individuals will be interdependent, and one will foresee what others might decide and use his foreseeing to guide his present decision. But quite apart from all the characters' thinking, foreseeing, and understanding of one another in the drama, the set of decisions of the participants is not the decision of any one of them. It is a set of decisions that leads from one situation to the next. Destiny is that linking of successive situations. There is something in the succession of human choices that is outside the range of human choice. Though everything in the drama is a product of the decisions, and though the decisions can be made with full consciousness of what the other characters are likely to do in response, still there cannot be any individual decision that constitutes the situation and the way one situation heads into the next. That logic between the situ-

---

57 LN 10 verso has, 'That is just a devitalizing blunder.'
58 LN 10 verso has, 'it *usually* needs to be purified, to be explained, above all, to be deepened, enriched, else disaster – but this process is to be guided by criteria of poetry – e contra, inferences from this poetic structure are to be resisted, as if it were a set of logical premises intelligence giving the gist of it in a manner that is perceptible will be understood, efficacious.'

ations is one way of conceiving destiny, one way of conceiving the manner in which God moves man's will even though man's will is free. This is expressed in the drama. Through the drama man can apprehend concretely his freedom, his capacity to decide, and the limitations upon his freedom. He cannot make other people's decisions for them, nor can he control his situation.[59]

5.3   The Lyric

Finally, the lyric, which originates from the chorus of the drama, stands to the drama as the statue stands to architecture. The lyric is the expression of the subject,[60] just as the statue is the visual expression of the space that actively feels, the space that is my body. On the other hand, the drama is the expression of destiny in the group, in group action, or in the action of different groups, just as architecture is the home of the people, the expression of their living.

6   Conclusion

What I want to communicate in this talk about art is the notion that art is relevant to concrete living, that it is an exploration of the potentialities of concrete living. That exploration is extremely important in our age, when philosophers for at least two centuries, through doctrines on politics, economics, education, and through ever further doctrines, have been trying to remake man, and have done not a little to make human life unlivable. The great task that is demanded if we are to make it livable again is the re-creation of the liberty of the subject, the recognition of the freedom of consciousness. Normally, we think of freedom as freedom of the will, as something that happens within consciousness. But the freedom of the will is a control over the orientation of the flow of consciousness, and that flow is not determined either by environment, external objects, or by the neurobiological demands of the subject. It has its own free component. Art is a fundamental element in the freedom of consciousness itself. Thinking about art helps us think, too, about exploring the full freedom of our ways of feeling and perceiving.

59 LN 10 verso adds, '*Grenzsituationen*: general old young, male female, opportunities limited from birth education temperament: struggle, suffering, guilt, death; Existenz: being in limiting situations.'
60 LN 10 verso has, '*subject* responds to nature, to "la condition humaine," to God.'

10

History [1]

I wish now to say something on the subject of history. First of all, from the viewpoint of education history is a subject that is totally different pedagogically from other subjects. It does not offer the opportunity for the training of a student's critical powers until its very latest stages. As Butterfield points out, there is all the difference in the world between teaching history and teaching mathematics. [2] The pupil, no matter how old, is able to see exactly what the reason is for each step as he goes forward in mathematics. But in history he will simply be told things and told things and told things, and he will read them in books; it is only when he gets to graduate work that he will have an opportunity to discover what are the sources, what are the criteria, and what is the type of value of the evidence available in history. It does not lend itself easily to the formation of the scientific mentality.

On the other hand, as perhaps you have already inferred from my earlier lectures on the good as object and as developing subject, and from the fact that philosophy of education has been a tool of people who are out to transform human society and human living, reflection on history is one of the richest, profoundest, and most significant things there is. In the past few centuries any great movement has been historical in its inspiration and its for-

---

1 The tenth lecture, Friday, August 14, 1959. The tapes begin with the opening of the lecture.
2 The reference may be to a book Lonergan has already quoted: Herbert Butterfield, *History and Human Relations* (London: Collins, 1951); pp. 168–69, together with pp. 91–92 and 154–57, come close to the view attributed to Butterfield in our text.

mulation. The liberal movement has been inspired by a doctrine of automatic progress, and it has dominated the English-speaking world and France. Germany has been dominated by historicist thinking. I believe that when the Americans had access to the archives of the German government after the last war, they discovered that the philosophy of Fichte had been an ultimate and controlling inspiration and criterion in top-level German politics and statesmanship. There has been very obviously an historicist inspiration in the Nazi and Fascist movements. Marxism is also a theory of history; it is the materialist conception of the dialectic of history. It is these movements that have exercised the profoundest influence on the modern world.

Books written on the subject are of all types.[3] I would note Ernst Troeltsch's study, *Der Historismus und seine Probleme.*[4] He has another work, *Der Historismus und seine Überwindung.*[5] It is a review of all theories up to about 1920, with a criticism of them. There are more recent works: Fr Martin D'Arcy, the English Jesuit, published *The Sense of History: Secular and Sacred.*[6] J.J. Mulloy edited from writings of Christopher Dawson a book entitled *Dynamics of World History.*[7] There is a paperback by Hans Meyerhoff, published by Doubleday Anchor Books, *The Philosophy of History in Our Time.*[8] It is a series of selections from notable authors, with further bibliographical indications. Maritain has a book on the philosophy of history.[9] Marrou has a book *De la connaissance historique.*[10] I have already mentioned

3 Lonergan mentioned a bibliography that he had supplied before the course. In his notes there is a bibliography (LN 48–50), partly typed and partly handwritten.
4 Ernst Troeltsch, *Der Historismus und seine Probleme*, Gesammelte Schriften III (Aalen: Scientia Verlag, 1961; the original was published by J.C.B. Mohr [Tübingen] 1922).
5 Ernst Troeltsch, *Der Historismus und seine Überwindung: Fünf Vorträge* (Berlin: Pan Verlag Rolf Heise, 1924); in English, *Christian Thought, Its History and Application: Lectures Written for Delivery in England during March 1923*, trans. ed. Baron F. von Hügel (London: University of London Press, 1923; New York: Meridian, 1957).
6 Martin D'Arcy, *The Sense of History: Secular and Sacred* (London: Faber and Faber, 1959).
7 Christopher Dawson, *The Dynamics of World History*, ed. John J. Mulloy (London: Sheed & Ward, 1957).
8 Hans Meyerhoff, ed., *The Philosophy of History in Our Time* (New York: Doubleday Anchor, 1959).
9 Jacques Maritain, *On the Philosophy of History*, ed. Joseph W. Evans (London: Geoffrey Bles, 1959).
10 Henri-Irenée Marrou, *De la connaissance historique* (2nd rev. ed., Paris: Editions du Seuil, 1955); in English, *The Meaning of History*, trans. Robert J. Olsen (Baltimore: Helicon, 1966).

Voegelin. There is also a book by Butterfield, *Christianity and History*.[11] There are all sorts of other works, but at least that will provide an indication of the extensive literature on the subject, especially if you check the bibliographies in these works.

1   The Problem of History

With regard to the problem of history, we may start from our discussion of human life as basically artistic, creative. Consciousness is not a function of external data or internal biological determinants, but a flow in which there are free acts that control the flow. Human consciousness is something that floats. Further, its orientation, what it grasps and what it chooses, is the source of everything distinctively human, of all there is that differentiates the distinctively human culture of the Pygmies both from a modern culture and from animals. The Pygmies spend most of their time singing and dancing. In that flow of human living a group memory is essential to any group.

Now what the historians started to do was to examine the contents of these group memories, or chronicles, or more elementary forms of reporting what happened. They attempted to go behind them; and they found that in many of the points the chronicles were almost certainly wrong. They developed methods of criticism of traditions. Their aim was to get behind the traditions to the facts, to what really happened. In the famous phrase of Ranke, the great German historian, the aim of history is to find out *wie es eigentlich gewesen,* how it really happened.

That enterprise ended up in difficulty, and the nature of the difficulty will become apparent if we revert to the three fundamental operations. Knowledge of fact arises with the judgment, when you say, 'That is so.' But before you have judgments there is an accumulation of insights, acts of understanding; and the insights arise upon experiences. Consequently, in any affirmation of fact, there is an enormous presupposition of acts of understanding. When the historians started criticizing the traditions, they gradually came to the discovery that the facts could be whittled down in any particular case to just nothing at all if one eliminated the way of understanding, the way people probably would be thinking and acting. History could be reduced to the barest bones. This produced, obviously, another revolt. Moving against the dry-as-dust historians who merely write monographs, finding out that less and less is really certain, there are the artistic historians

11 Herbert Butterfield, *Christianity and History* (London: Collins Press, 1958).

who try to give a vision of the past and present themselves more as artists than as scientists. This is perhaps the fundamental problem in the concept of history.

To say something on this problem, and to form a concept of history, I shall proceed, first of all, by considering the history of specialized science; secondly, the history of philosophy; thirdly, the history of theology; and fourthly, the problem of general history, which is the real catch.

2   The History of Specialized Science

Let us begin by thinking of what is conceptually the simplest type of history, namely, the history of a well-defined science such as mathematics, physics, chemistry, medicine.

It is immediately evident that to write the history of a science presupposes in the historian not merely familiarity with and mastery of all the techniques of the historian, such as how to use sources and how to criticize them,[12] but also a thorough knowledge of the particular subject on which he is writing. He has to be a mathematician if he is writing the history of mathematics. He has to be a physicist if he is writing the history of physics. He has to be a medical doctor if he is writing the history of medicine. Besides knowledge of historical techniques, then, he also has to know the subject; and he has to know that subject inside out. Without such knowledge he could collect masses of data that obviously have something to do with the history of mathematics or physics or medicine, but what he could not do would be to select out of his masses of data the key elements in the development of the subject; he could not discern the steps that made things jump forward, that had a broad, profound, enduring effect. Also, he would not be able to pick out the factors that retarded development, that proved roadblocks towards development, holding things up for centuries. He would not be able to order the whole into an intelligible picture and to distribute emphasis properly. He would not be able to indicate very briefly what is of no great significance but belongs to the picture, and so devote his main attention to what were the principal moments in the development of the science. Not only would the historian not be able to do any of these things that would be essential to a history of the science, but also, because he would not be able to do these

---

12 LN 51 mentions three names treated in some detail in *Method in Theology*, namely, Bernheim, Langlois, and Seignobos. See Lonergan, *Method in Theology* 199–201.

things, he would not notice the holes in his selection of data. He started off frantically to collect masses of data; but to be able to determine or recognize that a particular datum really is relevant to the subject, he has to know the subject. Because he would not be able to order the materials, he would not know where he should start searching for something that will account for a step that otherwise is unaccounted for in the process of the development of the subject.

We see from the example of the history of a well-determined and well-developed science that a knowledge of the subject is of essential importance in the whole historical task. The general criteria for the investigation and criticism of sources are a necessary but not sufficient condition of history. To put the matter differently, in a specialized history, by which I mean a history of a determinate subject, there is an a priori, and that a priori is knowledge of the subject itself in its contemporary form. The historian has to know the subject as it exists today and understand it thoroughly. From his own experience of learning the subject, he has to know about the nature of the development of the subject in himself. He will have to use the analogy of his own learning of the subject to make intelligible the history of the development of the subject.[13]

From this there follows a corollary. If a history of a subject is written with complete mastery of the sources and of historical technique and a complete mastery of the subject at a given time, and later the subject itself develops, then the history will have to be revised. There will now be a new a priori for collecting, ordering, and selecting the earlier facts. That new a priori may introduce smaller or perhaps larger changes. To take an example, histories of economics written prior to 1930 were written under the guidance of an economic science that, with the Depression, became discredited. There was a radical change in economic thinking that became generally accepted with the Depression, but that had not been generally accepted prior to the Depression. That change in the view of economists as scientists changes historical evaluations of what was going on in the nineteenth century and earlier periods.[14]

Furthermore, the more extensive and the more radical the development of a subject, the greater the likelihood of an extensive and radical revision

13 LN 51 phrases the matter somewhat differently: 'By understanding subject, one can understand one's own development, one can formulate relevant and exclude necessarily irrelevant hypotheses on past.'
14 LN 51 adds a second example: 'discovery of penicillin, revision history medic[ine].'

of the history of the subject. What had not been significant becomes significant, and what had been significant sinks to secondary importance.[15]

So much, then, for a first step, the history of a particular subject.

3   The History of Philosophy

We move to greater complexity when we consider the history of philosophy. Just as one has to be a mathematician to write the history of mathematics, so one has to be a philosopher to write the history of philosophy. All the same considerations recur. But there is a further consideration that has to be added. Until we reach the millennium, philosophers are not going to agree. The three basic operations lead to three modes in which the subject is organized, and that organization of the subject expresses itself in three fundamentally different types of philosophy: empiricist, idealist, or realist. The category into which a given philosopher really falls will depend on the degree of his self-appropriation. Further, it will depend upon the clarity and inner coherence of a given philosopher's thought, whether he really belongs to one of the pure cases or, for example, thinks himself a realist but has all sorts of empiricist assumptions in his thinking.[16]

Consequently, there will be a plurality of histories of philosophy. There is not just one philosophy at the present time, as one might say there is one mathematics. (It is not really true at the present time that there is just one mathematics, because the disputes about the foundations and conception of mathematics continue; but it is not quite as radical a type of dispute as in philosophy.) And so one can expect a plurality of histories of philosophy: a history of philosophy for empiricists, a history of philosophy for idealists, and a history of philosophy for realists, with possibly further types for people who are confused mixtures from among the three basic types.

On the other hand, philosophy is not a subject that admits radical revision.[17] This becomes clear simply by considering the meaning of the word 'revision.' If one were to suppose a radical revision, what would one be supposing? One would be supposing that new data have come to attention. There would be experiences of the data of consciousness or of the data of

15 This paragraph is taken almost verbatim from LN 51. It was not included in the lecture itself.
16 LN 52 has, 'Until millenium [sic], three basic types of philosophy to which must be added muddled types.' In an aside Lonergan referred to the muddled types: 'He can be mixed up.'
17 In place of this material on revision, LN 52 has the following: 'Historical facts can supply difficulties that mistaken philosophies cannot handle satisfactorily.

sense that do not fit into any existing theory. These data would be understood as not fitting into existing theories and demanding a new theory. There would have to be a judgment in which one affirms that the new theory is better or more probable than the older ones. In other words, revision presupposes the three basic operations; the philosophy is a function of the three basic operations, and so it cannot be changed by any revision, because revision presupposes those three operations.

Consequently, while we can expect a plurality of histories of philosophy for the same reasons as we can expect a plurality of philosophies, there are not to be expected radical revisions in the history of philosophy. You can expect a series of developments in which the notion of a history of philosophy is discovered and diffused. For example, on the Scotist theory of knowledge there cannot be development in any subject. The concept is the *species intelligibilis* that is impressed upon possible intellect, and it corresponds to the nature of the thing. There is not, between the thing and the concept, a developing understanding that expresses itself in ever more perfect concepts, as is possible on the Thomist theory. The concept is tied to the thing; so unless there is development in the thing, there cannot be development in the concept. Such a philosophy is nonhistorical; it implies that there is no such thing as history, that there are no concepts developing in time because of the development of understanding. Consequently, there will not be a history of philosophy in any area that holds that type of philosophy to be true. One may talk to Scotists about development, but they have no idea, *can* have no idea, at least coherently with their position, of what development in philosophy or in science could possibly mean. For them, there are the eternal truths; you know them or you do not know them, and that is all there can be to it.[18]

But this inadequacy of the same order of difficulty of apprehension as true philosophy. And easier for opponent to offer to do more research, to invent new hypotheses, than to correct his philosophic error.' Then: 'Pluralism of histories of philosophy offset by fact that philosophies not capable of radical development: family resemblance of empiricists, idealists, realists of all ages: they differ in the scientific and cultural and historical background from which they emerge; in the greater precision and wealth from which they go beyond predecessors; but they express same basic orientations possible to polymorphism of human consciousness.'

18 On this material, LN 52 reads, 'There have been philosophies (Scotist conceptualism, modern logicism) incapable in principle of historical thinking; unless concept function of understanding, development of understanding involves no basic developments in concepts, and so history fitted on Procrustean bed of immobility.'

So in the field of philosophy there is the situation that we can expect many different histories of philosophy that will see things in quite different perspectives. But we are not to expect radical revisions in the history of philosophy. The one development will be the discovery that philosophy has a history, and as philosophy becomes more refined, it will be able to do more refined and detailed work on earlier periods with greater security and conviction. In other words, progress in the history of philosophy will be the same as the progress in philosophy itself.

It is important to note that exactly the same difficulty occurs in the history of philosophy as occurs in general history, which is the difficulty from which we started. It might be said that, if people get down and really read the author, they can pick out the main facts on his thought; and that, if they read objectively, they do not read their own minds into it. That is the positivist idea. But de facto it does not work. St Thomas himself is something like a Platonic Idea with all sorts of different realizations in the real world. The same is true of Kant or Aristotle or any other great philosopher. There are several interpretations because there are several fundamental and opposed mentalities.

If one, for example, defines the real as the 'already out there now,' his rejection of Kant has to consist in an affirmation of the real as the 'already out there now.' One will hold that Kant's view is phenomenalism, and will oppose it with some immediate sensitive or intellectual intuition of reality. On the other hand, if one holds that one knows the real when one makes a true judgment, one's reading of Kant will be entirely different. One will not find fault with Kant because he says that the sensible data are just phenomena. If he wants to call them that, let him do so; that is not the real issue. The real issue is whether there is in Kantian philosophy room for a judgment of fact, and whether that judgment of fact has the implications that de facto are found in the realist assertion of the judgment of fact.

The whole interpretation thus takes a different viewpoint. What is extremely important from a realist viewpoint is of no importance from an empiricist viewpoint, and vice versa. Knowledge of fact presupposes understanding, understanding presupposes experience, and where there is radically different understanding, there will be radically different facts.[19]

19 On this material, LN 52 reads, 'Neutralism (appeal to facts, plain facts) is not a solution; it will be an apparent solution for the obtuse, who can find in data only their own mode of understanding, and so include their own understanding (limited) as a component in the plain facts. NB: As judgement, so knowledge of fact presupposes understanding, and what can be understood by everyone no matter how stupid is a poor criterion for settling what was understood by Parmenides, Heraclitus, Plato, Aristotle, &c.'

4   The History of Theology

Let us now move to a third topic in our attempt to close in upon the notion of history. Let us consider the history of theology. There can be a history of theology insofar as theology exists as a science. The first problem to settle, then, is, when did theology become a science? Or to put the same matter more clearly, when does any subject become a science?

I think the answer to that question is that a science emerges when thinking in a given field moves to the level of system.[20] Prior to Euclid there were many geometrical theorems that had been established. The most notable example is Pythagoras's theorem on the hypotenuse of the right-angled triangle, which occurs at the end of book 1 of Euclid's *Elements*. Euclid's achievement was to bring together all these scattered theorems by setting up a unitary basis that would handle all of them and a great number of others as well.

Similarly, mechanics became a system with Newton. Prior to Newton, Galileo's law of the free fall and Kepler's three laws of planetary motion were known. But these were isolated laws. Galileo's prescription was that the system was to be geometry; so there was something functioning as a system. But the system really emerged with Newton. This is what gave Newton his tremendous influence upon the Enlightenment. He laid down a set of basic concepts, definitions, and axioms, and proceeded to demonstrate and conclude from general principles the laws that had been established empirically by his predecessors. Mechanics became a science in the full sense at that point where it became an organized system.

Again, a great deal of chemistry was known prior to Mendeleev.[21] But his discovery of the periodic table selected a set of basic chemical elements and selected them in such a way that further additions could be made to the basic elements. Since that time chemistry has been one single organized subject with a basic set of elements accounting for incredibly vast numbers of compounds. In other words, there is a point in the history of any science

---

20   LN 53 has, 'A science emerges with the discovery that gives it a well-defined field and method.' Several items appear on LN 53 before this material. 'Theology is "fides quaerens intellectum." In time it becomes a science: hence, necessary to distinguish periods of (1) simple faith, (2) emergence of scientific elements, (3) constitution of science. As a religious science, it has to contend not only with philosophic polymorphism of man but also with the further dimension of polymorphism that results from the acceptance, the partial rejection, or the total negation of faith.'

21   LN 53 has, 'Priestley Boyle Lavoisier before Mendeleev.'

when it comes of age, when it has a determinate systematic structure to which corresponds a determinate field.

If we ask when it was that theology took the step that with Euclid was taken by geometry, with Newton by mechanics, and with Mendeleev by chemistry, the answer is that this step, this fundamental step, was taken when theology became a unified subject with a sharply delimited field distinct from any other subject. This step came with the discovery of the systematic notion of the supernatural order by Philip, Chancellor of the University of Paris, about the year 1230. If you wish to settle whether a question is theological or not, you simply ask, Is it supernatural?

People, especially non-Catholics, are often greatly upset when we use the word 'supernatural.' In current English it has the connotation of 'spooks.' But the thing to emphasize is, not the word 'supernatural,' but the idea of an order. Just as Euclidean geometry selects and orders a domain, just as Newtonian mechanics selects and orders a domain, just as the periodic table selects and orders a domain that makes the science a single whole with a clear method, clear criteria, and full awareness of what pertains to it and what does not, similarly theology selects an order that consists in grace which is above nature, in faith which is above reason, in charity which is above ordinary human good will, and in merit for eternal life which is above any human deserts. There is an entitative order of grace, faith, charity, and merit that comes to us through Christ, that is known by faith, that is realized by charity, that is socialized in the mystical body which is the church.[22]

With the notion of the supernatural, theology became a subject all by itself with a domain of its own. It obtained its method. Throughout the twelfth century, 'grace' and 'nature' were terms that were constantly used, but the theologians could not figure out why it was that nature was not a grace too. After all, God gratuitously gives us our nature just as much as he gives us grace. The theologians were in all sorts of difficulties over that. Again, the relation between faith and reason constituted similar difficulties. There is in Anselm, in Abelard, in Richard of St Victor, who were men of great speculative ability, the difficulty of distinguishing between the mysteries of faith and the truths of natural reason. That distinction is self-evident when one knows about the supernatural order. But the people who were trying to do theology before that order was a clearly conceived systematic

22 On 'order' LN 53 has, 'a set defined by intelligible relations,' and on 'supernatural' 'involving God as He is in Himself: faith above reason, grace above nature, charity above good will, merit above human deserts.'

notion did not have that evidence at all. And so you find rationalist tendencies in really great theologians of the late eleventh century and the twelfth century. But with the notion of the supernatural there were settled the object or field of theology, the method of theology, the fundamental criteria of theology.

The discovery of the notion of the supernatural makes a fundamental dividing line in the history of theology. If you study the theologians after that point, you find that fundamentally they speak and think the way we do today. But when you study the theologians before that point, you have an entirely different problem on your hands. In other words, you have a period that is simply the history of a science, and that will be the history of theology from 1230 on. The science began then, and it has existed since. It may have had its darker periods, its periods of decline, but at least the fundamental modes of conception, the fundamental methods, the fundamental criteria were fixed then. Further developments were needed, but the history of that later period is something that is eminently manageable. There will be different theological schools for the same reason as there will be different philosophical schools. Moreover, there will be religious conflict insofar as people are rationalists, insofar as they refuse to submit their judgments to the wisdom of God and the enlightenment that God can give us by revelation. So there are different histories of theology for philosophic reasons and as well for religious reasons. But from 1230 on in the Catholic world[23] there is a really manageable field for historical investigation.

One may ask about the earlier period, and one can discern a series of points of inflection. Just as Euclid is the beginning of geometry as a science though there were theorems before Euclid, and just as Newton is the beginning of mechanics though there were theorems before Newton that go back to the Greeks (for example, Archimedes' lever), similarly, while the full emergence of theology as a science occurred about 1230 with Philip the Chancellor, there are emergences of technical thinking on particular points in the earlier period, and they form the basic points to be investigated and brought to light in the study of that earlier period.

Let us take as one example the word *homoousios*, consubstantial. The Council of Nicea defined the Son as consubstantial with the Father. Now if one compares the symbols, the creeds, of the church on this matter, one will find that there is the *Quicumque*, which used to be known as the Athanasian

---

23 In an aside Lonergan mentioned that there would be a different history of the question of the supernatural for Protestants.

Creed — it is of Latin origin and mentality — and there is the Creed of the First Council of Constantinople in 381 — the date on this creed is disputed, but it belongs to the fourth or fifth century — and there is Nicea in 325, and there is the Apostles' Creed about the year 200. What do we find in these different creeds?

In the *Quicumque* there occur technical terms. One is not to confuse the persons or divide the substance. In God there are three persons and one substance, and one is not to confuse the persons, that is, one is not to say that the three are really one. And one is not to divide the substance; one is not to say that there are two or three Gods. Then systematically the creed goes to work. It speaks in even terms of Father, Son, and Holy Ghost. Father, Son, and Holy Ghost are God. Each is Lord, each is omnipotent, each is eternal. And they are not three beings but just one being. The point is rammed home in every possible fashion.

The decree of Constantinople states, 'We believe in God, the Father almighty, Creator of heaven and earth.' (It is the creed that is sung at High Mass or recited in the Mass.) There is affirmed then the consubstantiality of the Son, in the same way as at Nicea; and then there is added, 'I believe in the Holy Ghost.' It does not say that the Holy Ghost is God. It says *simul adoratur et conglorificatur,* he is adored with the Father and glorified with him. But it is not stated that he is God.

In the Council of Nicea there is affirmed the divinity of the Father and, in all sorts of manners, the divinity of the Son. But of the Holy Ghost it does not even say *simul adoratur et conglorificatur.* It simply says, 'And in the Holy Ghost, the holy Catholic church,' and so on.

In the Apostles' Creed it says, 'I believe in God, the Father almighty ... and in Jesus Christ, his only Son, Our Lord ... conceived of the Holy Ghost, born of the Virgin Mary ...' It does not say that either the Son or the Holy Ghost is God.[24] In the New Testament the word 'God' is the personal name of the Father. There is, consequently, a development in the use of the name, when in the *Quicumque* and generally in the Latin tradition, the word 'God' is applied indifferently to Father, Son, and Holy Ghost.

There is, then, in the creeds themselves the evidence that at Nicea, when the consubstantiality of the Son was defined, 'consubstantial' was a technical term. It indicates reflection of a philosophic type. Prior to Nicea the word was used about the divine persons only by the Gnostics, and perhaps

---

24 The last sentence is an interpretation of the statement in the lecture, 'It does not say he is God.'

by a few Christians about the year 300; its antecedents are bad. What happened at Nicea in the fourth century? For fifty years the Eastern church was in complete turmoil, and the West was suffering from the repercussions of it. There was something big going on; there were divisions in all directions and many different schools of thought. What happened at Nicea was that Christian thinking about the Son utilized a technical category, *homoousios*, to clarify its meaning, to express itself.

Prior to that period there was belief in the divinity of the Son, but there was the greatest difficulty in expressing it happily. Take, for example, Tertullian's book *Adversus Praxean*. Praxeas had held that the one who died on the cross was God the Father. In other words, he was denying a real distinction between the Father and the Son; the Father and the Son were just the same. Tertullian was insisting both that the Father was distinct from the Son and yet that both were God. However, he had a terrible time trying to say it, because immediately they objected, 'You hold that there are two Gods.' And he replied, 'I will never say that there are two Gods. I will call the Father God, when I speak of the Father alone. When I speak of the Son alone, I will say that the Son is God. When I speak of them both together I will do as St Paul: I will call the Father God and the Son Lord.' Obviously, there was a logical problem. How could one say that both were God, that they were really distinct, and that there were not two Gods? There was no doubt in Tertullian's mind that the Son was God; but how to conceive it was beyond him.

The same problem arises in Justin in a different form. The way we know that these people really believed in the divinity of the Son is by their exegesis of the Old Testament. The apologists of the early church were taking over the literary heritage of the Jews of the Old Testament and reinterpreting it, giving it a Christian interpretation as prophecy of the things that were fulfilled in Christ Jesus. For example, Justin undertakes to prove that the one in the Old Testament who appears to the patriarchs and the prophets and is named God is not the Father but the Son. So he conceives of the Son really as God, if he is the God that appears in the Old Testament. There is no doubt about it.

But the problem of a technical, reflective expression of the truths of the Christian faith was met with a solution at Nicea; and that solution itself took fifty years to be accepted by the Eastern church. All Athanasius himself could say for the word *homoousios* was that we cannot get along without it. De facto Nicea was the first instance in which the church committed itself to the use of nonscriptural terms. After Nicea there never was any difficulty about doing that. But at that time the intention was not to set up a precedent, but simply to meet an emergency. According to Athanasius, things would be ever so much better if no rule of faith contained any word that was not in scripture, that was not simply scriptural doctrine. But to handle the Arians it was essential to find an expression that they could not get round, so that, if they accepted it, they would really have to believe that the Son was God.

Now one can study that period in far greater detail, but one sees there the first emergence of theological thinking. With the *homoousios* we are not at the point that we are at in 1230, when a theological system is emerging; but it is one beginning point. There is another beginning of theological think- ing with the condemnation of the Nestorians and the Monophysites, when Christ is affirmed to be one person in two natures and when the one person is affirmed to be divine. 'Person' and 'nature' are not words that occur in the New Testament; and they occur in that definition in a sense different from the way they were used by prior Fathers. And so, in the Council of Ephesus, the Council of Chalcedon, and the Third Council of Constantin- ople there is the emergence of another element in Catholic theology, an el- ement that is like Pythagoras's discovery of his theorem prior to Euclid's *Ele- ments*, or like Galileo's law prior to Newton's system.

Similarly, in the middle of the twelfth century there was the discovery of the definition of the sacraments. The definition of a sacrament was formed, probably by Peter Lombard, as an efficacious sign of grace. It signified grace and it gave grace. And once the definition was made it was possible to count the sacraments and to know that there were seven. Until we have a defini- tion of fingers and decide whether thumbs are fingers or not, we cannot know whether we have eight or ten fingers. Similarly, there were difficulties about the number of the sacraments because there was not a definition of a sacrament. But with the definition there is the emergence of clear technical thinking on the notion of the sacraments.

Again, there can be conflicts, as between the Pelagianism of the West and Augustine, that finally come to a clarification with the development of the notion of the supernatural in 1230.

What I am trying to say is that the history of Catholic theology is fairly plain sailing after the emergence of the system in 1230, that prior to that there is the beginning of systematic elements in a series of points: the affir- mation of the consubstantiality of the Son, of the one person in two natures, and of the definition of a sacrament. After those definitions, on each point one has a simpler time with the history. But in the earlier period one is in the origins. Those systematic notions with their clear definitions are lack- ing, and the historical problem becomes much more complex.

Now this is equivalent to thinking that besides the history of a science, there is a history of what is not science. The history of a science contains an a priori in the developed science. Insofar as the science can be definitive in its fundamental features as philosophy or theology, there will not be fundamental revisions in the history of the science. However, prior to the science as science in its systematic form there is an earlier period in which there emerge elements that will come together in a system at a later period. Again, the emergence of those elements involves a study in which there is a transition to a systematic, scientific point of view, a transition that begins from a commonsense, symbolic, intersubjective mode of apprehension. The differences we drew between science and common sense, between objectivity and intersubjectivity, between science and art are all relevant to the historical study of those transition points – the emergence of the consubstantial, the one person in two natures, the definition of the sacraments, the supernatural, and the longer and more complex development of the doctrine of the church. So while one can form a fairly clear, definite notion of what history is and how it can be scientific, as long as one is dealing with the history of a science, still there is another field that is, as it were, the bigger and more ordinary field of history that cannot be handled in that fashion.[25]

There is a corollary that follows from what I have said about theology, namely, that the teaching of religion and theology is an enormous problem, and particularly so at the present time. It is at the present time that the full impact of the development of the historical sciences during the past century is hitting theology, and theology has not thought its way through the problems yet. So there will be a difficulty finding satisfactory books and satisfactory ways of treating the matter.

I have given some indication that one can go back to the beginning of the thirteenth century, and then to the points at which theorems emerged at Nicea, at Chalcedon, with the definition of the sacraments and the development of the doctrine of the church. In scriptural theology you are dealing with the same truths as in systematic theology. Systematic theology is theology expressed in the light of technically formulated dogmas or theorems

25 The break was taken at this point, with Lonergan indicating that he would devote the next period to that 'bigger and more ordinary field of history.' In fact, he began the next period with a corollary of what he had been saying about theology. The connection between what he had said about theology, on the one hand, and general history, on the other, appears on LN 53: 'Faith has an understanding that is prior to theologic system; but the question of this prior understanding, which is the historical and the divine basis of the system, raises the question of general history.'

such as the supernatural, one person in two natures in Christ, or the consubstantiality of the Son in the Trinity. Theology puts the whole of Christian doctrine on the reflective, technical, systematic level.

The advantage of theology is that it provides the church, which teaches all nations, with a mode of thought and expression that is independent of the cultural differences of the different nations of the world at any given time, and of the cultural differences at different times. Just this last July I was examining young men from Nyasaland, the Cameroons, and central Africa, who had to make the terrific leap from what recently at least was pretty much a paleolithic culture or something very elementary, very primitive. They had to learn Latin and learn theology and learn the history of theology, and so on. I have the greatest admiration for these people who make that leap. And one could not expect of them what one could expect of people coming from the older cultures of Europe. But the possibility, the significance of theology is that it provides a Catholic expression of the Catholic faith. It is difficult of access. People have to work to understand the exact meaning of technical theology, even in its basic propositions. They have to develop concepts that were hammered out in great controversies that stirred the whole church for notable periods of time: in the fourth century, on the mode of conceiving the divinity of the Son; in the fifth century, on the two natures in Christ; and so on. But there is in the church a mode of thought and expression that is independent of cultural differences. Not only does that provide a center of unity, it also provides a solid basis for reexpression in terms of the mentality of any age. If one knows theology, one is not tied down to the technical terms. One has the habit of understanding. One can express the same truth in other words and do so securely, hitting off exactly what is meant. If one does not have that habit of understanding, all one can do is repeat the formulae, or else run the risk of teaching error instead of truth when one attempts to reexpress it in a way that a teacher must, really to communicate to pupils.

The mode of teaching religion with the old Baltimore Catechism, which expressed, in answering questions, what were really theological propositions, has been attacked on pedagogical grounds, and we will not go into a discussion of that. But there is at the present time a great movement of biblical theology and an attempt to utilize the obvious fact that the mode of thought and expression in the New Testament and in the Old Testament is something much closer to the average man than technical theology can be. The differentiation between the mode of thought prior to the great councils and prior to the development of technical theology, on the one hand,

and the theological mode of thought, on the other hand, is a theological problem that has come into prominence in our time. The older generation of living theologians handles scriptural proofs in a manner that is simply unacceptable to other theologians.

The contemporary theologian, for example, in handling the question of the divinity of Christ as expressed in the New Testament, will distinguish a series of modes of apprehending the divinity of Christ, starting from the way St Peter speaks of Christ in the second chapter of Acts: Jesus was a good man, approved by God by wondrous deeds and miracles; God raised him from the dead on the third day, and that is something that he did not do for David; and manifestly, from the resurrection of the dead, it is clear that he has been made Christ and Lord. That is a mode of expression that would not, could not be used after Nicea. As a matter of fact, it is not used in other parts of the New Testament. But it is an apprehension of Christ. Peter knew Christ first of all as a man, and in the resurrection there was a manifestation of the difference between Christ and other men. There was not in Peter's mind the idea of God that you obtain from reading St Thomas or the Vatican Council. God for the Jews was the God of Abraham, Isaac, and Jacob, the God that led them out of Egypt, the God that spoke to them through the prophets. The Jewish concept of God has been described as a political anthropomorphism. In the New Testament there is a development in that idea of God. When St Paul speaks to the Jews he speaks in that manner, but when he speaks to the Greeks he speaks of the one who created all things, in whom we live and move and have our being. He is moving to a different apprehension of God. Without that different apprehension of God, God simply means 'the one who' — the one who did this and this and this. And when St Peter says that Jesus has been made Christ and Lord, you must not attribute to his expression the metaphysical implications that that expression would have later on.

So you can move through different strata, approaches, ways of speaking about Christ in the New Testament. In St Paul's letter to the Philippians, chapter 2, there is not merely the matter of Christ being man and then being raised to the level of Lord, judge of the living and the dead; he also speaks of him as preexistent, as one who was in the form of God and took on the form of a servant. In the opening of Hebrews there is an account of the Son; a series of Old Testament texts are knitted together; and while the element of the Son's preexistence is not, perhaps, so strongly emphasized as in Philippians, still it is manifest from the texts employed that the author of the epistle to the Hebrews is thinking of the Son as divine.

The full transition occurs with St John, who speaks of the *Logos* first and of his becoming man afterwards. You can start from the man and move up to the divinity, or you can start from God, the Word — 'and the Word was made flesh' — as in the prologue of St John.

The whole of the systematic theological treatise *De Verbo incarnato* is a further expansion of the Johannine conception. For that very reason it is difficult to connect it with texts in the New Testament, which usually start the other way, from the man. There is largely absent in the New Testament a systematic conception of God such as emerges in St Thomas or the Vatican Council. And similarly for a systematic conception of the divinity of Christ. These have to be perceived through indications of various kinds.

The proper teaching of religion and theology is a matter of mastering the biblical theology and the transition from biblical theology to the dogmas of the church. And one has to understand the lot in the light of a systematic theology. To teach such a theology is to teach a science of enormous complexity and sweep. People who take on the teaching of religion have a task that is not for me to break down, simplify, and clarify. I wish just to indicate the problem. It is a problem in historical thinking, and the danger is a one-sided approach. If one teaches simply biblical theology, there is the danger of undermining the dogmas of the church. Why should the church have gone on to these definitions that cause a division of Christians? On the other hand, if you teach simply the theological formulations, you are not easily in contact with the real meaning of the words in the New Testament, and you are not easily in contact with the concrete living of the religious life of the person you are attempting to form.

5   **The Problem of General History** [26]

Now we will attempt to move on to the big problem, general history.

History can be broken into a group of specialized histories on specialized topics: mathematics, physics, chemistry, biology, medicine, philosophy, the-

---

26 Lonergan's notes on general history are quite sparse, just a few lines on an unnumbered page between LN 53 and LN 54. That more existed can be surmised from the fact that a subdivision (A) is indicated, without any further subdivisions. At any rate, what we have reads as follows: '(A) General History without any conscious a priori; General History with no a priori except a critical historical method for penetrating and going behind the "existential" history that is group memory and functions as a common basis and vehicle of meaning for group action; General History with the double a priori of a philosophy and theology of man; a method of scientific historical research.'

ology, military history, legal history, constitutional history, technological history, and so on. All these subjects can be handled, and they can be handled very competently, from the time in which systematic reflection on the subject begins. But there will be difficulties with the period of origins, where systematic thinking does not exist yet. The problem of general history is that it moves throughout on this presystematic level, the same level as that of the origins of science and more technical matters.

I believe that the scientific approach to general history has to be of the same type as the history of science. In other words: all science is a matter of a scissors action − from above downward and from below upward; data, alone, lack significance; principles and leading ideas, alone, lack reality; it is by the coming together of the two that a science is developed. I have indicated this in physics and in chemistry, and I have indicated it again in the history of particular subjects. You have to know mathematics to write the history of mathematics; and similarly for other subjects. The matter is evident. And so we come to the question, What has one to know to be able to write general history?[27] What is its a priori? What stands to general history as knowledge of mathematics stands to the history of mathematics?

Christopher Dawson speaks of regional cultures.[28] Regional cultures belong to or become elements in extended areas of communication. Consider the grouping of small dialect groups of Greece into the Greek nation. This also occurred in Italy, where the Tuscan dialect became the Italian language, and in Spain, where Castilian is dominant. The one language simply means that one dialect acquired dominance. There are also multilingual areas of communication, for example, the Western culture − Europe and the Americas. Finally, outside this area cultural differences are so great that communications break down. The stages, then, are: (1) a single dialect; (2) a single language with many dialects; and (3) a single culture with many languages.

Let us try, then, to grasp this notion of regional culture, first, positively, in the light of art as an exploration of fuller ways of living. Regional culture is the simplest realization of a way of life. What is a way of life? Externally, it is a series of observable actions. Internally, it is a flow of consciousness, and

27 From this point to the words 'the flow is organically united' two paragraphs below, there is a gap on the tape. The material is constructed from the notes of F. Crowe.

28 Dawson's introduction (pp. xii–xx) to *The Age of the Gods* (London and New York: Sheed & Ward, 1933, first published 1928) gives what we might call a context for the idea. We have not been able to locate a reference for the specific term.

the flow is organically united. It does not have the unity of a system of thought, of a theorem, of a demonstration, of a type of intellectual synthesis. It is the coming together in vital organic unity of percepts, images, and affects, of insights and judgments, of decisions and choices. They all form part of a total flow. The past is the origin out of which comes the present, and the present leads on into the future. When we speak of images, percepts, and affects, we are distinguishing moments in a concrete totality.

If we want to apprehend this unity, this organicity, we have to think in artistic terms. It is the unity, not of an intellectual theorem, but of a style, a mode, an orientation. There is an old saying that style is the man. That is fundamentally true. Living is an art, and the artistic product is an expression of that living; it expresses and puts forth a pattern that is isomorphic with the pattern of the living.

Now this artistic living is simply living. It is not a purely individual affair. The individual grows up and develops under the influence of the example of others, under the influence of admiration and ridicule, of precepts and prohibitions, of praise and blame. And the individual is extremely sensitive to all this. His living takes its inspiration, its guidance, and its justification from the opinions of others. Consequently, the style that is the man is not something individual; it belongs to the group. There will be individual variations, but there is something common to all. There is something similar in the tone, the color, the way of doing things, the attitudes that are said to be characteristic of the regional group.

The regional group will be under the influence of geographic, economic, and hereditary determinants. There is a notable French sociologist of the last century, LePlay, who studied the family as the basic unit. His categories included the physical geography, the influence of the place, the seacoast, the mountains, the plains, the valleys, the rivers. One can think of the Eskimos determined in their mode of life by their Arctic habitat. Similarly for the people in the Sahara. The influence of geography provides one great determinant of what the mode of living will be. There is also the technological and economic determinant: the way they work, the tasks they have to perform in their way of life. Finally, there is the influence of heredity and historical memories, their culture, their religion. These three elements — the external determinants of nature, the determinants that come from the mode of subsistence, and the determinants that come from the memories of the past and the tradition, the expressions of values in a religion and in stories — are realized in a single whole, in an organic way of living. It is this regional culture that provides the basic unit in thinking about history. It is a basic harmony. It is not something that can be taught. There is culture that can be taught, and education is concerned with that. But culture on this earlier, simpler, more organic level of the region is something that is lived. You come into it by being born in it and by living with the people. The historian can get in touch with it simply through long familiarity with the documents and monuments of the past age. It is acquired in the way that common sense is acquired, not through any scientific study, but simply by an accumulation of insights that keep occurring; and though you are not noticing that they are occurring, finally they influence your whole way of thinking and conceiving.

Again, we can think of the regional culture in terms of its negation, the slum. The slum is not properly simply a poorer quarter, but a place where there congregate the failures of our industrial society, the people who have no hope and so no ambition, no stimulus. They exist from day to day and are all thrown together by chance. They pull out of it as quickly as they can if they retain the capacity to do so. The existence of the slum as the negation of the regional culture is, of course, a fundamental educational problem, because children are born into slums as much as, if not more than, elsewhere. The problem of the slum, of the breakdown of human dignity, human cohesion, and human standards is a consequence of the attempt that has been going on in recent centuries to remake man. The idea works so far, but there are people who are just not the type to fit into this plan, this idea, and they are driven out below.

I have attempted to state what I mean by the regional culture and its negation in the slum. To take a phrase that may throw some light upon the idea, Dawson has remarked that one can learn more about Byzantine life from the churches of Ravenna than from reading all the books on the topic.[29] In the churches a person with the requisite artistic sensibility will understand from the art — the mode of expression, of building and decorating — the tone of feeling, the orientation, the mentality of the people on a level that cannot be put into words. The regional culture is human living at a level that has not been conceptualized. And history, which is a conceptualization, is not going to be able to conceptualize it. It can only describe it, intimate it, communicate it artistically.

29 Christopher Dawson, *The Dynamics of World History*, ed. John J. Mulloy (New York: Sheed & Ward, 1956) 69: 'We can learn more about mediaeval culture from a cathedral than from the most exhaustive study of constitutional law, and the churches of Ravenna are a better introduction to the Byzantine world than all the volumes of Gibbon.'

This is the fundamental problem in general history: the reality with which it deals is not a conceptualization, not the realization of clearly formed concepts, and consequently it cannot be adequately represented by a conceptualization. It can be communicated artistically rather than conceptually. We are back at the problem that was evaded by speaking of the history of the sciences. The history of the sciences is the history of a movement that is strictly conceptual. But general history deals with intelligence living in the concrete. In the concrete there is not the separation of percept and feeling, of understanding and willing, of judging and deciding and choosing. They are organically one, and consciousness is undifferentiated.

We have an example of an extended area of communication in Voegelin's second volume of *Order and History, The World of the Polis*.[30] It is a discussion of the development of Greek order and its breakdown. It certainly is an extremely interesting presentation.[31] He traces the influence of Homer and Hesiod, the tragedians, Pindar, the philosophers, the Sophists, the historians, and finally, in the following volume, he goes on to Plato and Aristotle. There also is a recent book by Mary Renault, *The King Must Die*,[32] that has been very highly praised. It is a re-creation of the story of Theseus, and it is written from within the mythic consciousness of the time. It is the sort of book that perhaps could not have been written prior to the last fifteen years. The story is told by Theseus himself right through. Everything is taken for granted — all the doctrine of the gods, and so on — and it is all extremely plausible in a way. (Of course, she has underlying it her naturalistic explanations, but they do not intrude; they appear in an appendix.) The way the mythic consciousness finally involved a deception of Theseus himself is also there. But it is all there implicitly. It is a very brilliant piece of work. (I do not want it to be said that I recommend the book. It also exemplifies a statement made by Christopher Dawson that the achievement of Christianity was the transference of religion from the id to the superego.[33] Pagan religion is

30 See above, chapter 1, note 50.
31 Lonergan added that he was not sure just how good Voegelin's presentation is, and that he probably should ask one of the participants in the audience, Fr Hetherington, for his opinion.
32 Mary Renault, *The King Must Die* (New York: Pantheon, 1958).
33 See Christopher Dawson, *Understanding Europe* (New York: Sheed & Ward, 1952) 14: 'Even today very little thought is given to the profound revolution in the psychological basis of culture by which the new society of Western Christendom came into existence. Stated in the terms of Freudian psychology, what occurred was the translation of religion from the sphere of the Id to that of the Super-Ego.'

mixed in with sexuality, and that element is also present in the book; consequently I do not want to give any general recommendation of it. It may be difficult or offensive for some people.)

Now, when we move to this extended area of communication, our earlier analysis of the good as a developing object provides us with a set of categories of what really there is to go forward. We set forth an invariant structure of the good and the differentials that bring about change on the level of civilization and on the level of cultural values. Again, we noted the principles of decline and the different manifestations of sin, and then the principle of redemption. Finally, we set forth the levels of integration. In that concrete idea of the human good, that categorization of the human good as containing invariants, differentials, and integrals, one has a philosophic a priori for the study of history. And without something similar, the historian has nothing to write about.

In other words:[34] (1) The complaint in the relativist view of history is that, just as economic history changes with a new view in economics, so that the history of the nineteenth century will be written differently in 1910 and in 1950 because the science of economics has changed within that interval — what is generally accepted in one period is not at all generally accepted in the other, and vice versa, and that will profoundly influence what is thought to be significant — so in general history there are as many histories as there are nations. There is not merely the history of Germany. There is the German history of Germany, the French history of Germany, the Italian history of Germany, the English history of Germany, and so on. That is true for every country. Moreover, there are several German histories of Germany according to the different periods. Things that were not thought important in a previous period are thought important now. The history of the country is rewritten again, and rewritten again, from the viewpoint of as many different cultures and nations as the people who happen to write it. And so one moves into a complete historical relativism. This is a fundamental problem of historians at the present time.

(2) Historians have been thinking out techniques and ways of getting around relativism, and the problem can be eliminated up to a certain point. There is really an elimination of the problem to a certain extent insofar as one is moving from the data upward. Just as there are correlations on the level of natural laws, so there is something similar in the field of history, something that can be ascertained as matter of fact independently of the

34 The numbering here represents our editing.

viewpoint of particular historians. For example, one can set down what are simply facts concerning what Justin, Tertullian, Origen, Novatian, Alexander, Dionysius of Alexandria all had to say about Christ. And then there are the different schools and the controversies. The data of themselves exclude a number of accounts of what was going forward. They provide a determinant. But alone they do not suffice. There is also needed the movement from above downward. You are writing about man, and what you think of man cannot be neglected in your account of man's history. And if people have entirely different notions of what man is and of what is significant in human life, they are going to write history differently. There will be in general history the same difficulties as there are in a history of theology or of philosophy. There is going to be a pluralism, and I think that pluralism is more honest and more fruitful than any attempt to select out what everyone can agree on and disregard the rest. That attempt stems from simply accepting the positivist position, the secularist position.

There is a further point to be touched on. I have said that historically there do arise from the data, simply as data, correlations. Now I want to draw attention to the precise type of intelligibility that is to be found in historical data. You will remember that in the image of the circle intelligence grasps necessity. If the radii are equal the curve *must* be perfectly round; if they are unequal it *cannot* be perfectly round. However, from the particular data, from the graph that can be drawn as a result of scientific measurements after a period of experience, experiments, or observations, what intelligence grasps is not 'It *must* be this law, this formula,' but 'This formula is *possible*, and it is the simplest we can think of.' There is a difference between insight grasping possibility in the data and insight grasping necessity in the data. The intelligibility grasped by the historian will contain elements of necessity. There are particular mechanisms that amount to necessity. However, in general it is the same type of intelligibility that is possibility. Human action is a matter of insight into situations. The insight yields possible courses of action. And we are free because there is no way of demonstrating that one must take this course rather than that course.[35] The *operabile* can be determined, not by demonstration, but only by dialectical and rhetorical syllogism. That is why the action is free.

Moreover, not only is historical intelligibility a de facto realization of intelligibility, but also one must note that it is not without the surd. That notion

---

35 Lonergan referred at this point to Thomas Aquinas, *Summa theologiae*, 1, q. 83, a. 1.

of the surd I developed earlier.[36] In other words, sin is going against reason. The sinful action is similarly against reason, against intelligence. The situation produced by sinful action will be nonintelligible, nonrational; and the nonrational situation will provide objective evidence for false principles. There will result the dissemination of false principles. Historical intelligibility is dealing not merely with the intelligible but also with the surd, just as mathematics deals with numbers, some of which are real and others of which are imaginary, such as the square root of minus one.

Again, historical intelligibility is not without mystery. Human history is the realization of a divine idea; it is the exact realization of just what God intends and permits. It is free. That this intelligibility should be realized is a product of human freedom. The catch is that there are several different individuals, several different peoples, exercising their freedom. That is how there can be an element of historical inevitability, namely, the multiplicity of the peoples. There is an interlocking, an interdependence, of the different exercises of freedom. I spoke yesterday of the notion of destiny as exhibited by drama, and that is the idea I am speaking of here.

Finally, the possibilities of resisting the mechanisms and the determinisms that can emerge historically are heightened almost to an unlimited extent by Christianity. The death and resurrection of Christ express the victory of truth and goodness in spite of every kind of suffering: physical, in reputation, and in every other way. The example of Christ and the grace of God that comes to us through Christ constitute a historical force that, in Christ's own words, amounts really to this: Fear not, I have overcome the world.[37] Christ himself overcame the world by resisting the powers of evil in suffering everything they would inflict upon him. And he rose again the third day. It is this Christian hope that is a supreme force in history. It is a fundamental and unchangeable ground that enables ordinary mortals to stand by the truth, and stand by what is right, no matter what the consequences.

I wish to thank you all for your very kind attention during these two weeks.

36 See above, chapter 3, § 1.2.
37 See John 16.33. NRSV: '… take courage; I have conquered the world!'

Appendix

Our short appendix consists of five quotations from Lonergan's notes for the lectures on education. We judged these quotations too long to place in footnotes. But references to their appearance in an appendix are given at the relevant places in the footnotes, and here we provide an indication for each quotation as to where it fits in the text of the lectures. Our italics indicate underlining in the notes; where we judged it helpful, we have filled out in square brackets Lonergan's abbreviations; square brackets are used also for a sentence inserted in the middle of § A.

A.   **Philosophy of Education / Philosophy of ...**[1] (chapter 1, § 3, at note 60)

LN 20:

Any subject involves a set of basic terms and relations.

---

1 Lonergan not only worked out the concept of 'philosophy of ...'; he also contributed significantly to the philosophies themselves in various areas. There is an unpublished essay, 'Philosophy of History,' in his student papers (File 713 in the Archives), and years later in 1960, he lectured at Thomas More Institute, Montreal, on that topic. That same year he published a paper to answer the question, 'How should I conceive philosophy of religious experience?' (*Collection* 185). In 1973 he published his lectures on Philosophy of God, and Theology, and in 1980 wrote 'A Post-Hegelian Philosophy of Religion' (*A Third Collection* 202–23). Other lectures and papers, without 'philosophy of ...' in their title, nevertheless contribute quite directly to philosophies of mathematical logic, of existentialism, of science, and of course of education.

Every subject has developed and will develop: the basic terms and relations are not a unique set but a changing set.

Man is polymorphic: there are basic orientations that modify the distribution of emphasis, the hierarchy of values, the direction of development, in the basic sets of terms and relations: empiricist, idealist, realist; aesthetic, ethical, religious; sensate, idealistic, ideational; *mixed-up* or *immature and developing.*

Philosophies are pure expressions of human polymorphism; '*philosophies of* ...' are applied expressions of the same polymorphism ...

Philosophy of maths, natural science, human science, history, religion, education.

Philosophy of education is concerned the [sic] polymorphism of man in educational *theorists*, colleges for teachers, administrators, teachers, parents, pupils, *society.*

1 *Not philosophy* in sense of Wolff: abstract ens ≡ possible; logic ontology cosmology ... But *ens* ≡ comprehensive, omnia de omnibus (as notion 'concrete') underpins, penetrates, relates, goes beyond all contents

2 *Not philosophy*, as general concepts, principles, relevant to some abstract aspect, but philosophy as *comprehensive,* as grounding and unifying all particular disciplines

3 *Not philosophy* as a dam across river of life, growth, development but as the bed in which the river flows

4 *Not philosophy* as opposed to, exclusive of, theology. Christian philosophy: potentially (prior to concrete) formally (in concrete)

5 *Not philosophy* as prescinding from technical, practical: *hedgehog* and *owl*[2] but as grasping nature, value, limitations of techniques ... as concerned with putting technical questions in correct form, perspective.

[A second set of notes on the same topic appears on the next page.]

LN 21:

Philosophy of ... understands judges transforms specialized contributions by natural, humanist; not just application of general abstract rules but enters into, diversified by, more concrete issues

e.g. of maths, of nature, of history, of education

---

2 There is a Greek proverb (Archilocus, Fragment 103) according to which 'The fox knows many things, but the hedgehog knows one big thing.' It is possible, and seems highly likely, that in Lonergan's memory many years after his study of the classics, the fox became an owl; certainly the context in this note is not unlike that of the proverb.

261 Appendix

Contra – Philosophy is itself a subject. Logic Metaphysics (Ontology) Cosmology Natural Theology Ethics – Wolff – H. St Denis (on Insight and indigestion)[3]

A Wisdom judges basic concepts, orders sciences (objects)

B Insight *Ens* underpins, penetrates, goes beyond all contents; not abstract but comprehensive (like word 'concrete')

Metaphysics total heuristic structure; desiderium naturale – basic concepts of all sciences – order between sciences – the general account of the reality they know – the basis of knowledge of God – the open structure into which revelation, faith, theology may be inserted – enlarged metaphysics –> Philosophy of theology

C Xtian philosophy: a – distinguishes metaphysics proportionate being and total metaphysics; b – distinguishes less than intelligible, intelligible ..., *mystery* more than int ...[4] c – enlarges truth: not just immanent product of human mind but true for God

D Opposition to Xtian philosophy – potentially Xtian and specifically Xtian. Science specified by objects (formal) and deals with universal, necessary (self-evident, demonstrable); formal object not intelligibility in reality but *concept*, formality

E Basis of Xtian philosophy [Objectifier and Objectified]

Objects: God, angels, man, animals, plants, chemical elements, physical elements (universe);

Subject qua subject: objectifier: Logic Maths Method Metaphysics as proceeding from experience, understanding, reflection.

B.   Operations and Culture (chapter 3, § 2.2.4, at note 84)

LN 40 recto and verso:

'*Operations*

'*Sequences* (unilinear, multiple) of individual operations in the individual (*biography*), in the imagined group (*drama*), in existing social groups, subgroups, totality (*history*)

---

3 Henri Saint-Denis, reviewing *Insight*: 'The overabundance of material and side issues ... is such that some readers are likely to get intellectual indigestion' (*Revue de l'Université d'Ottawa* 29 [1959] 120–23, at 120).

4 The 'less than intelligible ... intelligible ... more than intelligible' were a fundamental schema and guiding structure for Lonergan from his student days; see 'Analytic Concept of History' (File 713 in the Lonergan Archives), p. 8: 'unintelligible ... intelligible ... too-intelligible.'

'*Schemes* of kinds of operations are concrete potentialities to elicit a significantly ordered sequence of operations

'*Group* of schemes: an intelligibly interrelated interdependent mutually complementary set of schemes which together are sufficient to meet a rounded totality of goals ends needs tasks exigences

'*Grouping* can emerge on natural, spontaneous, artistic, or reflective level; it can occur on several levels at once:

'Natural: intelligible but not intelligent

'Spontaneous: the creativity of Dasein; drama imitated by actor

'Artistic: objectification of grouping in song and dance, religious cult, myth and legend, architecture and statue, drawing and picture, epic drama lyric, wisdom literature (cf. Dawson on knowing Byzantine culture by studying the churches of Ravenna)

'Reflective: objectified in concepts theories systems; debated not only practically but also theoretically

'A *culture* is a way of life (American, British defended in ww II)

'It is a grouping of schemes of operation, where the grouping is embedded in the skills, the intellectual and moral habits, and the institutions and memories (existential history) of a social unit

'*Division of cultures*

'*A* Common sense mode of understanding: the group of sehemes of operations may be possessed by the social unit

'1) totally or almost so by each of its members

'2) only partially by any member, totally only by all together

'Hence, undifferentiated and differentiated common sense with differentiation through division of labour (or exceptional powers, cf Eliade Le chamanisme)

'Hence, difference between primitive cultures and early high civilizations (Sumer Egypt Crete Indus valley Hoangho Maya Incas)

'*B* Scientific mode of understanding (reasoning definition sets of definitions totality of deductive conclusions)

'1) Liberal culture: development of intellectual pattern of experience sought for its own sake and its spontaneous benefits; apt to [be] praised as useless, contrasted with banausic arts

'2) Contemporary culture: intellectual development turns to domination of nature and transformation of human society; what man has made of man can be remade and should (?); philosophies of politics, economics, education; applied science; sociology with an eye to social engineering

'*Types of Cultural Problems*

'Primitive: poverty, myth, magic; hard brutish short

'Early civilization: myth and magic remain; thought remains collectivist on level of truths and values

'Liberal: divides society into upper cultivated classes and lower uncultivated; has wealth of early civilization but lacks wealth of contemporary

'Contemporary: the products and projects of reflective thought fail to integrate with the natural artistic schemes; alienation of man from society and of social process from man; inhumanity, depersonalization, Jaspers, Heidegger, psychiatrists, sociologists; the slum'

C.   Dimensions of Choice and Apprehensions of Obligation
(chapter 4, § 3.3.3, at note 72)

LN 46:

Dimensions of choice

Object: A or Not-A; A or B

Act: decisive person chooses; drifter, conformist, consents to, chooses to, not make up his mind, be another instance of the average man in a given milieu

Act has to result from the subject: it is not determined by external circumstance, by biology, by psychic flow, by arguments, reasons, that demonstrate the operabile (rhetorical and dialectical syllogisms only); it results from my will, ut quo, from me, ut quod

I do it: to do it is a self-affirmation self-acceptance self-realization

My doing it cannot be based on complete and exhaustive knowledge; it cannot be free from all risk; I have to accept consequences, be ready to accept consequences, if I choose

If issue left to mere balancing of motives, impulses, then I am choosing, not to be *my*self, but just to drift, to conform, to be like everybody else – an obnubilation, an escape

My choosing not merely settles object of act, A and not B, but also settles an element, a disposition, a component of habit, that predetermines my future tendencies, my permanent orientation. By my choosing I make myself the kind of man I am to be

Good of order results from the goodness of persons that compose the order: what people make of themselves determines their concrete immediate world, its good and its evil. Good of order = order of personal relations; clear in feudal

But people make themselves by their choices; hence, the very act of choosing is a higher good than finite objects

Moral teaching should inculcate, dramatize, not merely good objects but also the goodness that lies in choosing itself, in the consciously autonomous personality — else mass-mind, plastercast of a man,[5] rank and file but not leaders, lack of civic virtue in Catholics

Still, resolute decisive man need not be a good man; he may be just a dangerous man, a Mussolini, Lenin, Stalin

The object of resolution, of decisiveness, is supremely the ever broadening horizon: it is the movement from the world of my limited concern to the world God made, from the order I understand to the order that God in his wisdom and goodness chose and in his omnipotence brings about. He brings it about through us, and what he intends is not a world without evils, but a world in which evil is permitted but good brought out of it.

Apprehensions of obligation[6] — Why should I? What is 'should' for me, in me?

(a) pure nexus: coherence between knowing and doing ≡ Major
Minor premises:

(b) realization A: I am involved; choosing; hence, I am obliged to coherence of doing with knowing

(c) realization B: We are involved: it is not only my good but also the good of others: parents friends associates country mankind history — good of order apprehended in personal relations, charity

(d) realization C: this is world God wills; conscious free instruments.

D. Group Theory (chapter 5, § 2.5, at note 42):

LN 73 verso:
Complete domination of subject
Operations related to one another: form a group; reversibility

---

5 See *Understanding and Being* 34, 35, 184, 264, 269; the phrase comes from Kant, *Critique of Pure Reason* A 836/B 864 (Norman Kemp Smith translation, 655–56).

6 This schematic presentation, while fully in line with the position of *Insight* that doing must be consistent with knowing (the major premise here), is nevertheless remarkable for its set of minor premises. The linkage of self, others, and God in the apprehension of obligation is established and set forth with a concise clarity that we have not seen previously in Lonergan; it also points directly toward the more elaborate notion of the human good that he will develop later.

Terms multiply related by sets of operations

Not merely prove but prove possibility or imposs of proving

Expansion: add new operations; operate on new materials (number: ordered set, lattice); represented by number (space-time, physics, chemistry, etc)

Identity: equivalence of different sets of operations: binomial

Invariance: what is unchanged by any operations of a group: tensors as defined by transformation properties; law as what is unchanged by spatio-temporal variation: Riemann Einstein

Isomorphism: same set of operations on different materials result in similarity of structure in different materials

Within maths: isomorphic fields (fruit of symbolic logic)

Arithmetical and physical applications

Eg form square with 1764 marbles; take square root of 1764; why does arithmetic technique yield result, $10^2a^2 + (2 \cdot 10a + b)b$

Learning: active method as differentiation of consciousness increases, operate on marbles, natural numbers, symbols

Form: as grasped by insight into image of sequence of operations; as governing sequence of operations; as expressed in implicit definition; as expressed in definition by form + common matter; as expressed in group of instances with form and individual matter

Classical view of intelligence

An initial stage of pure development, not a limiting definition

Greater reflectivity: not eternal abstract objects; but form in series of concrete activities and products

Break with faculty psychology: concrete consciousness operating in more highly differentiated pattterns.

Levels of Logic: manipulating symbols

analysing concepts: approfondir as phil, method

self-appropriation as ground of logic metaphysics epistemology.

E.   The Transformation of the Notion of Science
(chapter 6, § 2.7, at note 29)

LN 76:

Fundamental notions. Nature of Science.

1. The concept of science develops with the development and attainment of scientific knowledge.

2. Science is 'certa rerum per causas cognitio'
Aristotelian meaning: res: decem genera entis
    causae: end agent matter form
Chemistry: res: 3.10^5 compounds
    causae: periodic table of elements
    not certain but extremely probable
    Newton, causes
    Einstein, field theory
    Hamilton

3. Essence and properties: logical analysis
Valid in Natural theology; applied to universe by Spinoza
Qua logical, universally valid
Qua scientific: to know essence one must know properties: upward spiral
Human science: the essence of man is to become a man

4. Analytic propositions
Experience of ontological argument. Tautology.
Aquinas: I-II 66 5 4m[7]
Scotus, Ockham: intuition of existing and present as existing and present; Nicolas of Autrecourt

5. Scientia est de necessariis.
There are instances of necessity. C G. [*Summa contra Gentiles*] II 28–30
Science is of the intelligible: necessary, possible, de facto or empirical
Scotus, voluntarism. Aquinas, understand this universe.

6. Law and system
Galileo: system is geometry
Newton, Enlightenment: system is mechanics
Modern: state and probabilities

7. Science is gradual actuation of intelligence with respect to empirical data

7 '... cognitio principiorum indemonstrabilium dependet ex ratione terminorum: cognito enim quid est totum et quid pars, statim cognoscitur quod omne totum est maius sua parte.' This passage, a familiar one in Lonergan's writings, seems to be taken here as a Thomist sample of an analytic proposition.

Data are internal and external

The actuation involves the two moments of hypothesis and verification

The two moments are interdependent: hypothesis guides the activities of verifying; verifying brings to light further data which lead to the revision of hypotheses

The process contains an element of continuity: earlier successful organizations of data reappear in later organizations

There are upper limits to the process: it is always a matter of experiencing, understanding, judging

Hence the process is one of increasing probability and it converges toward ultimate truth.

8. State of science: system on the move

Lindsay & Margenau: axiomatic presentation of Q.T. 1937

David Bohm:[8] give origin and significance of components so that one will know how to change it.

---

8 In a long review of *Insight* in *The Modern Schoolman* 35 (1957) 236–44, James Albertson critiques, among other things, Lonergan's views on probability, and in this connection (p. 244) draws on a work of David Bohm which appeared in 1957. Lonergan would not therefore have seen it when he wrote *Insight*; it is possible that Albertson's reference introduced him to Bohm's work.

Lexicon of Latin and Greek Words and Phrases

The single purpose of this lexicon is to help readers unfamiliar with Latin and Greek to understand the lectures. Translations given by Lonergan (indicated by quotation marks) are therefore used where that is possible; even though they be not literally accurate, they show the sense in which he used the particular term in question. For his explanation of certain Aristotelian and Thomist terms, the reader should consult pages 94 and especially 170–72 above.

Latin Words and Phrases

actus exsistentis in potentia inquantum huiusmodi: the act of something existing in potency, insofar as it is in potency

actus imperfecti inquantum huiusmodi: the act of an imperfect being, insofar as it is imperfect

adaequatio: correspondence (for example, of mind and object in truth; also, in Lonergan's philosophy, metaphysical equivalence)

an sit?: is it?

animal rationale: 'the animal that is a logical animal'

animal symbolicum: 'symbolic animal' (in the active sense: an animal that uses symbols)

bonum et malum sunt in rebus: 'good and evil lie in the concrete'

bonum particulare: 'the particular good'

causa essendi: the cause of being

certa rerum per causas cognitio: 'certain knowledge of things by their causes'

Cogito, ergo sum: I think, therefore I am

de auxiliis: about (divine) help [in reference to a Dominican vs Jesuit dispute on the way grace operates]
Deus est: 'God is'
differentiae: (specific) differences
docta ignorantia: (knowledge of) 'the known unknown'

ens: 'being,' 'the real,' 'something that is affirmed'
ens dicitur ab esse: ' "Being," the noun, is said from "to be" '
ens et bonum convertuntur: 'being and the good are convertible'
ens per essentiam: 'a being that in virtue of its own intelligibility *is*'
ens per participationem: 'a being by participation'
ens quo: 'a component in a being'
ens quod: the being which
entia: beings
esse: 'existence,' being, the 'metaphysical equivalent' of 'veritas'
est: 'it is'

foras: see 'non foras'

gratia operans: operative grace

Hypotheses non fingo: 'I do not fabricate hypotheses'

id quod est: that which is
id quod omnia appetunt: 'what everything seeks or runs after'
indocta ignorantia: (the field of) 'the unknown unknown'
intellectus agens: 'the agent intellect, intellectual light'
intellectus possibilis: 'the possible intellect'
intelligere in phantasmatibus: to understand (something) in the (presented) images
intelligibile in sensibilibus: the intelligible (component) in what can be sensed
intelligere: 'understanding'
intentio entis: 'the intention of being'
intus: see 'non intus'

motus intelligitur [cognoscitur] ex termino: 'a movement is understood from its end [term]'; **motus cognoscitur non solum ex termino sed magis ex via ad terminum si est terminus:** a movement is known not only from its term but even more from the way to the term if there is a term

non foras: 'not without'
non intus: 'not within'

numerus et mensura motus secundum prius et posterius: number and measure of motion in respect of before and after
nunc: now

omni et nullo: (what is verified) in every instance (of the defined) and (is falsified) in none
omni et soli: (what is verified) in every instance (of the defined) and only in instances (of the defined)
omnia: 'everything'
omnis scientia est nobis naturaliter indita in lumine intellectus agentis: 'all science is naturally, virtually given to us in the light of agent intellect'
operabile: the doable

philosophia perennis: 'a perennial philosophy'
potens omnia facere et fieri: able to create all things and to become all things
prius et posterius: before and after

quid sit?: 'what is it?'

realitas: reality
reductio ad principia: 'a reduction (of the definition) to its principles'

sensibile: 'what is given to sense'
simpliciter: simply
simul adoratur et conglorificatur: together with (the Father and the Son) is adored and glorified
species intelligibilis: intelligible species

verbum: word
veritas: 'truth'
Verum est medium in quo cognoscitur ens: 'The truth is the medium in which one knows being'

Greek Words and Phrases

aisthêta: (plural of 'aisthêton')
aisthêton: 'what is given to sense'
aition: cause
aition tou einai: the cause of being, 'the reason why [the materials] are [something]'
alêtheia: truth

eidos: 'form'
einai: to be (see 'aition tou eivai')
epaktikos: (see 'logos epaktikos')
epistême: understanding

homoousion (neuter, or masculine accusative), **homoousios** (masculine nominative): 'consubstantial'

isos: 'equal'

kalokagathia: nobleness and goodness

logos: word, reason
logos epaktikos (plural: **logoi epaktikoi**): inductive reasoning, 'arguments that lead up'

morphê: 'form'

noêta: (plural of 'noêton')
noêton: known, understood

ousia: essence

sophia: wisdom

thanatos: death
ti esti, estin?: 'what is it?'
ti estin ousia?: 'what is being?'
to on: the existing (thing), the real

zôê: life
zôon logikon: 'the animal that is a logical animal'

Works of Lonergan
Referred to in Footnotes

We list here only those works of Lonergan that are referred to in our footnotes. Some of the works are published, some are in the semipublished state of notes issued for students, some are not published in any sense, but all are available in the Library and/or Archives of the Lonergan Research Institute, Toronto. We have indicated the number (anticipated or actual) for volumes appearing in the Collected Works (CWL).

'Analytic Concept of History.' Lonergan Archives paper (in File 713: History [CWL 21]).

Caring about Meaning: Patterns in the Life of Bernard Lonergan. Ed. Pierrot Lambert, Charlote Tansey, Cathleen Going. Montreal: Thomas More Institute Papers/82, 1982.

Collection (2nd ed.). Ed. Frederick E. Crowe and Robert M. Doran. Toronto: University of Toronto Press, 1988. Articles: 'Dimensions of Meaning,' '*Existenz* and *Aggiornamento*,' 'Openness and Religious Experience,' 'The Role of a Catholic University in the Modern World' (CWL 4).

'The Concept of *Verbum* in the Writings of St. Thomas Aquinas' (series of five articles). *Theological Studies* 7 (1946) to 10 (1949). (CWL 2).

De Deo trino. Vols. 1 (2nd ed.), 2 (3rd ed.). Rome: Gregorian University Press, 1964 (CWL 9).

De ente supernaturali: Supplementum schematicum. Notes for students, Collège de l'Immaculée-Conception, Montreal, 1946 (CWL 16).

De ente supernaturali: Supplementum schematicum. Revised edition. Toronto: Regis College, 1973 (CWL 16).

De intellectu et methodo. Notes by students of theology course, Gregorian University, 1959 (CWL 19).

De systemate et historia. Notes for theology course, Gregorian University, 1960 (CWL 19).

Existentialism. Notes for lectures, Boston College, 1957 (our references from counting pages in typescript made at Thomas More Institute, Montreal [CWL 18]).

'Gilbert Keith Chesterson,' *Loyola College Review* (1931) 7–10 (CWL 17).

Grace and Freedom: Operative Grace in the Thought of St. Thomas Aquinas (ed. J. Patout Burns). London: Darton, Longman & Todd, 1974 (CWL 1).

'The Human Good,' *Humanitas* 15 (1979) 113–26 (CWL 14).

Insight: A Study of Human Understanding. 5th ed. (ed. Frederick E. Crowe and Robert M. Doran). Toronto: University of Toronto Press, 1992. First edition, London: Longmans, Green and Co., 1957 (CWL 3).

Mathematical Logic. Notes for lectures, Boston College, 1957 (CWL 18).

Method in Theology. London: Darton, Longman & Todd, 1972 (CWL 12).

Moral Theology and the Human Sciences. Unpublished paper for the International Theological Commission, 1974.

Notes on Arnold J. Toynbee, *A Study of History.* Lonergan Archives paper (in File 713: History).

'The Original Preface of *INSIGHT.*' *METHOD: Journal of Lonergan Studies* 3:1 (1985) 3–7 (CWL 21).

Philosophy of God, and Theology: The Relationship between Philosophy of God and the Functional Specialty, Systematics. London: Darton, Longman & Todd, 1973 (CWL 14).

'Philosophy of History.' Lonergan Archives paper (in File 713: History [CWL 21]).

The Philosophy of History. Lecture at Thomas More Institute, Montreal, September 23, 1960. Transcription of tape-recording (CWL 6).

Review of George Boyle, *Democracy's Second Chance. The Canadian Register* (Quebec edition), June 20, 1942, p. 5 (CWL 17).

Review of Francis Stuart Campbell, *The Menace of the Herd. The Canadian Register* (Quebec edition), April 24, 1943, p. 5 (CWL 17).

A Second Collection: Papers by Bernard J.F. Lonergan, s.j. Ed. William F.J. Ryan and Bernard J. Tyrrell. London: Darton, Longman & Todd, 1974. Articles: '*Insight* Revisited,' 'An Interview with Fr. Bernard Lonergan, s.j.,' 'The Subject, ' 'Transition from a Classicist World-View to Historical-Mindedness' (CWL 11).

'Subject and Soul.' *Philippine Studies* 13 (1965) 576–85. Written as introduction for the English and French editions in book form of the *verbum* articles.

'Theories of Inquiry: Responses to a Symposium.' American Catholic Philosophical Association convention, March 28–29, published as 'Response' in the *Proceedings* 41 (1967); reprint, *A Second Collection* (CWL 11).

A Third Collection: Papers by Bernard J.F. Lonergan, s.j. Ed. Frederick E. Crowe. New York: Paulist, 1985. Articles: 'Natural Right and Historical Mindedness,' 'The Ongoing Genesis of Methods,' 'A Post-Hegelian Philosophy of Religion,' 'Prole-

gomena to the Study of the Emerging Religious Consciousness of Our Time'
(CWL 13).

Understanding and Being: The Halifax Lectures on INSIGHT. 2nd ed. (ed. Elizabeth A.
Morelli, Mark D. Morelli, Frederick E. Crowe, Robert M. Doran, Thomas V.
Daly). Toronto: University of Toronto Press, 1990 (CWL 5).

Verbum: Word and Idea in Aquinas (ed. David B. Burrell). Notre Dame: University of
Notre Dame Press, 1967 (CWL 2).

'Was G.K.C. a Theologian?' *The Canadian Register* (Quebec edition), February 20,
1943, p. 8 (reprint, under new title, of an article, 'The Theologian,' in symposium on Chesterton, ibid., November 13, p. 5).

Index

Note. The index does not include all the names of persons mentioned by Lonergan in his notebook, for some have little direct bearing on the text. I have been much more liberal in regard to topics, including even ideas to which Lonergan makes only passing reference. R.D.

Evidence, and virtually unconditioned, 185

Evil: aspects of e. opposite to those of good, 44–48; e. and civilizational development, 51; e. and evidence for false philosophies, 64, 257; e. and God, 29–30, 264; e. and human good, 27, 28, 68–69; e. a negation, 29, 43–48; particular and organized e., 43–44

Existentialists, 77, 187

Existenz, 190–91, 232 n. 59

Experience: and artistic and literary work, 178; e. a component in apprehension of reality, 216; e. defined in terms of group of operations, 176–77; e. and inquiry, 160, 177; instrumentalization of e., 213–14, 216, 221; e. and materialist, empiricist, positivist, pragmatist, modernist philosophies, 178; e. and particular good, 41, 177; e. and patterns, 211–14; e. on its own, 216; possible e. criterion for Kant, 184–85 & n. 22; e. and release, 215

Experience-Understanding-Judgment, 41, 176–77, 235; an interrelated whole, 176–77; and levels of good, types of value, types of culture, 179; parallel to matter-form-*esse*, potency-form-act, 41, 172, 177; and philosophic differences, 177–80. *See also* Consciousness, levels of

Experiential pattern. *See* Pattern

Expression: differences of e. in different periods, 116–18; inquiry and e., 117

Extension, for Descartes, 182, 186

Extension/duration, and explanation, 144

Externalization, and active method, 104–5

Extrapolation, and analogy, 172; e. and interpolation in science, 135

Fact(s): historical f., 235, 237, 238–39 n. 17; Kant and f., 185, 240; knowledge of f., 235, 240 n. 19; f. and neutralism, 240 n. 19; f. and revision, 93; f. and understanding, 235, 240

Faculty psychology, 83 & n. 16, 209–10, 265

Faith: f. answer to sin as aberration, 67; f. and reason, 242 & n. 22; rule of f., 245; f. and supernatural order, 242

Falling bodies, law of. *See* Body, bodies

False philosophies, 63–64, 257

Familiarity, and view of whole, 149

Family, and good of order, 34, 36, 41; and personal status, relations, 36, 41

Family resemblances in history of philosophy, 95, 96, 238–39 n. 17. *See also* Philosophic differences, Schools

Fascination, 214

Fascism, 234

Feeling(s): art and f., 214, 228, and chap. 9 passim; body is f. space, 162, 225; f. and music, 228; f. and notion of space, 162–63; release of f. in art, 215; f. and sensitive operator, 214

Fichte, Johann, 234

Field, of a science, 241–43 & n. 20

Field theory, 154–55

'Figures of speech,' 220

Finite: f. being composed of potency (matter), form, act (*esse*), 41, 172; f. being and good, and analogy, 30–31, 172; and criticism and choice, 32, 39–40; good of order f., 39; f. truth, 32; f. wisdom, 151

Flesch, Rudolf Franz, 5 n. 15

Form: f. and act in angels, 177; f. and concept, 113; inevitability of f. in art, 215, 219; f. known by understanding, 113, 177; f. and matter, 113–14, 124, 126, 150, 171–72 (*see also* Act, Matter, Potency); nonconceptual f. in art,